Sexual Homicide

Sexual Homicide

Patterns and Motives

Robert K. Ressler
FBI

Ann W. Burgess
University of Pennsylvania

John E. Douglas
FBI

With chapters by

James L. Luke, M.D.
Horace J. Heafner
Daniel L. Carter, Robert A. Prentky, and Ann W. Burgess

THE FREE PRESS

Fp

THE FREE PRESS
A Division of Simon & Schuster Inc.
1230 Avenue of the Americas
New York, NY 10020

THE FREE PRESS and colophon are trademarks
of Simon & Schuster Inc.

First Free Press Paperback Edition 1995

Manufactured in the United States of America

printing number
10 9 8 7 6 5 4 3 2

Library of Congress Cataloging-in-Publication Data

Ressler, Robert K.
  Sexual homicide.

  Includes index.
  1. Homicide—United States.   2. Sex crimes—United States.   I. Burgess, Ann Wolbert.
II. Douglas, John E.   III. Title.
HV6529.R47 1988   363.2'5   87-45495
ISBN 0-02-874063-7

Contents

Figures and Tables

Figures

Tables

Preface

This book is about sexual killers—many of whom have repeated their murderous acts multiple times. The book examines two aspects of sexual murderers: (1) characteristics of this group and of the subgroups within it, and (2) responses to sexual killers by the factions of society affected by them—law enforcement investigators, forensic pathologists, mental health clinicians, the legal system, surviving victims and their families.

A New Perspective

During the early 1970s, Special Agents of the FBI's Behavioral Science Unit (BSU) began profiling criminals on an informal basis by using crime scene information to deduce certain offender characteristics. Because these characteristics proved useful in identifying offenders, local authorities requested such assistance in increasing numbers. As a result, the FBI's criminal profiling service became available to all law enforcement agencies.

The agents involved in criminal profiling were able to classify murderers as either organized or disorganized in their commission of the crimes. Generally, an *organized* murderer is one who appears to plan his murders in a conscious manner and who displays control of the victim at the crime scene. The *disorganized* murderer is less consciously aware of a plan, and his crime scenes display haphazard behavior. Sometimes an offender has elements from both categories and can be called *mixed*.

The organized/disorganized distinction, which may also prove applicable to other types of crime, is especially practical for several reasons. It provides an immediate mental picture of the differences between the two classifications, and it is objective in its connotations. In addition, it avoids the technical psychological terminology that is often confusing to investigators.

Because this method of identifying offenders was based largely on a combination of experience and intuition, it had its failures as well as its successes. Nevertheless, a 1981 FBI evaluation questionnaire sent to field offices regarding the profiling service revealed that the criminal personality assessment had helped focus the investigation in 77 percent of those cases in which the suspects were subsequently identified.

The FBI Study

With the development of the criminal profiling project, a study of crime scene analysis was proposed by involved FBI agents. Using case record review, direct observation, and firsthand investigative interviews, the study would fill the gap left by earlier research that was not law–enforcement–oriented and would examine convicted, incarcerated offenders from a law enforcement perspective. In addition, it would be the first project to analyze the overall crime, paying particular attention to the crime scene. After completion of a pilot phase, the study was formalized in 1982 with a grant from the National Institute of Justice.

The study had both quantitative and qualitative approaches to data collection and analysis. Qualitative objectives were to describe the characteristics of the study population of murderers, the manner in which they committed their crimes, and the crime scenes. The descriptive data obtained would make an important contribution to the documentation of the sexual killer.

Quantitative objectives were somewhat more complex. Because the organized/disorganized classification was the only law–enforcement–developed classification to aid in the apprehension of sexual killers, its viability and potential for expanded use in criminal profiling was important to determine. Thus, the study had two quantitative objectives. First, it would test, using statistical procedures, whether there are significant behavioral differences at the crime scene between crimes committed by organized sexual murderers and those committed by disorganized sexual murderers. Second, it would identify variables, or specific characteristics, that may be useful in profiling sexual murderers and for which organized and disorganized sexual murderers differ statistically.

Study Sample

To meet these objectives, the study examined thirty-six convicted, incarcerated sexual murderers. To our knowledge, this is the largest compiled sample of sexual killers interviewed for research purposes. All of the murderers were males, most were white. Prior to interview, these men had exhausted their initial appeals and had consented to participate in the project. All cases were available for record review. Seven of these men had been convicted of killing one person, while the remainder had been convicted of killing multiple victims.

At the time of data collection, these thirty-six men represented a group of sexually oriented murderers who were available for research purposes. They do not represent a random sample, but we believe these thirty-six offenders, who came from geographic areas throughout the United States, can be used to indicate general characteristics of sexual murderers. Although some murderers in the study have been extensively written about elsewhere, our study is the first to examine them collectively as a subpopulation of murderers and from the law enforcement perspective.

Data were collected for a total of 118 victims, primarily women, of these 36 murderers. Nine victims survived and were treated as attempted-murder victims. For each killer, data were collected for each victim that the offender was convicted of killing. However, several offenders in the study are suspected of additional murders for which they were never brought to trial.

Data Collection

Data collection, which took place between 1979 and 1983, was performed both by agents from the FBI's Behavioral Science Unit and by Special Agents trained by the BSU. The data set for each murderer consisted of the best available data from two types of sources: official records (psychiatric and criminal records, pretrial records, court transcripts, interviews with correctional staff, and/or prison records) and interviews with the offenders. Thus, the information collected mainly reflects events as recalled by the murderers. Information was requested about the offender and his background, about the offense, about the victim, and about the crime scene. For some variables, data were not available because of incomplete records, conflicting responses, and offender unwillingness to respond to certain questions. The majority of offenders consented to be interviewed. Interviews were all conducted in prisons with the cooperation of officials at the various correctional institutions.

The participating offenders agreed to the interviews for several different reasons. Some of the murderers who admitted their crimes believed the interviews provided them with an opportunity to contribute to increased understanding or to clarify other people's conclusions about them. Offenders who would not admit to their crimes cooperated in order to point out why it was impossible for them to have committed the murders. Yet other murderers consented in order to "teach" police how the crimes were committed and motivated. Those who refused interviews had reasons ranging from the advice of an attorney to their own psychotic states.

The type of room used by the agents for the interviews was dependent upon the "status" of the offender. For example, one offender was the chief plumber for the prison and had his own office; other offenders were teachers to inmates and had an office attached to a classroom. Not all locations were so comfortable. Interviewing inmates living on death row, the most secure area in a prison, required that the agents walk through cell blocks. Requests, threats, and complaints were commonly made to the agents on such visits. Conducting interviews with offenders who are serving multiple life sentences in maximum security penitentiaries and who have committed violent and brutal homicides was not accomplished without tense moments. Often the murderers were not allowed to leave the more secure areas of the prison to be interviewed in the traditional interview room commonly used by family visitors, defense attorneys, and medical and psychological practitioners. Thus, some of the interviews were conducted on death row. As a general security rule, even special agents of the FBI are not allowed to possess firearms inside the walls of a prison. In the early stages of the interview program, some offenders were interviewed by one agent alone when additional agents were not available. In addition, after an initial interview by two agents, one agent alone would occasionally conduct follow-up interviews. However, one particular incident involving an agent conducting a solo interview resulted in a change in interviewing procedure.

On returning for a third session with a particularly violent serial murderer who had killed nearly one dozen victims, a veteran FBI interviewer was about to conclude a final, four-hour visit. As previously instructed by the attending guard, the agent pushed a button to alert the guard outside the room that the interview was over. The agent pressed the buzzer to summon the guard three times over a period of fifteen minutes; it became apparent that the guard was not responding. The offender, six feet nine inches in height and weighing 295 pounds, told the agent to "relax" because it was shift change time and also because the guards were feeding the inmates in the secure areas nearby. The murderer further indicated, with a note of intimidation in his voice and with a facial grimace, that it might be fifteen to twenty-five minutes before any guard would respond.

Noting the discomfort of the agent, the offender mused, "If I went ape-shit [berserk] in here, you'd be in a lot of trouble, wouldn't you? I could screw your head off and place it on the table to greet the guard." (The man's crime patterns included the dismemberment and beheading of most victims.)

The agent stated that such actions would cause him difficulty by landing him in more trouble. The inmate was then serving a sentence for seven counts of first-degree murder. The offender indicated that the status he would gain by killing an FBI agent would more than offset the punishment. The agent responded, "Surely you don't think we come in here without some method of defending ourselves!"

The inmate, in obvious disbelief, said, "You know as well as I weapons are not authorized in here!"

The agent then focused on self-defense and martial arts as a topic of conversation designed to stall for time, a method he had learned from his hostage negotiation training. The stalling technique worked, and the guard appeared at the door. As agent and inmate left the small interview room, the offender placed his arm on the agent's shoulder and said, "You know I was just kidding don't you?" He winked.

"Sure," the agent replied and let out a deep breath.

After this episode, policy was changed to require that two agents be present during interviews. The incident also demonstrated why in-depth research involving convicted murderers has not been conducted in the past. The lack of secure facilities for interviews and the nature of violent offenders are not conducive to the exchange of information. In fact, many penal institutions insist that FBI agents sign waivers stating that they will not be negotiated for in the event of a hostage-taking incident and that the state is not liable for injuries or death that may occur as a result of allowing agents to enter the prison beyond routinely used interview areas. As a matter of routine security procedure, most penitentiaries allow only law enforcement officers beyond the traditional interview rooms.

Definitions

For purposes of this book, *sexual homicide* describes murders with evidence or observations that indicate that the murder was sexual in nature. These include: victim attire or lack of attire; exposure of the sexual parts of the victim's body; sexual positioning of the victim's body; insertion of foreign objects into the victim's body cavities; evidence of sexual intercourse (oral, anal, vaginal); and evidence of substitute sexual activity, interest, or sadistic fantasy.

Crime scene characteristics are those elements of physical evidence found at the crime scene that may reveal behavioral traits of the murderer. The crime scene can include the point of abduction, locations where the victim was held, the murder scene, and the final body location. Examples of crime scene characteristics may include the use of restraints, manner of death, depersonalization of the victim, possible staging of the crime, and the amount of physical evidence at the crime scene.

Profile characteristics are those variables that identify the offender as an individual and together form a composite picture of the suspect. Profile characteristics are usually determined as a result of analysis of the crime scene characteristics and can include sex, age, occupation, intelligence, acquaintance with the victim, residence, and mode of transportation.

Organization of the Book

This book includes fifteen chapters. The first six chapters present a review of the literature on murder and a conceptual framework for the book—that is, the motivational basis for sexual homicide. Within the framework, various aspects of the murderer himself are described: his childhood and family background, his preoccupation with murder and development of deviant fantasies for murder, his decision to kill, his commission of the murder, and his escalation to increased or repeated violence. A case illustration is included. Chapter 7 describes the FBI's National Center for the Analysis of Violent Crime. Chapter 8 reports the research results of a law enforcement typology of organized and disorganized murderers. Chapter 9 describes criminal profiling, and in Chapter 10, Dr. James L. Luke outlines the role of forensic pathology in criminal profiling. Chapter 11 includes interviewing convicted murderers, and in Chapter 12, Unit Chief Horace J. Heafner discusses the police artist and composite drawings. Chapters 13 and 14 discuss the victim's perspective and implications for defensive strategies in confronting sexual assault. The final chapter reports on the murderers' prison status and presents implications from the study.

Our results have implications not only for law enforcement personnel who are responsible for the investigation and prevention of sexual homicide, but also for professionals in other disciplines addressing this problem. These groups include criminal justice professionals directly involved with the legal aspects of sexual homicide; correction institution administrators and staff personnel, who not only have custody of sexual killers but also are responsible for decisions regarding these individuals' return to society; for mental health professionals, both those involved with offender treatment and those assisting victims and families affected by these crimes; for social services personnel working with juveniles, as they detect the early signs and characteristics of violent individuals and seek to divert these individuals from criminal activity; for criminologists who study the problem of violent crime; and for public policy makers who attempt to address the problem through their decisions. It is our hope that this book will advance the knowledge base of these professionals as they seek increased understanding of the nature of sexual homicide and of the individuals who commit this shocking crime.

Acknowledgments

Many people have helped with this project. We wish to acknowledge past FBI Director William H. Webster and Executive Assistant Director John E. Otto for their early support of the criminal personality research project efforts of the Behavioral Science Unit, as well as current FBI Director William S. Sessions for his continuing support. We also wish to acknowledge James D. McKenzie, former Assistant Director of the FBI Training Division, and James W. Greenleaf, current Assistant Director of the FBI Training Division, and James A. O'Connor, Deputy Assistant Director of Training for their encouragement of the research.

We are especially appreciative for the grant monies received from the Department of Justice. We are indebted to many Department of Justice officials, including James K. Stewart, Director of the National Institute of Justice, for the initial project support and for his belief in the need to study serial murderers; and to former Office of Juvenile Justice and Delinquency Prevention (OJJDP) administrators Alfred Regnary and James Wootten for the additional monies to extend the data analysis on the role of early childhood sexual abuse in the life histories of sexual murderers. We wish to acknowledge Robert O. Heck for his belief in the criminal profiling concept. We thank our project staff from Boston City Hospital: Albert J. Belanger, Allen G. Burgess, Holly-Jean Chaplick, Marieanne L. Clark, Ralph B. D'Agostino, Carol R. Hartman, Arlene McCormack, Caroline Montan, and Karen Woelfel; our project staff from the FBI Academy: Richard L. Ault, Jr., Alan E. Burgess, Roger L. Depue, Robert R. Hazelwood, Kenneth V. Lanning, and Cynthia J. Lent; the University of Pennsylvania faculty and staff: Ellen Fuller, Barbara Lowery, Christine Grant, and Denise Scala; and our advisory committee: James L. Cavanaugh, Jr., Herman Chernoff, Charles R. Figley, Thomas Goldman, William Heiman, Marvin J. Homzie, Vallory G. Lathrop, Joyce Kemp Laben, Richard Ratner, Kenneth Rickler, Eileen E. Rinear, George M. Saiger, Stanton E. Samenow, and Marvin Wolfgang. We would like to thank them for all their comments, suggestions, and hard work. We gratefully acknowledge the Department of Corrections staffs at the various prisons and penitentiaries where the research interviews were conducted for their support of the research. We also wish to acknowledge the many FBI Agent Field Criminal Profile Coordinators for their valuable assistance in gathering data in the prisons and institutions throughout the United States.

We thank the following journals for permission to reprint sections of our published articles: *American Journal of Psychiatry, Behavioral Sciences and the Law, Journal of Interpersonal Violence*, and the *FBI Law Enforcement Bulletin*.

1
The Study of Murder

Interpersonal violence spans a wide range of human behaviors of which murder represents one of the terminal disruptions in the equilibrium of a society. Sexual homicide, a crime of increasing concern in our society, is the killing of a person in the context of power, sexuality, and brutality. Such crimes often receive widespread publicity, and they create a great deal of fear because of their apparent random and motiveless nature. Particularly in cases of serial sexual homicide, law enforcement officials feel public pressure to apprehend the perpetrator as quickly as possible.

Apprehension of the sexual murderer is one of law enforcement's most difficult challenges. Because sexual killings often appear motiveless and random, they offer few clues about why the murder occurred or, consequently, about the identity of the murderer. Even the sexual nature of these murders is not always immediately obvious, for conventional evidence of a sexual crime may be absent from a crime scene.

The Scope of the Problem

The number of sexual homicides occurring in a given year is difficult to assess, partially because of the manner in which crimes are investigated. In obvious cases of sexual assault and murder, the crime most often is reported as a homicide, not as a rape assault (Brownmiller 1975; MacDonald 1971). In other cases, conclusive evidence of sexual assault may be inadequate or lacking (Groth and Burgess 1977). Investigators may not recognize the underlying sexual dynamics of what appear to be either ordinary or motiveless murders (Cormier and Simons 1969; Revitch 1965). In addition, investigators often fail to share their findings, limiting the collective pool of knowledge on the subject (Ressler et al. 1980).

The difficulty in determining the scope of the problem of sexual homicide is reflected in official reports on murder. The FBI's Uniform Crime Reports (UCR) publication, *Crime in the United States*, presents statistics for crimes committed in the United States within a given year. For example, a survey of the statistics in the UCR for all murders committed in the period 1976 through 1986 shows that the number of murders in the United States has fluctuated from 16,605 in 1976 to a peak of 21,860 in 1980, dropping to 20,613 in 1986

(*Crime in the United States* 1986). The UCR also gives information about age, race, and sex of victims and offenders, about types of weapons used, and about situations in which killings took place. However, there is no differentiation in these official reports between homicides that included initially undetected sexual assault and those that did not.

The dearth of incidence statistics for sexual homicide promotes other approaches to evaluating this crime's magnitude. One of these approaches is to examine statistics for murders with unknown motives as indicators of the sexual homicide. Murder with unknown motive is one of five homicide categories for which the UCR annually provides data. These categories are as follows:

1. Felony murder (occurs during the commission of a felony).
2. Suspected felony murder (elements of felony are present).
3. Argument-motivated murder (noncriminally motivated).
4. Other motives or circumstances (any known motivation that is not included in previous categories).
5. Unknown motives (motive fits into none of the above categories).

Because sexual homicide so often appears random, motiveless, and with its sexual aspects obscured, some experts argue that many sexual homicides may be reported in the unknown motive category.

Figures for most categories of motives, except the unknown category, have remained relatively stable over the past decade. For example, felony-connected murders represented 17.7 percent of all murders in 1976, 17.2 percent in 1981, 18.0 percent in 1984, and 19.4 percent in 1986. The percentages for those murders placed in the "other" category are as follows: 1976, 18.6 percent; 1981, 17.1 percent; 1984, 17.6 percent, and 1986, 18.6 percent.

However, the number of murders committed for unknown motives has risen dramatically. These murders represented 8.5 percent of all murders in 1976, 17.8 percent in 1981, 22.1 percent in 1984, and 22.5 percent in 1986. This trend is of particular interest in the study of sexual homicide. Opinion has varied on the importance of this problem. Sociologists Wolfgang and Ferracuti proposed that the vast majority of murders are committed for a specific reason and that "probably less than 5 percent of all known killings are premeditated, planned, and intentional" (1982, 189). On the other hand, in a 1969 article psychiatrists Cormier and Simons cite studies observing that dangerous sexual offenses are both rare phenomena and nonescalating in aggression; in contrast, their data suggest that sexual murderers may be more common than we wish to acknowledge and that they do in fact have progressively violent records. The rapid increase in the unknown motive category, while most categories have held relatively steady, is an indication that the Wolfgang and Ferracuti proposition, first noted in 1967, may no longer be valid. Reporting methods for the unknown motive category have remained constant since 1976 and thus do not account for the dramatic increase in motiveless murder.

Although the incidence of sexual homicide may be difficult to ascertain, its effects are less unclear. Many sexual homicides are difficult to solve precisely because of the lack of clues. Law enforcement investigators note that solution rates may be misleading and should be scrutinized closely, since some crimes reported as unsolved are, in fact, solved after the figures have been reported. It is the belief of both investigators and clinicians that the majority of serial murders are sexual in nature (Lunde 1976; Ressler et al. 1985; Revitch 1965).

Veteran investigators say that sexual homicide is not a new phenomenon, although its apparent increase is. Public awareness of the problem has also increased, largely because of news media attention to these often bizarre, sensational crimes. People fear these crimes precisely because of the seemingly random nature of the murders.

Studies of Murder

Because of society's view of murder as both abhorrent and pervasive, the many aspects of murder have been studied by various disciplines. Law enforcement, the newcomer to the research arena, has added over the past decade its growing expertise in crime scene analysis.

Studies of murder have offered different perspectives on this violent crime. Epidemiological studies report on demographic data concerning victims and perpetrators (Constantino et al. 1977) and patterns of homicide (Rushforth et al. 1977; Wolfgang 1958). All disciplines have tried to categorize murderers. They have been typed in terms of motive (Revitch 1965), intent (Kahn 1971), number of victims (Frazier 1974), and type of victim (Cormier and Simons 1969). However, the majority of studies do not specifically address sexual homicide but rather study murder without differentiating between sexual and nonsexual crimes (Perdue and Lester 1974).

Studies examining murder divide into the various disciplines focusing on the subject: (1) individual case reports by journalists, (2) studies of the psychological aspects of the individual who committed the murder, (3) studies investigating murder and murderers within a sociological context, (4) legal aspects of the crime, and (5) crime scene patterns.

The Journalist's Perspective

The first category represents a mass communication mechanism for informing the public of crimes being committed. As such, the possible mechanisms include newspapers, magazines, and books. The writers are usually journalists, and on occasion they may have additional training like Joseph Wambaugh, formerly a police detective, who wrote *The Onion Field*, which depicts the murder of a police officer.

The news of a murder in general and a sexual homicide in particular arouses strong emotion in the public. Newspaper headlines highlight the bizarre aspects ("Body-hack Case," "Vampire Killer's Trial Begins"), the victim ("The Victim's Last Hours"), the serial aspect ("Killer Strikes Again"), the outcome ("Next Stop: The Electric Chair") and the twenty-year anniversary ("July 14, 1966").

Detective magazines are another mechanism for communication and often contain the facts learned at trial or during a journalist's investigation. In addition, journalists (Keyes 1976), as well as mental health professionals (Brussel 1968; Schreiber 1983), write books aimed at the general population.

The Psychological View

The second category includes studies that examine the individual murderer in terms of psychiatric diagnoses, childhood antecedents to criminal behavior, and criminal behavior as the result of learned responses to particular stimuli. Also in this category are studies designed to determine techniques for treating incarcerated violent offenders.

Study focus on the characteristics of individual murderers was evident as many as two hundred years ago. In the late eighteenth century, Swiss mystic Johann Kaspar Lavatar developed the art of physiognomy, whereby an individual's facial features were held to reveal his or her character. At about the same time, Franz Josef Gall contended that phrenology, the study of the formation of an individual's skull, could disclose both character and mental capacities. Physiognomy and phrenology were both used to study criminals, and death masks of murderers' heads were examined in an attempt to explain criminal acts (Attick 1970).

Among more recent theories that seek to explain violent human behavior through examination of individual physical characteristics is the approach based on the finding that certain violent criminals have a rare chromosomal abnormality called XYY (Jacobs, Brunton, and Melville 1965). According to this theory, the presence of an extra male, or Y, chromosome results in a greater likelihood that the individual will engage in aggressive and violent behavior. This idea received a great deal of attention in 1968, when it was reported that Richard Speck, the man who one night murdered eight student nurses, had the XYY abnormality. It was later found that Speck did not have the extra Y chromosome. Subsequent research demonstrated that although the XYY abnormality is four times more likely to show up in the male criminal population than in the general male population, most individuals with this condition display no abnormally violent behavior (Bootzin and Acocella 1980).

In the last decade, the field of psychiatry has paid increasing attention to brain function in all types of psychological problems. Neurological, genetic, and biophysiological components are being studied in the murderer (Lewis et al. 1986; Morrison 1981).

Psychological theories and explanations of violent behavior are substantially more common than those based on physical characteristics. As do studies based on individual physical attributes, these psychological studies focus on the characteristics of the individual murderer. According to Bootzin and Acocella (1980), psychological theories can be categorized as having either (1) a psychodynamic perspective (that unconscious childhood conflicts give rise to abnormal behavior), (2) a behavioral perspective (that inappropriate conditioning results in abnormal behavior), or (3) a humanistic-existential perspective (that abnormal behavior results from a sense of personal failure).

Although individual-focused studies of violent behavior may be widely divergent in terms of their theoretical bases, they often have one thing in common: they group individuals into various categories. By producing taxonomic schemes to aid in understanding the causes of human violence, researchers seek to clarify methods of treating violent individuals and eliminating violent behavior.

Among recent general studies of human violence, several propose typologies having many categories. For example, Wille (1974) groups murderers into ten types: (1) depressives, (2) psychotics, (3) murderers with organic brain dysfunction, (4) psychopaths, (5) passive-aggressive individuals, (6) alcoholics, (7) hysterical personalities, (8) child killers, (9) mentally retarded murderers, and (10) murderers who kill for sexual satisfaction. In contrast, Guttmacher (1973) suggests six categories of murderers: (1) "average" murderers free from prominent psychopathology but lacking societal values, (2) sociopaths desiring revenge on the population at large for maltreatment during childhood, (3) alcoholics who kill their wives over fear of losing them, (4) murderers avenging a lover's loss of interest, (5) schizophrenics responding to hallucinations and delusions, and (6) sadists who kill to achieve sexual pleasure.

Other researchers have suggested fewer types of murderers. Megargee (1966) claims that there are only two types of extremely assaultive individuals (1) undercontrolled persons, who respond with aggression when frustrated or provoked, and (2) overcontrolled persons, who, despite rigid inhibitions against the expression of violence, build up an aggression that eventually results in violence. Simon (1977) studied thirty murderers and classified them into three groups: type A murderers had a tendency to murder impulsively, often with a weapon present and under the influence of alcohol. Type B murderers were more likely to be involved in a victim-induced homicide, with the victim usually a woman with whom the murderer had formed a relationship. Type AB murderers were able to sustain enduring, though sadistic, relationships with their victims and posed the greatest risk of future homicidal acts. Tanay (1972) has classified homicidal behavior into three categories: (1) ego-syntonic homicide, compatible with the offender's thinking and fulfills a consciously acceptable wish for the perpetrator; (2) ego-dystonic homicide, noncompatible with the offender's thinking and occurs against the conscious wishes of the perpetrator (who is in an altered state of consciousness); and (3) psychotic homicide, which occurs while the murderer is in a delusional state.

The few studies that specifically address sexual homicide suggest the existence of two types of sex murderers: the rape or displaced anger murderer (Cohen et al. 1971; Groth, Burgess, and Holmstrom, 1977; Prentky, Burgess, and Carter 1986; Rada 1978), and the sadistic, or lust, murderer (Becker and Abel 1978; Bromberg and Coyle 1974; Cohen et al. 1971; Groth, Burgess, and Holmstrom 1977; Guttmacher and Weihofen 1952; Podolsky 1966; Prentky, Burgess, and Carter 1986; Rada 1978; Ressler 1985; and Scully and Marolla 1985). Podolsky notes that rapists who murder kill after raping their victims, primarily to escape detection. These murderers, according to Rada, rarely report sexual satisfaction from their murders or perform postmortem sexual acts with their victims. In contrast, the sadistic murderer kills as part of a ritualized, sadistic fantasy (Groth, Burgess, and Holmstrom 1977). For this murderer, aggression and sexuality become fused into a single psychological experience—sadism—in which aggression is eroticized. According to Brittain (1970), subjugation of the victim is of importance to this type of sexual killer; cruelty and infliction of pain are merely the means to effect subjugation.

The various systems for classifying murderers have themselves been categorized. According to Athens (1980), the first system type assumes there is a uniformity, or pattern, to the characteristics of a particular violent crime. In theory, once such a pattern is discovered it will reveal the cause of the crime. The second type of system assumes that violent crimes are committed by individuals with psychopathic personality makeup; according to the third classification type, a combination of social and psychological factors results in violent behavior.

These studies represent a small sample of the many different classification systems of violent individuals. Nevertheless, they demonstrate that there is little relationship between the many different taxonomic schemes. Thus, as Megargee and Bohn (1979) have stated, they have limited use in providing information to those whose task it is to deal with the problem of violence and are instead designed more for theoretical discussion. A similar criticism has been voiced by Tanay (1972), who expresses concern that significant innovations in homicide control have not been developed, despite the many descriptions of the crime. Studies attempting to provide both a new description and a new solution for criminal behavior are based in learning theory (Samenow

1984). Researchers (Yochelson and Samenow 1976) spent many years studying criminals committed to a mental institution and found that specific thinking patterns separate hard-core criminals from society at large, regardless of background. In other words, criminal behavior is the result of the way criminals think, not of their environment or of other factors that are commonly used to explain this behavior. Thus, say the researchers, changing violent behavior must involve changing the way an individual thinks rather than changing that person's environment.

The Sociological View

In contrast to studies and classification systems based on the individual murderer, other research has examined homicide as a social phenomenon. Included in this third category are sociological studies examining violent crime within the context of the society in which it occurs. These studies consider cultural factors and social characteristics that might contribute to aggressive behavior. Like sociologists, historians have also studied murder with the belief that an analysis of the patterns of violence within a given society at a given time is a unique method of demonstrating many characteristics of that society (Buchanan 1977).

One such approach to understanding violent crime has been offered by Wolfgang and Ferracuti (1982). These researchers suggest that because the sociological approach to criminology, with its emphasis on cultural aspects, and the psychological approach, with its emphasis upon the individual, are apparently divergent, criminology must integrate the different ways of studying a homicide. Although an understanding of the social structure within which a murderer acts is as important as an understanding of the individual murderer, the valuable information to be gleaned from sociological research is not readily available for practical application. In addition, individuals who deal with the practical matters of homicide are unable to confirm researchers' theories.

With this need for integration as their starting point, Wolfgang and Ferracuti studied homicides that result from passion or from an intent to harm but not to kill. They theorized that within many cultures a subculture of violence exists and contended that homicide rates are highest among a homogenous subcultural group. In a subculture of violence, the use of force disrupts the values of society at large. Although the idea that values are actually motives for specific behaviors can be criticized as an oversimplification, it may be true that specific acts can reflect a basic value system.

The sociological literature has also looked at the victim. One of the most pervasive ways of analyzing victims has been through the concept of victim precipitation and victim participation. The victim is one of the causes of a crime, suggests Hans von Hentig. In 1948 he stated, "In a sense the victim shapes and molds the criminal. . . . To know one we must be acquainted with the complementary partner." Mendelsohn (1963, 239–241), in writing of the biopsychosocial personality of the accused and of the victim, elaborated on the doctrine of victimology while preparing for the trial of a man who, had it not been for "the perversity of his former wife," would never have been found guilty of murdering her and her lover. Wolfgang (1958, 252) has used the concept of victim precipitation in his well-known studies of criminal homicide, applying it to those cases in which the "role of the victim is characterized by his having been the first in the homicide drama to use physical force directed against his subsequent slayer." An example is the husband who attacked his wife with a milk bottle, a brick, and a piece of concrete block while she was making breakfast. Having a butcher knife in her hand, she stabbed him. Wolfgang (1958) found victim-precipitated homicides represented 26 percent of a total of 588 homicides studied through police reports in Philadelphia. Adding to this concept, Schafer (1968, 152) concluded that "it is far from true that all crimes 'happen' to be committed; often the victim's negligence, precipitative action, or provocation contributes to the genesis or performance of a crime."

Modern researchers have stated the importance of sociological examinations of murder not only to understanding homicide, but also to understanding society's interrelationships, particularly those of the past. In a study of several sensational murders that took place during the Victorian era, Attick (1970) focuses on the social detail revealed through these cases. Statistics quoted by Attick indicate that although the characteristics of an individual murder may change from one historical period to another, patterns of murder do not. For instance, during the period 1837 through 1901, Attick analyzed that most murders were domestic in nature, while the next largest group was homicides committed during the course of a felony. A comparison of these statistics with the 1986 *Crime in the United States* figures shows that descriptive categories are fairly consistent with the addition of the unknown motive: arguments (37.5 percent); unknown motive (22.5 percent); felony (19.4 percent); miscellaneous nonfelonies (18.6 percent); and suspected felonies (2 percent).

The Legal View

The fourth category includes the mechanisms through which the legal community communicates its work, often in professional journals and occasionally through textbooks (Heymann and Kenety 1985).

The problem of murder has been described from the legal perspective, most often written from the trial perspective. In fact, law reviews often focus on specific cases. Emphasis is usually given to trial strategies from the prosecution or defense perspectives.

Law Enforcement's View

The last category of law enforcement's perspective looks at the investigation, suspect identification, and suspect apprehension as critical to homicide study. Law enforcement, whose responsibility it is to combat violent crime, has looked carefully at homicide analyses. Unlike other disciplines concerned with human violence, law enforcement does not, as a primary objective, seek to explain the actions of a murderer. Instead, its task is to ascertain the identity of the offender based on what is known of his actions. Described by one author as an emitter of signals during the commission of a crime (Willmer 1970), the criminal must be identified as quickly as possible to prevent further violence. While studies explaining why certain individuals commit violent crimes may aid them in their search, law enforcement investigators must adapt study findings to suit their own particular needs. Criminal profiling and criminal personality assessment are ways in which law enforcement has sought to combine the results of studies in other disciplines with more traditional investigative techniques in an effort to combat violent criminal behavior.

Criminal profiling has been used by law enforcement with success in many areas and is viewed as a way in which the investigating officer can narrow the field of investigation. This assessment does not provide the identity of the offender. Instead, it indicates the kind of person most likely to have committed a crime having certain characteristics.

Airport antihijacking measures and drug courier apprehension have been aided through law enforcement's use of basic profile characteristics. Screening techniques apply groups of characteristics to differentiate between the flying public and potential hijackers and drug traffickers.

Criminal profiling techniques have also been used in identifying anonymous letter writers (Casey-Owens 1984) and persons who make written or spoken threats of violence (Miron and Douglas 1979). In cases of the latter, psycholinguistic techniques have been used to compose a "threat dictionary," whereby every word in a message is assigned, by computer, to a specific category. Words as they are used in the message are then compared to those words as they are used in ordinary speech or writings, and the vocabulary usage of a particular author or speaker may yield "signature" words unique to that individual. In this way, police may not only be able to determine that several letters were written by the same individual, but they may also be able to learn about the background and psychology of the offender.

Rapists and arsonists also lend themselves to criminal profiling techniques. Through careful interview of the rape victim about the rapist's behavior, law enforcement personnel may be able to build a criminal personality profile of the offender (Hazelwood 1983). The theory behind this approach is that behavior reflects personality, and by examining behavior the investigator may be able to determine what type of person is responsible for the offense. Common characteristics of arsonists have been derived from an analysis of the Uniform Crime Reports data (Rider 1980). Knowledge of the arsonist's psychodynamics can aid the investigator in identifying possible suspects and in developing techniques and strategies for interviewing these suspects.

Profiling has been found to be particularly useful in investigating sexual homicide because, as was discussed earlier, many of these crimes appear motiveless and thus offer few obvious clues about the killer's identity. In murders that result from jealousy, a family quarrel, or commission of a felony, the readily identifiable motive generally provides vital information about the identity of the killer. Because many sexual homicides fail to provide this information, investigators must look to methods that supplement conventional investigative techniques in order to identify the perpetrator.

Criminal profiling uses the behavioral characteristics of the offender as its basis; sexual homicide crime scenes yield much information about the killer's behavior. A new dimension of information is available to the investigator through profiling techniques. For example, the apparent lack of motive in many sexual homicides is illustrated by the murderer's seemingly random selection of victims. Yet as Lunde (1976) points out, selection is based on the murderer's perception of certain victim attributes that are of symbolic significance to him. Although the victims are probably unaware of this significance, the murderer may assume the victims do indeed know of their place in his delusional scheme. Thus, an analysis of similarities and differences among victims of a particular murderer may produce important information concerning the motive in apparently motiveless crime. This in turn may provide information about the perpetrator himself.

The idea of constructing a composite of a murderer is not new. In 1960 Palmer published results of a three-year study of fifty-one murderers who were serving sentences in New England. Palmer's "typical murderer" was twenty-three years old when he committed murder. With a gun, this typical killer murdered a male stranger during an argument. He came from a low social class and achieved little in terms of education or occupation. He had a well-meaning but maladjusted mother, and he experienced physical and psychological frustrations during childhood.

Similarly, Rizzo (1982) studied thirty-one accused murderers during the course of routine referrals for psychiatric examination at a court clinic. He concluded that the average murderer was a twenty-six-year-old male who most likely knew his victim and for whom monetary gain was the most probable motivation for the crime.

Criminal profiling as used by law enforcement today seeks to do more than describe the typical murderer, if in fact there ever is such a person. Law enforcement investigators must assess the crime scene in terms of what it may reveal about the type of person who committed the crime. Although Lunde has stated that the murders of fiction bear no resemblance to the murders of reality (1976), a connection between fictional detective techniques and modern profiling methods may indeed exist. For example, it is an attention to detail that is the hallmark of famous fictional detectives; the smallest item at a crime scene does not escape their notice. As stated by the famous Sergeant Cuff in Wilkie Collin's 1868 novel *The Moonstone*, widely acknowledged as the first full-length detective story,

> At one end of the inquiry there was a murder, and at the other end there was a spot of ink on a tablecloth that nobody could account for. In all my experience along the dirtiest ways of this dirty little world I have never met with such a thing as a trifle yet.

This attention to detail is equally as essential to present-day profiling. No piece of information is too small; each detail is scrutinized for its contribution to a profile of the killer.

In contrast, criminal profiling methods do not share with fictional techniques the reliance on one specific clue to solve a case. The broken matchstick that leads police to the killer's door simply does not exist. Instead, experienced profilers look at the overall picture of the crime. Obvious as well as implied clues are used together, not individually, to provide information about the murder.

Criminal profiling is best viewed as a way for law enforcement to focus its efforts in a particular area. Profiling has been described as a collection of leads (Rossi 1982), as an educated attempt to provide specific information about a certain type of criminal (Geberth 1981), and as a biographical sketch of behavioral patterns, trends, and tendencies (Vorpagel 1982). Geberth has also described the psychological profile as particularly useful when the criminal demonstrates some form of psychopathology, and has stated that the crime scene often reflects the murderer's behavior and personality in much the same way as furnishings reveal the homeowner's character. Criminal personality assessment helps investigators identify those patterns of behavior and personality.

Notes

Athens, L.H. *Violent criminal acts and actors*. Cambridge, Mass.: Routledge and Kegan Paul, 1980.

Attick, R.D. *Victorian studies in scarlet*. New York: W.W. Norton, 1970.

Becker, J.V., and Abel, G.G. Men and the victimization of women. In J.R. Chapman and M.R. Gates (eds), *Victimization of women*. Beverly Hills, Calif.: Sage Publications, 1978.

Bootzin, R.R., and Acocella, J.R. *Abnormal psychology: current perspectives.* 3d ed. New York: Random House, 1980.

Brittain, R.P. The sadistic murderer. *Medical Science and the Law,* 1970, 10:198–207.

Bromberg, W., and Coyle, E. Rape! A compusion to destroy. *Medical Insight,* 1974, April, 21–22, 24–25.

Brownmiller, S. *Against our will: men, women and rape.* New York: Simon and Schuster, 1975.

Brussel, J.A. *Casebook of a Crime Psychiatrist.* New York: Bernard Geis, 1968.

Buchanan, J. *Society and homicide in 13th century England.* Stanford, Calif.: Stanford University Press, 1977.

Casey-Owens, M. The anonymous letter-writer—a psychological profile? *Journal of Forensic Sciences,* 1984, 29:816–19.

Cohen, M.L., Garofalo, R.F., Boucher, R., and Seghorn, T. The psychology of rapists. *Seminars in Psychiatry,* 1971, 3:307–27.

Collins, W. *The Moonstone.* 1868; New York: New American Library, 1984.

Constantino, J.P., Kuller, L.H., Perper, J.A., and Cypress, R.H. An epidemiologic study of homicides in Allegheny County, Pennsylvania. *American Journal of Epidemiology,* 1977, 106:314–24.

Cormier, B.S., and Simons, S.P. The problem of the dangerous sexual offender. *Canadian Psychiatric Association,* 1969, 14:329–34.

Federal Bureau of Investigation. Internal memorandum from Howard Teten to William H. Webster, 1981

Frazier, S.H. Murder—single and multiple aggression. *Aggression,* 1974, 52:304–12.

Geberth, V.J. Psychological profiling. *Law and Order,* 1981, 46–49.

Groth, A.N., and Burgess, A.W. Sexual dysfunction during rape. *New England Journal of Medicine,* 1977, 297:764–66.

Groth, A.N., Burgess, A.W., and Holmstrom, L.L. Rape: power, anger and sexuality. *American Journal of Psychiatry,* 1977, 134:1239–43.

Guttmacher, M. *The mind of the murderer.* New York: Arno Press, 1973.

Guttmacher, M.S., and Weihofen, H. *Psychiatry and the law.* New York: Norton, 1952.

Hazelwood, R.R. The behavior oriented interview of rape victims: the key to profiling. *FBI Law Enforcement Bulletin,* 1983.

Heymann, P.B., and Kenety, W.H. *The murder trial of Wilber Jackson: a homicide in the family.* 2d ed. St. Paul, Minn.: West Publishing Co., 1985.

Jacobs, P.A., Brunton, M., and Melville, M.M. Aggressive behavior, mental subnormality and the XYY male. *Nature,* 1965, 208:1351–52.

Kahn, M.W. Murderers who plead insanity: A descriptive factor-analytic study of personality, social and history variables. *Genetic Psychology Monographs,* 1971, 84.

Keyes, E. *The Michigan Murders.* New York: Pocket Books, 1976.

Lewis, D.O., Pincus, J.H., Feldman, M., Jackson, L., and Bard, B. Psychiatric, neurological, and psychoeducational characteristics of 15 death row inmates in United States. *American Journal of Psychiatry,* 1986 143:838–45.

Lunde, D.T. *Murder and madness.* San Francisco: San Francisco Book Co., 1976.

MacDonald, J.M. *Rape offenders and their victims.* Springfield, Ill.: Charles C. Thomas, 1971.

Megargee, E. Undercontrolled and overcontrolled personality types in extreme antisocial aggression. *Psychological Monographs, General and Applied,* 1966, 80:1–29.

Megargee, E., and Bohn, M.J., Jr. *Classifying criminal offenders.* Beverly Hills: Sage Publications, 1979.

Mendelsohn, B. The origin of the doctrine of victimology. *Excerpta Criminologica,* 1963, 3:239–44.

Miron, M.S., and Douglas, J.E. Threat analysis: the psycholinguistic approach. *FBI Law Enforcement Bulletin,* 1979, 49:5–9.

Morrison, H.L. Mass murderers: patterns of behavior and developmental deviations. Paper presented at the American Academy of Psychiatry and the Law, San Diego, Fall 1981.

Palmer, S. *A study of murder.* New York: Thomas Crowell, 1960.

Perdue, W.C., and Lester, D. Temperamentally suited to kill: the personality of murderers. *Corrective and Social Psychiatry,* 1974, 20:13–15.

Podolsky, E. Sexual violence. *Medical Digest,* 1966, 34:60–63.

Prentky, R.A., Burgess, A.W., and Carter, D.L. Victim responses by rapist type: an empirical and clinical analysis. *Journal of Interpersonal Violence,* 1986, 1:73–98.

Rada, R.T. Psychological factors in rapist behavior. In R.T. Rada (ed.), *Clinical aspects of the rapist.* New York: Grune & Stratton, 1978.

Reiser, M. Crime-specific psychological consultation. *The Police Chief,* 1982, 53–56.

Ressler, R.K., Douglas, J.E., Groth, A.N., and Burgess, A.W. Offender profiling: a multidisciplinary approach. *FBI Law Enforcement Bulletin,* 1980, 49:16–20.

Ressler, R.K. (ed.) Violent crimes. *FBI Law Enforcement Bulletin,* 1985, 54:1–31.

Revitch, E. Sex murder and the potential sex murderer. *Diseases of the Nervous System,* 1965, 26:640–48.

Rider, A.O. The firesetter: a psychological profile, part 1. *FBI Law Enforcement Bulletin,* 1980, 49:1–23.

Rizzo, N.D. Murder in Boston: killers and their victims. *International Journal of Offender Therapy and Comparative Criminology,* 1982.

Rossi, D. Crime scene behavioral analysis: another tool for the law enforcement investigator. *The Police Chief,* 1982: 152–55.

Rushforth, N.B., Ford, A.B., Hirsch, C.S., Rushforth, N.M., and Adelson, L. Violent death in a metropolitan county: changing patterns in homicide (1958–74). *New England Journal of Medicine,* 1977, 274:53–58.

Samenow, S.E. *Inside the criminal mind.* New York: Time Books, 1984.

Schafer, S. *The victim and his criminal.* New York: Random House, 1968.

Schreiber, F.R. *The Shoemaker.* New York: Simon and Schuster, 1983.

Scully, D., and Marolla, J. "Riding the bull at Gilley's": convicted rapists describe the rewards of rape. *Social Problems,* 1985, 32:251–63.

Simon, R.E. Type A, AB, B murderers. *Bulletin of the American Academy of Psychiatry and the Law,* 1977, 5:344–62.

Strauss, M.A., and Baron, L. *Sexual stratification, pornography, and rape.* Durham, N.H.: Family Research Laboratory, University of New Hampshire, 1983.

Tanay, E. Psychiatric aspects of homicide prevention. *American Journal of Psychiatry,* 1972, 128:49–52.

U.S. Department of Justice. *Uniform Crime Reports.* Washington, D.C.: U.S. Government Printing Office, 1986.

von Hentig, H. *The criminal and his victim*. New Haven, Conn.: Yale University Press, 1948.

Vorpagel, R.E. Painting psychological profiles: charlatanism, charisma, or a new science? *The Police Chief*, 1982:156–59.

Wille, W. *Citizens who commit murder*. St. Louis: Warren Greene, 1974.

Willmer, M. *Crime and information theory*. Edinburgh: University of Edinburgh, 1970.

Wolfgang, M.E. *Patterns of homicide*. Philadelphia: University of Pennsylvania Press, 1958.

Wolfgang, M.E., and Ferracuti, F. *The subculture of violence: towards an integrated theory in criminology*. 2d ed. Beverly Hills, Calif.: Sage Publications, 1982.

Yochelson, S., and Samenow, S.E. *The criminal personality: the change process*. New York: Jason Aronson, 1976.

2
Growing Up to Murder:
The Social Environment and
Formative Events

FBI agents who are investigative profilers examine a crime for information that reveals the characteristics of the offender. Although not quite the same as fingerprints, certain patterns of the offender's personality can be detected through examination of crime scene evidence. In our study of thirty-six sexual murderers, we were able not only to identify some of these patterns but also to examine factors believed to influence the development of these patterns. The background information we collected, through offender interviews and records, made it possible for us to draw certain conclusions about these men.

This chapter presents what we learned about the social environment and formulative events of the thirty-six murderers we studied. These characteristics were analyzed in terms of what they tell us about the men themselves. Through an understanding of some of the dynamics behind sexually deviant behavior, we better understand the roots of the developing motivation to murder.

Readers should recognize that we are making general statements about these thirty-six offenders. Not all statements are true for *all* offenders, although they may be true for *most* of the thirty-six men or for most of the offenders for whom we obtained data. Responses were not available from all offenders for all questions.

Childhood Attributes

At first glance, it appears the thirty-six murderers began their lives with some distinct advantages (see table 2–1). All male and almost all (thirty-three) white, they were usually eldest sons. Four offenders were the only child in the family, and four were adopted as infants or as very young children. Most of them grew

Sections reprinted with permission from Sage Publications: Ressler, R.K., Burgess, A.W., Hartman, C.R., Douglas, J.E. and McCormack, A. Murderers Who Rape and Mutilate. *Journal of Interpersonal Violence* 1 1986, 273–87.

Table 2–1
Childhood Attributes

Attribute	Number/Total	Percent
Male	36/36	100
White	33/36	92
Eldest son	20/36	56
Average or better intelligence	27/34	80
Both parents present initially	20/35	57
Mother's occupation housewife	16/31	52
Stable family income	20/27	74
Self-sufficient economic level	30/35	86

up in the 1940s and 1950s (birthdates ranged from 1904 to 1958), a period when attitudes in the United States favored the oldest, white, male child.

Most of the offenders had unremarkable appearances at the time of our interviews, suggesting that as boys they were not unattractive. Their heights and weights were within norms, and few had distinguishing handicaps or physical defects to set them apart in a group of boys or men. With regard to appearance, there was little to distinguish them from other groups of males.

The offenders were of good intelligence, with only seven having IQ scores below 90, or less than average. Sixteen were classified in the average to bright normal range (IQ scores of 90 to 119). Of real interest is that eleven of the responding murderers had superior to very superior intelligence, with IQs over 120.

The majority began life in a two-parent home. Half of the mothers were homemakers and did not work outside the home. The majority of fathers (58 percent) worked at unskilled jobs, while thirteen fathers had skilled jobs. Of greater importance is that three-quarters of the fathers earned stable incomes. Over 80 percent of the offenders described their family socioeconomic levels as average (self-sufficient) or better; only five men believed their families lived below marginal economic levels (see table 2–1).

Thus, mothers were in the home raising the children, and fathers were earning stable incomes; poverty was not a factor in the socioeconomic status of families. The subjects were intelligent, white, eldest sons. Yet despite such positive personal attributes and social factors, these male children became not successful participants in society but convicted murderers.

Social Environment

Delving further into the backgrounds of these offenders provides possible answers to the critical question of what went wrong. Is there evidence to suggest what may have contributed to the development of homicidal behavior?

Factors concerning the social environment of family backgrounds
ships and treatment of the offender as a child and concerning personal se.
experiences as a child and adolescent are examined.

Family Functioning

Although the families initially appear to be functional with both parents
present, a number of problems appear within the parents' backgrounds to
indicate they had their own stresses and problems to deal with in addition to
raising children. The family histories of the thirty-six murderers revealed that
multiple problems existed in family structure. First, substance abuse was a
major problem among family members. Nearly 70 percent of the families had
histories of alcohol abuse, and one-third of the families had histories of drug
abuse. In describing his father's alcoholism, one offender revealed how the
alcohol abuse was repeated in his own life.

> *Offender*: Every time I was suspended from school, I would explain to my
> father what happened, even if it was my fault. That was when he was deep into
> his alcohol problem. So he'd go to school with me and wait for the teacher to
> show up and start cussing me out. [My father] didn't appreciate that and he'd
> go off [and] cuss [the teachers] out, threaten them and everything . . . He'd
> make the teachers back down, then make me go back to school.
> *Agent*: How long did you stay in school?
> *Offender*: I stayed until tenth [grade when] they started putting out false
> rumors that I was extorting the other students.
> *Agent*: What were you doing?
> *Offender*: At that time my problem was with alcohol. [The alcohol
> problem] was really picking up then.

It is of interest that the offender does perceive the extortion but he tries to avoid
the issue by changing to another problem.

Family backgrounds also contained psychiatric problems. Over half of the
families had histories of psychiatric disorders: ten mothers, seven fathers, four
brothers, and one sister all had psychiatric histories. In several cases, a
mother's psychiatric hospitalization absented her from the family. These
histories were often combined with problems involving aggression. The
background of one offender abstracted from the criminal history of his father
revealed how psychiatric problems and aggression were intertwined.

> The offender's father shot and killed one of his own brothers when the subject
> was thirteen. Prior to this crime, the father had been investigated concerning
> acts of arson and insurance settlement fraud. The father was tried for the
> murder but found not guilty by reason of insanity. He was diagnosed during

the trial as suffering from paranoia. The father was also suspected in the killings of two other persons, including a trespasser on his property and a foster child who had disappeared. After the murder, the father was committed to a state mental hospital; however, two years later he escaped with the help of the subject's mother. He was later captured by authorities in a neighboring state, but because officials declined to extradite him he was released.

In some cases the mix of psychiatric disturbance and aggressive acts was also present in the offender as a child. Twenty-five of the men for whom data was available had histories of early psychiatric difficulties. Some of the men claimed not to remember these problems, as in the following case:

Offender: My mom said she took me to see a psychiatrist when I was young, but I don't remember it. She said it was about getting in so many fights at school. I did hit a teacher one time. I was running down the hall, I didn't know it was a teacher [who] grabbed me by the back of the coat and told me to slow down and quit running. I hit her. By the time I was fourteen or fifteen I hit a few others.

Half of the offenders' families had members with criminal histories. The illegal behavior could be known within the family ("My mother was a beautician and numbers runner and my father was a carpenter and sold drugs") or it could be a family secret as in the following case.

Offender: My father did five years in the penitentiary and he changed his name after that. He even had one sister [who] never spoke to him after that.
Agent: It was a big secret?
Offender: I don't know why he fell [what his offense was].

A review of the record confirmed our suspicion that the father had been convicted of a sexual crime against the child of his sister.

In addition, almost half of the reported cases of criminal activity involved sexual problems among family members. One such problem involved observed indiscriminate sexual behavior by the mother as in the following case record.

The offender's relationship with his mother was one of love-hate. He states his mother was an alcoholic and he frequently saw her go out with men so that he came to "hate anyone who goes out with one's mother." He reports at age sixteen he brought a man home and his mother became involved with the man. The offender later reported assaulting this man with intent to kill.

In an example of a father's extramarital behavior, it appears that the subject focused more on the mother's anxiety than the father's affairs.

When I was older my father told me, in a general and humorously irreverent fashion, stories about affairs he'd had when I was ten or younger. I never suspected my mother was unfaithful . . . rather, my mother feared she was losing my father and that a separation or divorce might happen.

Relationship with Parents and Siblings

It is often suggested by child and family theorists that the structure and quality of family interaction is an important factor in a child's development, especially in the way the child perceives family members and their interaction with him and with each other. For children growing up, the quality of their attachments to parents and to other members of the family is most important to how these children as adults relate to and value other members of society. Essentially, these early life attachments (sometimes called bonding) translate into a map of how the child will perceive situations outside the family. Because of the importance of these early life attachments, we were especially interested in specific factors within family relationships that best suggested the offenders' levels of attachment to other people (see table 2–2).

The multiple family problems we observed suggest not only inconsistent contact between some family members and the murderer as a child, but also inadequate patterns of relating. Thus, the possibility that most of the offenders experienced positive interactions with family members seems unlikely. As one father observed of his son growing up, "As long as I knew him, he seemed to be

Table 2–2
Family Background Characteristics

Characteristic	Number/Total	Percent
Family history of problems		
Family alcohol history	20/29	69
Family history of drug abuse	9/27	33
Family psychiatric history	16/30	53
Family criminal history	16/32	50
Family sexual problems	12/26	46
History of abuse and neglect		
Physical abuse history	13/31	42
Psychological abuse history	23/31	74
Relationship with parents/siblings		
Instability of residence	23/34	68
Father leaves before age twelve	17/36	47
Mother dominant parent	21/32	66
Negative relationship with male caretaker figures	26/36	72
Negative relationship with mother	16/36	44
Perceived treated unfairly	15/28	53
No older sibling role model	16/36	44

satisfied to be by himself. I did not think that was natural." Another parent described the son as being sullen and going for days without talking to his parents.

When examining the patterns described by the murderers regarding their own families, one is impressed by the high degree of instability in home structure. Only one-third of the men reported growing up in one location. Seventeen said they experienced occasional instability, and six reported chronic instability or frequent moving. In addition, over 40 percent lived outside the family home before age eighteen. These residences included foster homes, state homes, detention centers, and mental hospitals. The histories of frequent moving illustrate that the families had minimal attachment to a community, thus reducing the child's opportunities to develop positive, stable relationships outside the family, relationships that might compensate for family instability.

As was stated earlier, both parents were present in over half (twenty) of the cases, with the father absent in ten cases, the mother absent in three cases, and both parents absent in two cases. However, of importance is that in seventeen cases the biological father left home before the boy reached twelve years. The absence was due to a variety of reasons, such as death or incarceration, but most often the reason was separation and divorce. In six cases of thirteen divorce situations, the natural father left when the boy was under age six and in seven cases when the boy was between ages seven and eleven. There generally followed a two-to-five-year period before the mother remarried and a new stepfather entered the home. Sometimes the boy never saw his natural father again as in the following case:

> The offender's mother married at age fifteen and had two sons before separating and having the marriage annulled. The father was reported to have served time in the state prison for the criminally insane. Immediately after the mother remarried, the second husband began adoption proceedings. These records were sealed so that the subject's natural father would be unaware of the adoptions.

Clearly, the loss of the father over a period of time, followed by an adjustment to a new male caretaker was required of the boy. Several offenders commented on the significance of parental separation and acquiring a new male caretaker. The following quote is from an offender who committed his first murder at age fourteen while his mother was honeymooning with her third husband.

Agent: Is there anything in your early life that caused you some real hard feelings over and over?

Offender: I believe it all started out as far as being confused and not understanding about the breakup between my mother and father. Because I love them both.

Agent: And that goes back to what age?
Offender: Seven.

In another case the murderer stated:

> When my parents were together, I could go to either of them. Then for some reason they started having problems with each other. So it got to the point where Pop wasn't home most of the time . . . That's where my problems started because even though they were separated, I never lost the love for my Pops either, and Mom really didn't appreciate that.

Given the departure of the father from the family, it is not surprising that the dominant parent to the offender during childhood and adolescence was the mother (for twenty-one cases). Some of the offenders were able to speculate on the meaning this had in their lives, as in the following case:

> The breakup of the family started progressing into something I just didn't understand. I always thought families should always be together. I think that was part of the downfall . . . I had no male supervision. My father and my stepfather never said whether I did anything good or bad. They left that totally up to my mom. We'd go out on boats and cycle riding and stuff like that, but when it came down to the serious aspects of parent-child relationship, never anything there from the male side . . . My brother was eighteen and moved in with my real dad. I was ten and stayed with my mother.

Only nine murderers said the father was the dominant parent, and two said both parents had shared the parenting role. The fact that twenty-two (63 percent) families remained intact and thirteen (37 percent) merged into reconstituted families suggests that absence alone does not account for the boy's sense of noninvolvement with his father. Rather, the lack of ability on the part of the father to project a positive sense of himself to his son or to express positive regard for the boy himself set the stage for an empty existence for the boy and the man he subsequently became. The psychological and social disengagement was experienced deeply by the boy. When this compounded an already ambivalent relationship with the mother, early signs of negative human attachment or the disregarding of potential positive ones might have been expected.

The low level of attachment among family members is indicated by the murderers' evaluations of the emotional quality of their family relationships. Perhaps the most interesting result was that most offenders said that they did not have a satisfactory relationship with the father and that the relationship with the mother was highly ambivalent in emotional quality. Sixteen of the men reported cold or uncaring relationships with their mothers, and twenty-six reported similar relationships with their fathers. The following observation of father-son interaction was noted in one murderer's record:

> According to the defendant's mother, the natural father remained in the picture after the divorce and had a consummate hatred toward his two young sons. On one occasion, this man struck the [offender] with a glass container when the [offender] was less than one year old. Another time, the father was stopped just short of choking the boy when the child was about four years old. Still another time, the father was observed shooting at his preschool son playing in the yard. The mother states that because of the dangers posed by her first husband, she and her second husband were forced to move frequently.

Concerning attachment to siblings, twenty offenders had no older brothers and seventeen had no older sisters. Thus, in terms of having a strong role model during formative years, these men lacked older siblings to fill in for parental deficiencies. Rather, they had to compete with younger siblings in an insufficient social environment. As one man said, "I was jealous of my [younger] sister as a kid. When we graduated in eighth grade, I got a sleeping bag and she got a grand piano." Or in the reconstituted families after divorce and remarriage, the offenders had their sibling order changed because of the new stepbrothers and stepsisters.

This lack of attachment carried over to peer relationships. Murderers often characterized themselves as shy or loners. They did not win the popularity contests in school; people generally did not remember them. A defense lawyer for one of the murderers realized that he and his client had been in the same high school class, but the lawyer remembered nothing about his client as an adolescent.

Formative Events

Increasing attention is being paid to the specific psychological reaction patterns of children experiencing both direct and indirect childhood trauma. Direct trauma includes experiencing physical and sexual abuse. Indirect trauma includes witnessing or observing disturbing interactive experiences. Pynoos and Eth (1985) identify common features found in the child's witness of rape, suicide, and murder as including the distressing intrusion of violent or mutilating imagery, the challenge to the child's own impulse control, the task of assigning human accountability, and the potentially debilitating effects of unexplored revenge fantasies.

History of Parental Discipline

Compounding the murderers' limited opportunities for positive attachments were their perceptions of parental discipline. Frequently they reported discipline as unfair, hostile, inconsistent, and abusive. The following example illustrates one murderer's linkage of parental discipline to his homicidal behavior:

> I believe what caused the rapes on the street was when I was a kid I never had a dad around. He was gone. My stepdad and me never got along. My half brothers and sisters could do things that I'd get whipped for because he said my mother was setting a bad example for me. That made me hate him. If those women weren't by themselves, that would stop a lot of rapes and murders.

Many of the murderers felt they were not dealt with fairly by adults throughout their formative years. The following quote from a serial murderer summarizes some of these feelings, with his violent thoughts linking family experiences to the world at large. These thoughts become fertile ground for revenge.

> See, if I had my way, you guys would never have grown up or become FBI agents. I wanted the whole world to kick off when I was about nine or ten. I didn't want my family to break up. I loved them both. There was a lot of fighting and that had me crying watching it at night. They divorced. I've got two sisters and my mother treated me like a third daughter, telling me what a rotten father I have. I'm supposed to be identifying with my dad and I never did. I've got an older sister that beat up on me a lot—five years older. I got a younger sister that lies on both of us and gets us punished. I had the instinct to feel like I'm getting a rotten deal.

History of Abuse and Neglect

Personal histories of abuse and neglect were present during the development of these murderers. Neglect was often subtle. For example, in one case, the boy was an only child of a first-generation American family, whose parents operated a small store that required their working seven days a week, twelve hours a day. The boy was left to the care of various family members or neighbors. It is suspected that he was sexually molested during this time by a caretaker. Further examination of this component of neglect and abuse in these murderers revealed something of its impact.

There was evidence of both psychological and physical abuse in the childhood histories. Psychological abuse was noted in twenty-three cases and generally included examples in which the child felt humiliated. In one case, the subject reported how he stopped bed-wetting at age sixteen.

> *Offender*: When we'd go places and I'd wet the bed, I felt ashamed of it
> . . . When they started to make fun of me, I quit.
> *Agent*: Who did?
> *Offender*: The whole family. That was their way of breaking me of doing it.

Physical abuse was reported in childhood histories for thirteen offenders. As one man reported, "My parents solved family disagreements by shouting and physical beating."

Sexual Experiences

We were particularly interested in the presence of sexual abuse in the background of the murderers, as it has been suggested in other studies as an important factor in later sexually violent behavior.

The individual development characteristics of the thirty-six murderers showed the presence of sexual problems and violent experiences in childhood and adolescence, and a dominant sexual fantasy life (see table 2–3). Because witnessing sexual activity/violence can have strong impact on a child, we asked offenders about these experiences. In nine cases, men reported witnessing sexual violence; in nine cases, men described witnessing disturbing sexual activity of a parent; in eleven cases, murderers reported witnessing disturbing sexual activity of other family members or friends ("I walked in on my girlfriend and another male friend naked").

The murderers were asked also about histories of sexual injury (that is, surgery) or disease (that is, sexually transmitted diseases). Six murderers reported contracting a sexual disease as an adolescent ("After my first experience with a hooker in the service, I got the clap") and other incidents, which included self-mutilation to the genitals as punishment for "bad

Table 2–3
Childhood Sexual Experiences

Experience	Number/Total	Percent
Witnessing sexual violence	9/26	35
Witnessing disturbing sex (parents)	9/26	35
Witnessing disturbing sex (other adults, friends)	11/26	42
Sexual injury or disease	9/25	28
Sexually stressful events	19/26	73
Childhood sexual abuse	12/28	43
Voyeurism	20/28	71
Pornography	25/31	81
Fetishism	21/29	72
Rape fantasies admitted	22/36	61
First rape fantasies occurred between ages twelve and fourteen	11/22	50
Consenting sex	20/36	56
No peer consenting sex	16/36	44
Sexual incompetence	14/32	44
Sexual aversion	13/30	43
Autoerotic practices	22/28	79

thoughts" and, in one case, shaving the hair from his body because it made him "feel dirty." Sexually stressful situations were present for nineteen offenders and included negative parental reaction to masturbation, verbal assaults on the gender identity of the boy, and/or observing the adolescent boy engaging in homosexual activity with peers.

When questioned about prior sexual abuse, twelve, or 43 percent, of those murderers responding (twenty-eight) indicated such abuse in childhood (ages one to twelve); nine, or 32 percent, were abused in adolescence (ages thirteen to eighteen); and ten, or 37 percent, as adults (over age 18). These forced and pressured direct sexual traumas occurred within the family ("I slept with my mother as a young child," "I was abused by my father from age fourteen," "My stepbrother tried to rape me") as well as outside the family ("I got picked up downtown one night by some guy when I was around seven or eight"), or as adults in a prison setting.

The adult sexual performance of the murderers often remained at highly visual and autoerotic, or sexually self-stimulating, levels. Although twenty men were able to state an age of first consenting sex to orgasm, they did not report extensive, peer-related sexual histories. For example, one man, who had an extensive history of masturbating to adolescent deviant fantasies, believed himself in his last year of college "to be a bit old to be a virgin" and, in response, began visiting prostitutes.

As adults, almost half of the offenders reported an aversion to sex. Sexual concerns and problems acknowledged in interviews predominated in more than three-quarters of the offenders. More than half described themselves as ignorant of sexual issues; almost 70 percent felt sexually incompetent; 56 percent experienced sexual dysfunction; 30 percent expressed concern with genital size. Many were concerned with other sexual problems ("I don't think I'm like other people"); some men preferred sex only with dead women. The interviewers suspected that of the sixteen offenders who did not report an age for first consenting sex, most never experienced consenting "normal" sex.

An analysis of the relationship between prior sexual abuse in childhood or adolescence and sexual problems shows that those sexually abused (in order of magnitude of difference) were more likely to report sexual conflicts (92 percent versus 40 percent; $p = .01$), sexual dysfunction (69 percent versus 50 percent), and sexual incompetence (77 percent versus 60 percent). There was little or no difference on sexual ignorance.

The strong reliance on visual sexual stimuli was noted in the offenders' ranking of sexual interests. Pornography ranked highest (81 percent, or twenty-five of thirty-one responses), followed by compulsive masturbation (79 percent), fetishism (72 percent, or twenty-one of twenty-nine responses), and voyeurism (71 percent, or twenty of twenty-eight responses). A smaller number reported bondage sex, indecent exposure, sexual contact with animals, making obscene telephone calls, rubbing against others, and cross-dressing.

An analysis of the relationship between sexual abuse in childhood and adolescence and sexual activities indicates that those sexually abused were (in order of magnitude of difference) more likely to engage in sexual contact with animals (40 percent versus 8 percent; p = .06), bondage sex (55 percent versus 23 percent), fetishism (83 percent versus 57 percent), obscene phone calls (36 percent versus 15 percent), indecent exposure (36 percent versus 21 percent), pornography (92 percent versus 79 percent), rubbing against others (27 percent versus 15 percent), and cross-dressing (18 percent versus 7 percent). There was little difference or no difference noted in the area of voyeurism.

Three offenders self-reported involvement in sexual asphyxial practices from age 12 through adulthood. In one case, the man described his early sexual fantasies (starting at age 4 to 5) and how they were intensified by his piercing his abdomen with such instruments as pins, small knife blades, and fishhooks while he was masturbating. One time when he was about age thirteen, in making a suicidal gesture, he shot himself in the abdomen with a .38 caliber pistol.

Role of Childhood Sexual Abuse and Family Relationships

The murderers with sexual abuse histories were compared with murderers without sexual abuse histories and the following family background variables: (1) the emotional-social quality of the subject's relationship with his mother; (2) the emotional-social quality of the subject's relationship with his father; (3) the dominant parent in the rearing home; (4) the socioeconomic level of the rearing home; (5) the continuity of the family residence; and (6) family structure. For most of these analyses, data is available for twenty-four to twenty-eight sexual murderers.

Relationship with Mother. Of twelve murderers who had been sexually victimized either as a child or adolescent, 42 percent report that the emotional-social quality of the relationship with the mother during early home life was poor. This proportion is larger than that reported by murderers who were not abused (21 percent). See table 2–4.

Relationship with Father. Of twelve murderers with childhood sexual abuse histories, 92 percent report that the emotional-social quality of the relationship with the father during early home life was poor. This is significantly different (p = .002) from the proportion reported by murderers who report no sexual abuse. See table 2–4.

Table 2–4
Sexual Abuse by Factors Related to Family Environment and Structure

Item	Sex Abuse (%)	No Sex Abuse (%)
Relationship with mother (n = 26)		
Warm, average, variable	58.3 (12)[a]	78.6 (14)
Cold, distant, hostile	41.7 (12)	21.4 (14)
Relationship with father (n = 25)[b]		
Warm, average, variable	8.3 (12)	69.2 (13)
Cold, distant, hostile	91.7 (12)	30.8 (13)
Socioeconomic status (n = 28)		
Advantaged, average	46.2 (13)	66.7 (15)
Marginal, submarginal	53.8 (13)	33.3 (15)
Dominant parent (n = 24)		
Father	27.3 (11)	30.8 (13)
Mother	72.7 (11)	69.2 (13)
Continuity of residence (n = 28)		
Stable through development	30.8 (13)	33.3 (15)
Occasional instability	46.2 (13)	46.7 (15)
Chronic instability	23.1 (13)	20.1 (15)
Family structure (n = 26)[c]		
Intact	53.8 (13)	84.6 (13)
Reconstituted	46.2 (13)	15.4 (13)

[a]A number in parenthesis = total number in sexually abused or nonsexually abused category.
[b]$p < .01$
[c]$p = .09$

Socioeconomic Level. The socioeconomic level of the murderer's rearing home was indicated by whether the home was average/advantaged or marginal/submarginal (sometimes on welfare). The results indicate that sexually abused murderers were more likely than those not abused to report that their rearing home was marginal or submarginal (54 percent versus 33 percent). See table 2–4.

Dominant Parent. Sexually abused murderers were no more likely than those not abused to report either the mother or the father as the dominant parent. See table 2–4.

Continuity of Family Residence. The results show that murderers with histories of sexual abuse were no more likely to grow up in families that are chronically unstable in terms of stability of residence (23 percent versus 20 percent). See table 2–4.

Family Structure. Twenty-six murderers described the structure of their families as either intact (two parents present) or as reconstituted (one parent plus stepparent). Murderers with histories of sexual abuse were more likely to report a reconstituted family structure than were murderers without such histories (46 percent versus 15 percent). See table 2–4.

In summary our findings support Hirschi's (1969) argument that attachment to conventional persons, commitment to conventional pursuits, involvement in conventional activities, and belief in conventional values reduce the likelihood that a youth will engage in delinquent conduct. Hirschi found that attachment to parent is strongly associated with resistance to delinquency.

Our study also suggests that instead of developing peer-related interests and activities, the murderers as adolescents retreated into their own sexually violent fantasy worlds. One begins to see how an early fantasy pattern used to cope with childhood abuse and unsatisfactory family life might turn a child away from reality and into a private world of violence where the child can exert control. The control of the fantasy becomes crucial to the child and later to the man. However, these are not fantasies of escape to something better, as is often seen in children recovering from sexual assaults and abusive treatment. These men did not overcompensate for the aggression in their early lives by idyllic thinking or creative interests. Rather, their energies were funneled into fantasies of aggression and mastery over other people, suggesting a secret, projected repetition of their own abuse and an identification with the aggressor. As one murderer said, "Nobody bothered to find out what my problem was, and nobody knew about the fantasy world."

Behavioral Indicators

The murderers' behaviors and experiences at various stages in their lives are, we believe, important indicators of what later motivated them to kill. As part of our study, we looked at these factors, which we call behavioral indicators of actions toward others, in connection with how they may have contributed to the men's violent acts. Our analysis of behavioral indicators used a checklist of symptoms and behavioral experience (see table 2–5). The checklist is based on a standard list of indicators used in psychosocial research and includes indicators of thinking patterns and behaviors derived from the FBI profilers' understanding of criminal behavior. However, readers should keep in mind that many of these behavioral symptoms have no consistent definitions or ways of measurement. For example, there is no method of measuring a pattern of masturbation.

Childhood. An analysis of twenty-four checklist items indicates that over 50 percent of the murderers reported the following present in childhood: daydreaming (82 percent), compulsive masturbation (82 percent), isolation (71

Table 2–5
Frequency of Reported Behavior Indicators in Childhood, Adolescence, and Adulthood for Sexual Murderers

	Frequency					
	Childhood		Adolescence		Adulthood	
Behavior	*n	(%)	*n	(%)	*n	(%)
Daydreaming	28	82	27	81	27	81
Compulsive masturbation	28	82	28	82	27	81
Isolation	28	71	26	77	26	73
Chronic lying	28	71	28	75	28	68
Enuresis	22	68	20	60	20	15
Rebelliousness	27	67	25	84	25	72
Nightmares	24	67	22	68	21	52
Destroying property	26	58	26	62	23	35
Fire setting	25	56	25	52	25	28
Stealing	27	56	27	81	25	56
Cruelty to children	28	54	28	64	27	44
Poor body image	27	52	27	63	26	62
Temper tantrums	27	48	26	50	25	44
Sleep problems	23	48	22	50	22	50
Assaultive to adults	25	38	25	84	28	86
Phobias	24	38	23	43	24	50
Running away	28	36	26	46	26	11
Cruelty to animals	28	36	26	46	25	36
Accident prone	24	29	22	32	22	27
Headaches	21	29	21	33	22	45
Destroying possessions	25	28	23	35	23	35
Eating problems	26	27	25	36	26	35
Convulsions	26	19	24	21	23	13
Self-mutilation	26	19	24	21	25	32

n = Number of subjects with data.

percent), chronic lying (71 percent), enuresis (bedwetting) (68 percent), rebelliousness (67 percent), nightmares (67 percent), destroying property (58 percent), fire setting (56 percent), stealing (56 percent), cruelty to children (54 percent), and poor body image (52 percent).

Adolescence. Over 50 percent of murderers reported various behaviors present during adolescence: assaultive actions toward adults (84 percent), rebelliousness (84 percent), compulsive masturbation (82 percent), stealing (81 percent), daydreaming (81 percent), isolation (77 percent), chronic lying (75 percent), nightmares (68 percent), poor body image (63 percent), cruelty to children (64 percent), destroying property (62 percent), enuresis (60 percent), and fire setting (52 percent). Almost half of the murderers (46 percent) described adolescent cruelty to animals.

Adulthood. Of the twenty-four checklist items, the following behaviors were reported present during adulthood by over 50 percent of the murderers: assaultive actions toward adults (86 percent), daydreaming (81 percent), compulsive masturbation (81 percent), isolation (73 percent), rebelliousness (72 percent), chronic lying (68 percent), poor body image (62 percent), stealing (56 percent), and nightmares (52 percent).

For descriptive purposes, we use the terms *internal* and *external* to classify the behavioral indicators. *Internal behaviors* include thinking patterns and experiences within or unique to the individual. The internal behaviors most consistently reported over the murderers' three developmental periods were daydreaming, compulsive masturbation, and isolation. *External behaviors* are those overt actions that can be observed by others. The most reported external behaviors include chronic lying, rebelliousness, stealing, cruelty to children, and assaultive actions toward adults.

Interviews with thirty-six convicted sexual murderers provided insights, particularly in terms of the criminals' inner, private worlds. As was discussed in the previous chapter, we found this world to contain attitudes, beliefs, and justifications that partially explain how murder can be committed. These attitudes and beliefs encourage fantasies that do not link the subject in any positive, sympathetic, or empathetic way with the victim. Rather, the murderer constantly uses fantasy to develop constructs and beliefs to justify violent acts and to discount its impact on the victim.

Outcome: Performance

Examination of the performance behavior of these murderers revealed another paradox. Despite their intelligence and potential in many areas, their performance in academics, employment, and military service was often poor. In all of these areas, expectations did not match potential (see table 2–6). Many offenders felt a sense of failure beginning at a young age. It appeared that what ultimately compensated for poor performance was fantasy, in which all factors could be controlled.

Although most of the offenders had the intelligence to perform well in school, several of them repeated elementary grades. One murderer, whose IQ was tested at 112, stated the following:

> I failed the second grade because I was uneducable. [My parents] wanted to take me completely out of school. They wanted me to stay home and work on the farm. But then I skipped the third grade because I passed the entire second grade and went on and excelled in many areas and dropped out in others. I excelled in math but couldn't spell.

Table 2–6
Performance Characteristics

Performance	Positive/Total Responses	Percent
Academic		
Grade repetition	11/30	36
Did not complete high school	17/36	47
Poor performance in high school	15/25	60
Employment (prior to murder)		
Steady employment	7/35	20
Unsteady employment	24/35	69
Unemployed	4/35	11
Military		
Criminal record in military	4/14	29
Honorable/general discharge	6/14	42
Undesirable/dishonorable/medical discharge	8/14	58

Only one-third did average or better in high school, with twenty-two achieving fair to poor academic performance. The majority did not finish high school. In addition, school failure was frequently mentioned by the men, suggesting that they related this early failure to their sense of inadequacy. As one murderer said:

> My education kept me back. I went to the penitentiary and one of the inmates was a college professor. He taught me more about reading than any man. He took the time and helped me with my vowels. He sat down and didn't treat me like some adolescent, dumb animal. He talked to me on a straight level.

In addition to looking at academic performance, we examined job performance. Although the murderers had the intelligence to perform skilled jobs, most offenders had poor work histories in unskilled positions. Only 20 percent had ever held steady jobs. For example, one offender had the following sequential work history for the three years prior to his apprehension for three murders: butcher (eight months), clerk/delivery boy (five months), various short-term jobs (eight months), radio repairman (three months), unemployed (ten months), television repairman (two months).

Military performance was also poor. Only four of the fourteen men who had been in the military service received honorable discharges. One of the men honorably discharged dates the onset of his deviant fantasies to the time following his military experience:

> My early adolescent deviant fantasies are importantly different than those following my return from Vietnam. I was only the victim in those of adolescence; the deviant fantasy expressions of rage and anger did not have external objects, women and society, until after Vietnam.

Two men received general discharges, three were dishonorably discharged, three had undesirable discharges and two received medical discharges. One of the discharges was a result of "intense murderous assaultive feelings toward women." In this case, military officials believed that because military stress was likely to cause the man's acting out of these feelings he should be discharged. Tragically, these feelings were later acted out through his murder of several women.

Conclusion

In evaluating the social environment and childhood formative events of the thirty-six murderers, it is helpful to think of them in terms of how they may have formed a foundation for later criminal behavior. Although the personal strengths of the murderers are usually positive attributes for successful people, they did not turn the men away from murder. Instead, the offenders were preoccupied with family and personal problems. Were these problems sufficient to lead to adult homicidal behavior? Such causal links are difficult to substantiate; nevertheless, it appears reasonable that the ineffective social environment extends to include outside interveners such as teachers, juvenile authorities, and clinicians who receive referrals to evaluate troubled children. It is noteworthy that twenty-five of the thirty-six men had some type of psychiatric assessment or confinement as a child or as an adolescent. Many people, including family, ignored the boy's behavior, were nonintervening and nonprotective, and supported the developing cognitive distortions (for example, boys will be boys).

In time, thinking patterns containing negative attitudes and beliefs developed; these became an ultimate justification for violent acts toward others.

Notes

Hirschi, T. *Causes of Delinquency*. Los Angeles: University of California Press, 1969.

Pynoos, R.S., and Eth, S. Children traumatized by witnessing acts of personal violence: Homicide, rape, or suicidal behavior. In S. Eth and R.S. Pynoos (eds.) *Post-Traumatic Stress Disorders in Children*. Washington, D.C.: American Psychiatric Press, 1985, 17–44.

3

Preoccupation with Murder: Patterned Responses

The thirty-six sexual murderers in our study, replying to the fundamental question of what triggered their first murders, revealed that, as a group, they were (1) aware of their long-standing preoccupation and preference for a very active fantasy life, and (2) devoted to violent, sexualized thoughts and fantasies. Most of these fantasies, prior to the first murder, focused on killing. This contrasts with the fantasies that evolved *after* the first murder; these advanced levels of fantasies often focused on perfecting various phases of the murder.

The role of thought and fantasy in the motive and behavior of suspects is a newly identified factor in violent crimes, especially in sexual murders. In the last twenty years, the role of sadistic fantasy has been explored in several studies (Brittain 1970; Reinhardt 1975; Revitch 1965, 1980; West et al. 1978), with MacCulloch and colleagues (1983) suggesting that sadistic acts and fantasy are linked and that fantasy drives behavior.

In analyzing the data we obtained through interviews with the murderers, we attempted to link our quantifiable findings with indications from the murderers themselves of aggressive thoughts and fantasies directed toward sexualized death. The findings suggest that these thought patterns were established early and existed in a context of social isolation.

The central role that fantasy plays in the thinking patterns of these men is noted in one of the subject's statements: "All my life I knew I was going to end up killing." It also was observed in the statement of a parent who, after her son was convicted of fetish robberies, feared the outcome of her son's moodiness and isolation would be "something really terrible and tragic."

Current understanding of how thinking patterns help maintain behavior patterns (Beck 1976), combined with investigations of sadistic fantasies (Brittain 1970; MacCulloch et al. 1983; Ressler et al. 1985), serve as foundations for our hypothesis that the motivation for sexual murder is based on fantasy.

Sections reprinted with permission from Sage Publications: Burgess, A.W., Hartman, C.R., Ressler, R.K., Douglas, J.E. and McCormack A. Sexual Homicide: a Motivational Model. *Journal of Interpersonal Violence*, 1 1986, 251–72.

The Role of Fantasy

Murder is compensatory in the fantasy world of the murderer. Because these offenders believe they are entitled to whatever they want and that they live in an unjust world, fantasy emerges as an important escape and a place in which to express emotion and control regarding other human beings. The preference for fantasy and its centrality in the life of these men marks it as a private and powerful reality.

One murderer stated, "Murder is very real. . . . You have to do all the practical things of surviving." This murderer contrasts the act of murder and what follows with his long-standing fantasy of violence and murder. His statement communicated that once the murder has been committed, the offender must cope with the reality of his actions. This sets into motion further development of his fantasy world. This phenomenon will be discussed in chapters 4 and 5 on the phases of murder.

What is the origin of the thought to kill? Thoughts are understood as ideas that have been processed from incoming stimuli received through the organization and functioning of the brain (Gardner 1985). Daydreaming has been defined as any cognitive activity representing a shift of attention away from a task (Singer 1966). A fantasy, as we define it, is an elaborate thought with great preoccupation, anchored in emotion and having origins in daydreams. A fantasy is generally experienced as thoughts, although the individual may be aware of images, feelings, and internal dialogue. Some people may be conscious only of thoughts, whereas others are conscious only of feelings. Fantasy is a normal way for adults as well as children to obtain and maintain control of an imagined situation.

However, the level of fantasy development may differ among people and is generally based on the individual's ability to identify certain thoughts as daydreams, to articulate their content, and retrospectively to recall this content. Singer (1966) observed that 96 percent of adults report that they daydream several times a day, and Beres (1961) noted that fantasy may either substitute or prepare for action. For various groups of people, fantasies may be sadistic (MacCulloch et al. 1983). It is not known how many people activate their sadistic fantasies and in what context this may occur, but Schlesinger and Revitch (1980) caution that once the fantasy builds to a point where inner stress is unbearable, the way for action is prepared.

Whereas psychological motives for violent behavior are usually conceptualized in the literature as having roots beginning with trauma, insult, and/or overstimulation in early childhood, our thesis is different. We theorize that these men are motivated to murder by way of their thinking. Over time, their thinking patterns emerged from or were influenced by early life experiences. For example, a child abused by an adult caretaker begins to think about being hit every time an adult comes near him, dwelling on the hitting. He may imagine (fantasize) about someone coming to help him by beating up the adult. This thinking pattern may bring relief, because someone has protected him in his fantasy. In addition, while being abused the child may psychologically remove himself from the pain. He may pride himself on his control over pain in the face of abuse; for example, while being beaten he does not flinch or blink. This thinking pattern gives the child a sense of control and, as a result, tension is relieved. The child can increase or decrease terror with different levels of arousal through fantasy. Development of this type of thinking pattern does *not* necessarily mean a child will grow up to be an abuser; our example illustrates the role of fantasy and its development.

In this section we document the importance of thoughts and fantasy as framework for and justification for killing. There is an early onset of fantasies that express aggression and create sadistic ideas. These fantasies are realized in private and peer play. Some take a repetitive pattern expressed later in patterns of murder.

Early Fantasy Development

Early expression of fantasy development is noted in children's play. As the child matures his use of language increases with the fantasy. Childhood fantasies are usually positive and aimed at promoting the child's learning through the repetitive thinking and rehearsal of actions. What is remarkable in the interviews of offenders is an absence of recounting of positive childhood fantasies. It is not clear whether such fantasies were actually absent or whether the early positive resources of the offender have been lost in the well of negative perspectives and behaviors. In discussing childhood fantasy development it is important to remember that not all children respond to their environment with violent fantasies and that not all children who fantasize violence act out and end up as killers. What the offenders indicate is the commitment to their fantasies and the secret reality of the fantasies for them. In the following example, school officials were aware of the pervasive nature of a child's daydreaming, but no one pursued the content of that daydreaming with the boy.

> I felt guilty for having those thoughts [toward family] and submerged them and built up lots of hostility and then it gets off into fantasy . . . They should have noticed it at school, so excessive was my daydreaming that it was always in my report cards . . . I was dreaming about wiping out the whole school.

Early Sexualization of Fantasy

Evidence for childhood sexual fantasies in the lives of the thirty-six murderers was gained from parents and caretakers as well as from the offenders. Play patterns were interpreted as the expression of dominant fantasies. Some offenders recalled latency age and pubescent fantasies and play activities. Parents provided information about preschool fantasies. In one case, a mother recalled finding her three-year-old son with one end of a string tied to his penis and the other end shut in a bureau drawer. This behavior suggests that this was not the first such incident and indicates the repetitive fantasy around the sexual and autoerotic behavior; it also seems most likely that the behavior was initially introduced and taught by an older person—in this case we believe it was a babysitter. Thus, one sees the dominance of the fantasy in a very young child carried over to the child's play without the babysitter present.

Aggressive Components of Early Fantasy

When the murderer is asked to describe his early favorite play activities, especially in the latency age period, he reveals a repetitive acting out of the core aggressive fantasy. This repetition is not just a mental construct. When we talk about childhood fantasies, we are talking about a fantasy so dominant that it is a persistent theme in the play of the child with other children or with themselves. The repetition can be the direct expression of an original violation or assault. For example, one subject at age fifteen would drag younger boys into the bathroom of the residential facility and force oral and anal sex on them, reenacting his own victimization at age ten but with his role reversed to the victimizer. He did not consciously connect his behavior with his own earlier assaults. Sexualized rituals of adolescence were not associated with the prior victimization. Rather, though at times bizarre, the rituals were manifest secondary attempts at mastery and control over people and types of situations.

Another offender as an adolescent openly masturbated in his home, especially in front of his sisters, using their underwear in his masturbation rituals. This behavior represented the hyperarousal state derived from his memory of his childhood victimization by an adult. He describes the punitive response from his mother to masturbatory behavior and his rejection by family members. Even upon recall, his pain and hurt at their ridicule was clear. He appeared oblivious to the inappropriate nature of his acts and instead remains offended by their response, feeling rejected and that they were intolerant and unfair.

From our interviews with offenders, we began to glimpse the high degree of egocentricity in their fantasy and play, which incorporate other children and family members as mere extensions of their inner world. There is little insight into the impact of their behavior on others. In one case, the twelve-year-old subject would play "gas chamber" repeatedly with his sister. This game required the sister to tie him up in a chair, throw an imaginary switch and when "gas" was introduced, the subject would drop over on the floor, writhe convulsively, and "die." This game combined a sexual and death theme fantasy.

The childhood onset of fetish interests is also noted in the subjects. Several subjects as very young boys of age five or six described strong interest and attraction to high-heeled shoes, female underwear, and rope. There is an awareness on the part of the subject of the advanced, repetitive sexual interest in these fetish items into adolescence and adulthood. Further, when the subjects began to murder, these took on importance in ritualized aspects of their murders.

Early Expressions of Sexual and Aggressive Fantasy

Early fantasies often give rise to behavior tryouts that are precursors to criminal behavior (MacCulloch 1983). These precursor behaviors have the capacity to move the child into pain-inflicting acts. These behaviors break through in subtle as well as overt ways. They may break through (in such behaviors as bullying younger children or putting pins in the rug for a sister to walk on), or they may be noted in the offender's earliest encounters with law enforcement. Although such encounters are often dismissed as adolescent adjustment problems, they may be evidence of an escalation in aggressive acts toward others.

Especially illustrative of such escalation of fantasy expression is the previously cited example of the three-year-old boy who was observed by his mother with his penis tied to a bureau drawer. As an adolescent, he was found by his parents in the bathtub practicing autoerotic asphyxia with his penis and neck tied to the cross-bar of the faucets. At age fourteen his parents took him to a psychiatrist after noticing rope burns on his neck. At age seventeen this same subject abducted a young teenager at gunpoint, took her to a deserted area where he kept her all night, and released her in the morning. The girl reported the situation and the adolescent was apprehended and released. The charge on his record was "girl trouble." The acts of aggression toward the victim included intimidation through showing a weapon and forcing her compliance in accompanying him. Of importance is the offender's shift in the object of aggression from himself to an easily controlled victim (a younger, smaller person who was controlled through a weapon). Not until late adolescence, when the offender began following women, confronting them with a knife, binding them, and fondling them was the offender sent to prison. After release from prison, his crimes escalated to the murder of three young women by asphyxia.

Interestingly, these early expressions of aggressive fantasies are often the more disturbing memories for the offender to reveal and are the ones he seeks to avoid discussing. We suspect that he realizes that he had control over these behaviors and that he was aware that he had crossed the line. That is, he learned that he could act violently and that he could kill with impunity because he has gotten away with these acts without anything really happening to him. He was not controlled by authority. The power of life and death and the realization that one decides whether to control, injure, or kill is a very early experience for these men.

Sadistic Behavior.   The early aggressive behaviors may be acted out first toward animals. Some murderers described childhood histories of sadistic behavior toward animals. In one case, the murderer as a young boy had acquired the nickname "Doc," apparently from his fondness of slitting open the stomachs of cats and observing how far they could run before they died. In another case, the murderer responded to a question about aggressive acts toward animals by telling both of his killing a cat and of his experience of losing his pet dog:

> I killed a cat once . . . I can't tell you why. I was just mad and the cat came at the wrong time and I strangled this cat. It's the only animal I ever killed. . . . I had a dog when I was young and somebody fed it ground glass and we had to put it to sleep. I was very shook up over that. It was the only dog I ever had.

This example illustrates several points: the displacement of anger to an animal; identification with the aggressor who fed ground glass to his dog; feelings of distress. When linked to the offender's deviant behaviors, this vignette illustrates the repetitive method used to torture and then kill (extracting fingernails and strangulation murders of women) and his statement of remorse after killing. He admits to the agents that he knows he will continue to kill, and though feelings of remorse are not a deterrent to killing, he still experiences remorse after the murders.

In another case, the murderer gives an example of blaming a cat for a situation (rather than what he did or did not do in the situation) and how this escalated into cruelty to animals:

> One time I found a kitten and it was raining. The kitten was shivering and I brought it home. About two weeks later the house was full of fleas. From there I just started hating cats.

When asked what happened to the cat he replied:

> I don't know what happened. My father thought I did something to it, and I thought my father did something to it because I came home from school one day and the cat just wasn't there . . . That's when I got to tying a cherry bomb to the cat's leg, light it, and watch the cat run down the street . . . Made a lot of one-legged cats.

The dominant thinking and play patterns of offenders are very aggressive and violent from childhood through adulthood. Offenders are aware of the intensity and elaboration of their fantasies. Each act that moves closer to the expression of intense emotion becomes incorporated into their imaginations. Acts fuel more elaborate and violent thoughts. What might appear to us to be an abrupt change of character in suddenly killing a cat or a person proves to be based on much more conscious and preconscious activity as well as on prior preparatory acts. This process reinforces the centrality of violence and murder in the lives of these men. Violence and killing are now natural and justified acts in their lives.

The sadistic behavior may extend beyond animals to other objects or to peers. The following instance demonstrates the power of early symbolic play. One subject connected his murderous acts to the adolescent behavior of decapitating his sister's dolls: "I used to do my sister's dolls that way when I was a kid . . . just yanked the head off her Barbie dolls." In another case, the offender described his actions toward a boy his own age: "When I was little, I got in an argument with a kid and chased him with a hatchet."

The time between the sadistic behavior toward animals and acting out murderous fantasies by killing a person was, in one case, quite short. The offender killed his grandparents when he was an adolescent. As an adult he does not connect his violent fantasies with his prior acts of killing animals and then killing his grandparents. Though he is not conscious of why he killed his grandparents, his unconscious associations are revealed in the interview.

> My stepbrother and I are running around the yard with sticks chasing the giant bluejay, trying to snuff him. He's running around squawking and we've got him wounded and we're trying to kill him before my stepdad finds out, because he'd skin us for snuffing his fine feathered friends. And my grandparents were the same way about small furry animals or the feathery animals, so I snuffed everything that flew, when I could get my gun trained on them.

The offender describes the aggressive and violent pseudoplay activity with a stepbrother in killing birds, an act he knows will enrage the stepfather. His use of the verb *skin*, which is usually used in reference to animals, to predict an action he believes his stepfather would take is revealing in terms of the language content of the fantasy.

This murderer went on to reveal that he was given a gun when he was twelve. He was required by his grandparents to give it up to them when he was fourteen because of indiscriminate shooting behavior. He subsequently shot and killed his grandparents. He is able to link the decision to kill with the use of a gun, but he does not link his grandparents' murder to their insistence that he not have a gun. The following excerpt from his interview as an adult demonstrates his lack of conscious insight into his overt violent behavior with his gun:

Agent: Do you think there is any correlation between a familiarity with guns and being able to kill?

Offender: It sure helps. It becomes an attribute.

Agent: From doing it once or twice?

Offender: No, I think it is independent until after you decide you can start killing people. Then it becomes one hell of a tool, unfortunately, just like a veteran that goes bananas.

Tragically, the grandparents take away the gun believing that that will stop the behavior rather than asking: What is going on with you that you use the gun in this way? What is in your head? We speculate that the murderer did not want his inner world exposed and he killed to keep the private fantasy intact. He is only aware of making a decision to kill people. He does not link the precursors to the decision. He only knows and states that he decided early that he would kill. This dramatic example demonstrates the early power of the boy's violent imagination and his strong desire to keep his thoughts private. When he was released from prison after serving time as an adolescent for his grandparents' murder, he knew he was going to kill again. Shortly after his release he began to murder women.

It appears that the early sexual aggression is established in the child's mind and is reinforced in ritualistic play with other children. There is an elaboration of the fantasy, and acting out becomes more circumspect. The pattern of aggressive arousal is acted out through play and, later, directly toward people and other forms of life, usually without fear of adult disapproval or restriction. These men learn early that they can get away with violent behavior. In essence they see nothing wrong with what they are doing. Many of them emphasize that they are doing exactly what everyone else thinks of doing.

Self-victimizing Behavior. Not only was sadistic behavior noted in childhood histories of the murderers we studied, but also self-victimizing behavior (sometimes called masochistic behavior).

One offender's early childhood fantasies indicated a fixation on his internal organs. At age five (a critical age for gender identification), he described the following event. He was sleeping between his mother and his pregnant aunt when the aunt had a severe hemorrhage, losing blood in the bed, bedroom, and bathroom, where she miscarried. Also, his grandmother had a hysterectomy at about the same time. We can speculate on how the experience of sleeping with two adult females could stimulate feelings of intimacy and closeness, which were then disrupted by a puzzling and frightening scene. The visualization of the blood and the miscarriage appears to have triggered some morbid curiosity about female internal organs as well as his own. The offender further reports one childhood fantasy around this time as stimulated by seeing an ant on his belly and feeling that he wanted it to bore a hole through him. He also reports a dream of his belly's growing out three to four times his body length and of unsuccessfully attempting to saw it off. In this example one notes both the pregnancy and abortion fantasy. This theme of having both alternatives is seen in his fantasies of being both male and female and of attributing a phallus to a woman ("I fantasized Amazon women capturing me, having sex with me and spearing me during orgasm"). The confusion over identification with the female dramatically carries over into adulthood. Further, it is acted out in his murders. However, he does not connect his early thoughts with his crimes. He reports having "normal" adolescent fantasies in relation to calendar nudes and junior high school girls.

The offender recalls his abnormal fantasies only on the bathroom floor and restricts his normal masturbatory activity to his bed. One might link this dichotomy to the early childhood experience in which he slept in the bed with his mother and aunt and saw the bathroom where the aunt miscarried. The subject advances his fantasies to behavior as an adolescent and claims not to remember abnormal fantasies after high school. When he reaches adulthood, rage and aggression is noted when there is a link to sexual frustration. He describes impulsively picking up a large kitchen knife in his girlfriend's apartment just after she had been "sexually teasing," thinking of stabbing her, putting it down, and dismissing the thought from his mind. This type of penetration fantasy is noted in his offenses, in which he mutilates his victims by disembowelment. In reviewing the total sample, the question regarding masochistic acts revealed that 13 percent of the offenders (15 victims out of 118 victims) committed such an act during the offense.

Aggression into Adulthood

The adult murderers incorporate their early remembered acts of play into their murders of adults. The offender who pulled off Barbie dolls' heads beheaded his victims; the one who chased his friend with a hatchet used a hatchet in his murders. In addition, subsequent murders by these offenders saw increasing mutilation of the victims.

The familiarity and acceptance of the strong sadistic and murderous impulses, as well as of bizarre sexual assaults, carry over into adulthood in a disconcerting manner. There is little concern that these behaviors are wrong. Rather, there is regard only for the expression of personal desires. One offender described such a situation:

> In the service one time, I was pulling guard duty and watched a guy crawl through the fence. He got caught in the steel wire and [when] I laughed and he grabbed me and threatened me. He said if I said anything he would beat me up. I had a carbine, and I cocked it off, and I started shooting. I chased him

through seven tents and I was honestly trying to kill him at the time. This guy grabbed me out of nothing because I laughed at him, and he made me mad.

Fantasy Development over Time

Interviews with the murderers in our study often revealed fantasy development over time. The following illustrates how an early fantasy of one of the serial murderers continued to develop up to and beyond several murders. This childhood fantasy followed the move of the offender's bedroom to a windowless basement room and seemed to introduce him in a conscious way to the fantasy life that occupied much of his later life.

Child fantasy:

I was eight years old, having nightmares, that's when I went off into the morbid fantasy and that's when the death trip started. The devil was sharing my bedroom with me, he was living in the furnace. The furnace was there battling away in the corner with an eerie glow in the middle of the night.

Adolescent fantasy. Later in the interview, the same murderer describes his motive to kill:

I knew long before I started killing that I was going to be killing, that it was going to end up like that. The fantasies were too strong. They were going on for too long and were too elaborate.

Adult fantasy. Following the first murder, the fantasy became reality. This required a change in the structure of the fantasy in order to repeat the crime. The same murderer tells of this fantasy development:

It was almost like a black comedy of errors, the first killings, two people, it was terrible because I made three fatal errors in the first twenty-four hours. I should have been busted . . . I saw how loose I was and I tightened it up, and when it happened again and again I got tighter and tighter and there weren't any more slips.

Rape Fantasies

Many of the murderers were able to describe the importance of a fantasy life in their early development. For nineteen of the thirty-six murderers who responded to a question about the age at which they began to fantasize about rape, the answers range from five to twenty-five years old. The results of a comparison of murderers with a sexual abuse history shows that murderers reporting childhood sexual abuse (11) began to fantasize at an earlier age than did those not reporting abuse (8), or ages 11.6 years versus 15.3 years.

Seven of these men acted out these fantasies within a year of becoming consciously aware of them. In addition, several of the offenders admitted that their first rape was also their first sexual experience. One offender who by age nineteen had raped and murdered five women told in this report of his first rape at age fourteen.

> The offender had fantasized about raping a twenty-five-year-old neighbor for whom he did errands. To carry out his fantasy, he scaled up her apartment building wall ("as a cat burglar and wearing a stocking mask") and entered the apartment through a patio door. He knew such an entrance was possible because he had practiced it before during burglaries he committed. He took a knife from the woman's kitchen and confronted her in her bedroom, where he robbed and then raped her. After the crime, police interviewed all the neighbors, including the offender. He told police an elaborate story of how he had seen a suspect in the parking lot when returning home from a party and how he fought with and succeeded in running off this suspect. Three weeks later he was arrested for the rape, after fingerprint evidence and clothing were found linking him to the crime.

This example illustrates the propensity of offenders to interject themselves into crime investigation activities. This is an interesting link between fantasy satisfaction and acting out behaviors—that is, between the crime itself and power within the law enforcement system.

Fantasy assumes a crucial role in sexual murders. When questioned about the murders themselves and about their preparation for the murders, the murderers identified the importance of fantasy to the rapes and murders. This chapter suggests that these men murder because of the way they think. The cognitive structure emerging from early trauma and neglect is primary to the way they think; however, their beliefs and actions are reflective, encouraging, reinforcing, and evolving the patterns necessary to commit sexual crimes and murders. Their fantasies reflect their actions based on their beliefs and patterns of reasoning. Extensive early childhood aggressive and sexualized vengeful preoccupations and sadistic acts either indulged in by reenactment of trauma or repetitive play not only develops their reasoning for murder but also rehearses the methods. These cognitive acts gradually lead to the conscious planning and justification for murderous acts.

Notes

Beck, A.T. *Cognitive Therapy and Emotional Disorders*. New York: Universities International Press, 1976.

Beres, D. Perception, imagination and reality. *International Journal of Psychoanalysis*, 1961, 41:327–334.

Brittain, R.P. The sadistic murderer. *Medical Science and the Law*, 1970, 10:198–207.

Gardner, H: *The Mind's New Science*, New York: Basic Books, 1985.

MacCulloch, M.J., Snowden, P.R., Wood, P.J.W., and Mills, H.E. Sadistic fantasy, sadistic behaviors and offending. *British Journal of Psychiatry*, 1983, 143, 20–29.

Reinhardt, J.M. Sex perversions and sex crimes: a psychocultural examination of the causes, nature and criminal manifestations of sex perversions. *Police Science Series.* Springfield, IL: Charles C. Thomas, 1975.

Ressler, R.K. et al. FBI Law Enforcement Bulletin, 1985, 54:1–43.

Revitch, E. Sex murderer and the potential sex murderer. *Disease Nervous System*, 1965, 26:640–648.

Revitch, E. Gynocide and unprovoked attacks on women. *Correctional and Social Psychiatry*, 1980, 26:6–11.

Schlesinger, L.B., and Revitch, E. The criminal fantasy technique: A comparison of sex offenders and substance abusers. *Journal of Clinical Psychology*, 37:210–218, 1980.

Singer, J.L. *Daydreaming*. New York: Random House, 1966.

West, D.J., Roy, C., and Nicholas, F.L. *Understanding sexual attacks*. London: Heinemann, 1978.

4

Antecedent Behaviors and the Act of Murder

P utting thoughts and plans of murder into action presents the murderer with various behavioral options. The manner in which he chooses to act reveals much about the man behind the crime; thus, it often forms the basis for law enforcement investigation of crime scene patterns. We view the act of murder as being divided into four distinct phases: (1) antecedent behavior and planning, (2) the act of murder, (3) disposing of the body, and (4) postcrime behavior. At each of these phases, the murderer's thinking patterns, as presented in chapter 3, influence his choice of how he will act. Although these phases are discussed as separate components, they are overlapping segments of one event: murder. In this chapter, we describe phases one and two and the range of behavioral choices exhibited by the thirty-six murderers in our study.

Phase One: Antecedent Behavior and Planning

The first phase of murder, the killer's antecedent behavior, forms the backdrop against which the crime occurs. Precrime stress factors, frame of mind, and planning combine to influence the murderer's actions during this stage.

Precrime Stress Factors

The killer's mental and emotional state, his frame of mind, and hence his behavior before he murders are influenced to varying degrees by what is happening around him. Murderers often cite certain precipitating stresses as the causes for their behavior. They are not necessarily aware of the basic issues behind these stress factors, issues that play a powerful role in motivation. Yet in the mind of the murderer, stress factors (such as a disagreement with parents) are more than sufficient to justify aggression toward others, even toward strangers. Stress factors described by the men in our study as being present immediately prior to murder include conflict with females, parental conflict, financial stress, marital problems, conflict with males, birth of a child, physical injury, legal problems, employment problems, and stress from a death.

Conflict with Females. The men were able to state in forty-eight (59 percent) of eighty-one murder cases with data that their perceptions of what set the stage for murder involved a conflict with a woman. In one instance, a murderer described meeting a woman in a bar and having some drinks with her. She began ridiculing him. He later picked up another woman and took her to his apartment where he brutally murdered her.

However, some murderers revealed that although stress initially appeared to be caused by conflicts with women, other factors were underlying. One murderer described this additional stress.

> I had broken up with my girlfriend three days before, and I was feeling a lot of anxiety and pressure. Then the day after this [the murder] happened, she called to say she was sorry and she wanted to see me. Knowing what I'd done and everything, I didn't want to see her. So I stayed away from her for about two weeks. . . . I didn't [commit the murder] just because I was mad at my girlfriend. . . . There was peer pressure; there was outside pressure from school. I had been slacking off in my studies because my girl and I started to have trouble a month or so before this all happened. I felt a combination of things as far as [causing] what actually took place. It was pressure from home to bring up my grades, to get a job, etc.

Parental Conflict. Another major stress factor for the murderers immediately prior to murder is conflict with parents. For forty-six (53 percent) of eighty-six murder cases, murderers described parental problems. In one case, the killer had numerous fights with his stepfather and tried to kill him with a .45-caliber gun. In another case, a young man who had been adopted at an early age contacted his natural mother after obtaining her name and address. He went to visit her, fully prepared to be accepted into her home. However, he was rejected by her and then learned that he had a sister whom their natural mother had raised. His unconscious rage over his sister's acceptance and his rejection was transferred to victims the age and general appearance of his sister.

Financial Problems. In 48 percent of eighty-six murder cases, the murderers stated that financial difficulties were present at the time of their crimes. Again, this stress factor may be closely related to another, as is revealed in the following example:

> I had some financial difficulties, [although] my wife and I were getting along pretty good. I was arguing with my parents because I was always drunk. I had

some conflicts with my mother-in-law, my father-in-law, and my brother-in-law. We'd usually end up in an argument [over] something.

The man's high level of aggression was linked with financial, alcohol, and family member problems, the factors contributing to his emotional state.

Employment Problems.   Difficulties with employment were given as precipitating stress factors in 39 percent of ninety murders and were suspected in an additional 26 percent. Employment problems involved situations in which the murderer was unemployed or was having difficulty at work. The employer of one of the murderers made the following report:

> [The offender] did not take orders or advice. He did not get along with other employees. He would usually get into arguments with other employees over nothing. The employees were afraid to say much to him or cross him in any way. He had bad body odor, and I could not get him to do anything about it. [Although] he did my delivery work well and I had few complaints from the customers, my trouble with him was his trouble with other employees.

Marital Problems.   Because only a minority of murderers were married, marriage was less frequently an identified cause of stress. However, in 21 percent of eighty-nine murders it was identified as a problem. For example, one murderer admitted he was seeing other women, and he had learned that his wife was also involved in an affair. During this time, his fantasies of rape and murder intensified.

Additional Stress Factors.   Other precipitating stressful events identified by the murderers included legal problems (28 percent of eighty-nine cases), conflict with a male (11 percent of eighty-one cases), physical injury (11 percent of eighty-three), death of a significant person (8 percent of seventy-eight), and birth of a child (8 percent of eighty-nine cases). The following excerpt from a prison record is an example of this latter event as a precipitant for murder.

> Shortly after learning of his wife's pregnancy, [the murderer] purchased a pistol he [later] kept at home, claiming he was afraid his wife might be assaulted or his home burglarized while he was at work. After the birth of this first child, there was a marked change in [the offender]. He became more preoccupied, complained of physical pain, his sleep was restless, and his relationships with others deteriorated. He had little interest in sexual relations with his wife. . . . Three murders were in specific reference to this birth. The first murder was committed six weeks after the birth of the child, the second murder occurred when his wife was pregnant with their second child, and the

third murder occurred on the day after the first birthday of the first child and coincided with the child's birthday party.

One final example of a precipitating stress factor illustrates the complexity of these factors.

The murderer, a drug user, reported a long-standing problem with depression, which was evidenced by his frequent need for psychiatric hospitalization. The man had aspirations to become an actor, and he expressed great disappointment in his failure to gain employment as such. Hospital records from several weeks before the crime was committed revealed the man was depressed, suffered from insomnia and diarrhea, and talked of suicide. The day after he was discussing discharge from the hospital with staff, he committed murder.

Frame of Mind

Frame of mind is a general descriptive term for a dominant emotional state that acts as a primary filter and interpreting mechanism regarding external events. The frame of mind of offenders just before the crime revealed highly negative emotional states such as frustration (50 percent), hostility and anger (46 percent), agitation (43 percent), and excitement (41 percent). Of equal interest are those symptoms and mood states associated with internalized distress— that is, nervousness (17 percent), depression (14.6 percent), fear (10 percent), calm (8.8 percent), or confusion (7 percent). These findings suggest that there is little emotion experienced by the killer that reflects any sense of vulnerability, thereby permitting the killer to interpret the behavior of the victim in the most negative manner. The frame of mind and mood states illustrate how the killer supports his negative cognitions and justification for the crime. There is no emotional reservoir to relate to the vulnerability, pain, and fear of the victim.

Precrime Planning

In relationship to precrime planning or premeditation, 50 percent of the murderers rated their act as intentional in planning who, when, and where they were going to murder. Another 34 percent recognized that they had a congruent mood state to murder and were open to opportunities. This figure suggests an aura of impulsiveness for the act; however, in the structure and organization of thinking, it fits in with the style of these killers. They know of places and strategies by which to obtain victims; when the right combination exists, they commit the crime and label it opportunistic. The remaining 16 percent of the offenders viewed their murderous acts as purely spontaneous and unplanned. These men were without self-appraisal or awareness of any thoughts or emotions building up to a murderous expression. Nevertheless, it appears that sexual murderers may preplan and be more intentional in their crime than has been previously reported in the literature.

Motivations for murder may include a conscious fantasy, plan, directive, or reason to kill. Murderers operating on a conscious motivational level usually remember their thoughts prior to the murder. One of the murderers we interviewed described his preoccupation with murder immediately prior to killing someone: "I had a compulsion during the day and hoped it would settle down—hoped I could wipe it out drinking."

These men have conscious, detailed plans for murder. Often the plans are improved upon with each successive killing; each new experience gives the offender insight into his next murder. Although the man who killed after breaking up with his girlfriend had no conscious plan for his first murder, he carefully planned subsequent murders to avoid being apprehended. With each new murder, the killer improved on his fantasy planning.

Other murderers may be motivated to kill by triggering environmental factors. Although their murderous actions are cued by external occurrences (which we address in our discussion of phase two) their plan for murder is *not* spontaneous. Some people, such as Samenow, question whether there is any such thing as a spontaneous homicide (Samenow 1984).

In one apparently spontaneous murder, the murderer met the victim in an apartment building hallway; as he passed her, he hit her and dragged her to a landing near the roof. However, crime scene evidence indicated that the killer had previously fantasized about such a murder. The victim's body was placed in a ritualized position, the victim had been tied up after death, and the crime scene displayed a certain symmetry, all of which pointed to a planned crime.

Precrime Actions

The precrime actions of the murderers in the days and hours before they killed provide clues to their mental states at the time of the murders.

In the days before they murdered, several offenders were involved in criminal or violent activities. At least two men committed fetish burglaries, breaking into homes to steal items that, for them, had sexual connotations. An offender who later killed three women assaulted and threatened his wife, forcing her to write a suicide note; another offender killed neighborhood dogs shortly before committing murder. One murderer, who killed five people within one week, set several fires and shot off his gun inside his apartment and from his car in the days preceding the murders. On the day of the first murder, homeowners in the area reported break-ins and thefts.

During the hours immediately before the murders, some murderers go looking for victims. Several described cruising the single bars, parking lots, gay bars, or the gay districts to locate victims. In other cases, they cruise the highways to pick up hitchhikers for victims. The men's actions sometimes involved alcohol and/or drug use. One murderer stabbed to death and eviscerated one woman and attempted to eviscerate another after spending the evening drinking beer and smoking marijuana with them.

The murderer's precrime behavior moves him toward the actual act of murder. In this phase, the murderer's selection of a victim and the onset of certain triggering factors culminate in the murder itself.

Victim Selection

For the murderer with a conscious plan or fantasy, selecting a victim begins the acting-out level of behavior. The plan or fantasy constructed earlier may call for a victim who meets certain criteria, and many murderers have been known to seek out a victim who is exactly right for the fantasy. The history and circumstances of the victim are often important. The victim may be symbolic of someone in the murderer's past, as in the case of the man who killed older women, close to his mother in age. Before his invalid mother died, the man exhumed female bodies from a graveyard and used the corpses in bizarre sexual activities. The man had been caring for his mother, and after her death he murdered the first of his two victims. In another case, the murderer had deep-seated conflicts with his mother, who often ridiculed his inability to form a relationship with a certain type of woman. The man sought and killed attractive, wealthy, female college students—the women his mother claimed were unattainable for him.

Other murderers may look for certain actions in their victims. One man who chose his victims from hitchhikers said, "She was playing up the role, the big beautiful smile and getting in the car, which was kind of tragic, but she had advertised to get blown away." Another murderer sought women to model hosiery and shoes for photographs; after forcing them to pose nude in high-heeled shoes, he killed them.

For the killer without a conscious plan or fantasy, a person may become a victim by eliciting certain responses. For example, someone may remind him of his belief in an unjust world. He may feel unfairly treated, and this sets into motion the justification to kill. One killer felt that his continued rejection by women was an injustice. In response to his frustration over this feeling, he shot and killed women who either were accompanied by men or were attractive enough to be sought by men. Other murderers respond to victims with rage and anger.

Triggering Factors

When discussing their first murders, the men we interviewed generally indicated that something happened to move them either to act out their fantasies of killing or to murder to preserve other fantasies. These occurrences, which we call triggering factors, are often closely connected with how the murderer selects his victim. The murderer with a well-rehearsed fantasy of murder kills to preserve the fantasy, as does the fetish burglar who kills when someone intrudes on his ritual. The murderer with a history of violent fantasies directed against women acts out these fantasies, often claiming that alcohol or the woman herself triggered the murder.

A variety of triggering factors can activate the violence, and the murderer's emotional state may leave him especially open to such factors. Many triggering factors center around some aspect of control. Often the killer's feeling of control and dominance is interrupted by the behavior of the victim. The victim's natural attempt to run away may enrage or upset the murderer because it indicates he may lose control. To another murderer, the victim's offer to comply with his demands may be inflammatory, as it indicates that the victim, rather than the attacker, has made a decision about how the assault will proceed.

The triggering factor in one case was that a victim's behavior did not match the rapist's fantasy of an exceptionally good sexual experience. This man kept giving orders to the woman, thus indicating his fantasy for how he intended the sexual assault to proceed. Her lack of "cooperation" shattered his fantasy. He became enraged and killed her. Another murderer recalled the triggering factor of the victim's trying to escape, although he did not recall the murder itself. His fantasy had centered around control and dominance; the victim's resisting behavior made him murder to preserve his fantasy.

> We were upstairs and I was taking my clothes off. That's when she started back downstairs. As a matter of fact, that's the only time I hit her. I caught her at the stairs. . . . She wanted to know why I hit her. I just told her to be quiet. She was complaining about what time she would get home and she said her parents would worry. She consented to sex. . . . then I remember nothing else except waking up and her dead in the bed. .

Some murderers kill to fulfill a specific fantasy. Several men mentioned going "hunting" every night for a victim. Because they had a specific type of victim in mind, they would wait until an appropriate one appeared. The victim's meeting the killer's criteria would, in fact, trigger the murder. The murderer may be looking for a woman with a male companion in a parked car or a woman alone driving a specific type of car. When such a victim appears, the murderous action is triggered.

Other killers become compelled by their fantasy of murder prior to committing the crime. One murderer, who killed seemingly at random, said he was ordered to murder by flying saucers. To these men, the identity of the victim is irrelevant; the act itself has primary importance.

> I'm all up to kill somebody. It's cold and it's cut and dried. I told the police the first [person] that got into the car . . . it didn't matter if it was male or female, I was going to blow somebody away.

In this case, just the accessibility of someone triggered the murder.

Although some of the murderers in our study did not report fantasies in a conscious way, their description of murders they committed reveal hidden fantasies of violence, often against women. Several of the men described the factors that triggered the killing as their not feeling well, depression, alcohol, or drugs. Out of 118 victim cases, half (49 percent) of the murderers said they had been drinking prior to the crime. The murderers were asked if their use of alcohol at the time of the offense differed significantly from typical drinking. Thirty percent said yes. Drug use at the time of the offense was 35 percent; however, only 12.5 percent said that drug use differed significantly from their typical drug habits. The following example illustrates the statement of a killer who had been drinking.

> It was the same as with the other one. I had been drinking at the bar. I don't even remember leaving. I don't know what made me kill her. I don't even know why I raped her. I had a good-looking wife at home. I saw her get into her car and I walked up and got in the car with her, yelled at her, took her down there where I raped her. I kept telling her I didn't want to hurt her, but I just started choking her.

We suspect that these murderers are preoccupied with a kind of internal dialogue that sustains anger, discontent, irritability, or depression. Use of alcohol or drugs is an attempt to moderate such internal stress, but the fantasy continues. Such an offender is often unaware of the extent of this internal dialogue. For example, when chastised by a teacher or boss, he may talk to himself: "If I ever got that son of a bitch, I'd rip him apart; I'd smash him up." One murderer, after performing poorly in the service and being intimidated by his sergeant, went AWOL on a drinking binge. While out on the street, he beat a drunk to death after the man grabbed him. The murderer felt justified in his actions and was unaware of the intensity of his rage or the impact of his blows. He then beat to death a second man. Finally, he abducted a female acquaintance. When he awoke the next morning, her dead body was beside him with a broomstick thrust into her vagina with such force that it had penetrated her lungs. Although he believes he killed her, he claims no recollection of the incident.

To the men with unconscious plans, violent thoughts are not acknowledged as serious contributors to their behavior. Rather, they believe external circumstances trigger the murderous behavior. One murderer described incarcerated men as "good guys." However, he alluded to a fantasy of dominance when he noted the sense of power bestowed by alcohol.

If it hadn't been for beer and whiskey, I wouldn't be here [in prison] today. I've seen a lot of men come in and out since I've been here. They go out and they come in. The only reason they do is that they get hold of a bottle. Ninety percent of the guys that are in here are pretty good people, but when they get hold of that bottle, it makes them feel like they are superman.

Phase Two: The Act of Murder

The Actual Murder

Killing the victim moves the murderer to the reality of murder. The victim may not die as in the fantasy or in the way the offender planned. He may have to use more violence, he may feel more frightened than he anticipated, or he may be startled by the fact that he feels excited. Some murderers are exhilarated—they broke the rules, they killed. This feeling will induce some to kill again, while others will, in horror over what they have done, turn themselves in to the police.

For some men the actual murder goes beyond their fantasies of killing. There is confirmation and reinforcement of the fantasy, and pleasure or triumph in the power of the act. One murderer described his heightened excitement when driving his car with the dead bodies of two victims inside.

> I drive up to my apartment with two murdererd girls in my car. The trunk is a mess, with one body stabbed to death. The other [body] is on the back seat. The landlord is [at my apartment] with two friends. I [drove] right up and they kept on talking and I thought, wow, would they freak out if I just got out and opened my trunk and back seat and just threw bodies out in front of them . . . I took the heads up to my room. I could sit there looking at the heads on an overstuffed chair, tripping on them on my bed, looking at them [when] one of them somehow becomes unsettled, comes rolling down the chair, very grisly. Tumbling down the chair, rolls across the cushion and hits the rug, bonk. The neighbor downstairs hates my guts. I'm always making noise late at night. He gets a broom and whacks on the ceiling. "Buddy," I say "I'm sorry for that, dropped my head, sorry." That helped bring me out of the depressions. I would trip on that.

Other murderers feel a surprising sense of horror over the act they committed. The following case illustrates how one murderer reacted to the second of his three murders.

> A thirty-year-old woman was strangled, stabbed, and shot. She had also been cleaned up and positioned in bed after death. Fingerprints were left at the crime scene, along with a message written in lipstick on the wall: "For

heaven's sake, catch me before I kill more. I cannot control myself." Six months later the murderer kidnapped and killed a six-year-old girl; a ransom note left at the scene matched the handwriting of the earlier message.

The Sexual Element of Homicide

Although all the murders in our study contained a sexual element, it is apparent that the execution of this element and its meaning to the offender vary. Some victims were raped and then murdered; others were sexually mutilated only after death. In one case, there were no obvious signs of sexual assault; however, the disembowelment of the victim was later found to have a sexual meaning for the killer. Rapists who murder, according to Rada (1978), rarely report any sexual satisfaction from the murder nor do they perform postmortem sexual acts. In contrast, the sadistic murderer (Brittain 1970), sometimes called the lust murderer (Hazelwood and Douglas 1980), kills as part of a ritualized sadistic fantasy.

Rape murder.   In our study, 56 percent of 108 cases with data had victims who were raped prior to death. One murderer recalled how he sexually assaulted the woman in one location and then transported her elsewhere to kill her: "We got to my apartment. Inside my apartment I tied her up. I wanted to have intercourse. . . . Afterwards we went out to my car, and I took her to a deserted area where I killed her."

The rape murder may be prompted by an emotional frame of mind, as in the following case in which the rage was evident in the stabbing of one of his victims.

> We were walking along, through the culverts, underneath the highway. That's when I pulled out the knife and without even saying [anything] I stabbed her. I had the gun in this hand and the knife came from my back pocket, and I just came around like this and hit her like this. She fell right there, and she screamed as she was falling. I kept stabbing. She fell down and landed on the ground. I kept on stabbing—maybe fifty to one hundred times.

Mutilation Murder.   The killer may rape a victim both before and after the victim dies, and these acts may often be sadistic and include mutilation and torture of the victim. For example, in one case the offender raped the victim and then slowly strangled her manually with a garrote. After death he also raped her.

A sexual act was committed only after the victim's death in 42 percent of ninety-two cases with data we studied. In one case, the murderer ejaculated into a knife wound he made into the victim. In another, the killer sexually assaulted both of his victims after he shot them.

Components of torture, mutilation, and overkill, or the infliction of more injury than is necessary to kill a person, are evident in many of these murders. Unusual or bizarre imagery or acts may be necessary to elicit feelings of sexual excitement in the killer. The level of complexity and bizarreness that is needed to obtain and sustain emotional arousal suggests that the ultimate expression of the murderer's perversion may be his mutilation of the victim.

FBI criminal profiling experience finds a frequent component of sexual murder to be the insertion of foreign objects into the vaginal and anal cavities of victims. This act is often combined with other acts of mutilation, such as slashing of the body, cutting of the breasts and buttocks, and biting of various parts of the body. It is noted that these acts, particularly in the case of the disorganized offender, do not coincide with completed acts of sexual penetration. Thus, evidence of sexual fluids are not present in the cavities of the victims. When sexual fluids do appear, they are more often found on or around the body and have been produced by masturbation rather than sexual contact with the victim. This indicates the homicide and assault have triggered a sexual fantasy that excited the killer. Since his sexual history is that of solo sex, and he finds interpersonal relationships difficult, if not impossible, he reverts to masturbatory acts even when a real partner (his victim) is available. Masturbation generally occurs after death, when the fantasy is strongest.

It is theorized by FBI research that the act of placing foreign objects into the victims by the disorganized offender may be a form of regressive necrophilia. This act, therefore, is a substitute for actual sexual intercourse. The insertion becomes the sexual act through fantasy, leaving no sexual evidence for the homicide investigator. It is for this reason that the sexual element of the crime is often missed by police investigators, psychologists, or psychiatrists who evaluate the case. Mental health professionals rarely have access to or examine crime scene photographs in their evaluations and rely solely on narrative descriptions of the murderous acts. Therefore, insertion of a foreign object in the vaginal cavity is often erroneously viewed as an act of mutilation rather than that of sexual substitution. The understanding of the sexual substitution concept provides a criminal profiler with a clearer and more accurate mental picture of the killer. (Turn to page 146, "A Case Example," for an example of a disorganized crime scene involving regressive necrophilia.)

One-third of the ninety-two victims with data showed evidence of torture. One killer picked up female hitchhikers and, after driving them to remote areas, first raped the women and then beat them on the head with a hammer. Victims of one murderer were also forced to perform fellatio on the offender while he forcefully inserted a hammer handle into their vaginas.

Mutilations often occur when the victim is already dead, a time when the killer has ultimate control over the victim. One victim was found with genitals mutilated and breasts amputated; the murderer had returned to the crime scene 14 hours after killing her and had cut off her breasts.

Another victim was found with stab wounds in the vagina and groin and with her throat slashed. Her nipples had been removed and her face severely beaten, and her cut-off hair was found hanging from a nearby tree branch.

Some murderers volunteered information on the intention of the mutilations. One murderer said that the mutilation after death was a way of disposing of the body, implying that he had a pragmatic reason. However, in addition to cutting up the body, he pulled out the victim's fingernails. The man later claimed not to remember this.

Depersonalization is one form of mutilation that was evident in several of the cases we studied. The term *depersonalization* is used to describe actions taken by the murderer to obscure the personal identity of the victim. These actions may occur before the victim is murdered, as in the case of the offender who mutilated nearly beyond recognition the faces of the young boys he sexually assaulted and killed. Another offender covered his elderly victims' faces with such items as blankets, pillows, towels, and bedspreads. However, not all depersonalization is as overt as these examples imply. The act of rolling a victim over onto his or her stomach so the face is not visible may be a subtle form of depersonalization.

The acting on the murderous thoughts and fantasies sets into motion the early phases of murder. Important to this action in the first phase are precrime stress factors, frame of mind, precrime planning and actions, victim selection, and triggering factors. The behaviors of the murderer confront him with the reality of his act and constitute the second phase of murder.

The third and fourth phases of murder include the disposal of the body and postcrime behaviors; they are described in the next chapter.

Notes

Brittain, R.P. The sadistic murderer. *Medical Science and the Law*, 1970, 10:98–207.

Hazelwood, R.R., and Douglas, J.E. The lust murderer. *FBI Law Enforcement Bulletin, April 1980,* 18–22.

Rada, R.T. *Clinical Aspects of the Rapist,* New York: Grune and Stratton, Inc., 1978.

Samenow, S.E. *Inside the Criminal Mind,* New York Times Books, 1984.

5
After the Murder

After committing the murder, the offender must decide what to do with the body. If this confrontation with reality has not been anticipated, the murderer may give himself up to the authorities. As one murderer said, "It blew my mind killing those people. I wasn't ready for that. The fantasies were there, but I couldn't handle the death trip and dead bodies. I freaked out and gave myself up." In contrast, for one murderer the high point of the crime was not the act of killing, but the successful dismemberment and disposal of the body without detection.

Some murderers cover the body, wash the wounds, or otherwise interact with the body, a reaction that demonstrates remorse or concern for the victim. Some murderers hide or bury the body, perhaps to keep the secret and maintain control. Other offenders openly display the corpse in a public area, hoping the body will shock and offend society.

Several aspects of this phase of murder contribute to our understanding of the crime. This chapter discusses phases three and four of the act of murder. Phase three, the means of disposal, the state of the body, and the body's final location provides insight into how and why the murderer responds to the fulfillment of his fantasy to kill. Phase four discusses the murderer's postcrime behavior.

Phase Three: Disposing of the Body

Patterns of Disposal

There were several different patterns of disposing of the body noted in this sample. Although it is not always clear why some murderers leave the victim's body while others use elaborate methods to dispose of it elsewhere, some murderers provided explanation. One offender described his internal dialogue as he confronted the body of this first murder victim.

> I got a dead body on my hands. People saw me come in here. How am I going to pack this out? Am I gonna put it in a double bag or sheet and carry it out of here? I figured the smaller the better. I chopped [the body] up . . . stuffed

some in the refrigerator . . . dumped guts in vacant lots . . . throwing pieces here and there, whatever came out of the bag first . . . I was scared.

After the first murder, the killer may be better prepared for dealing with the body. In a second case, the above murderer described a planned dismembering of the body after killing the victim in a car. He then carried the body in a bag up two flights of stairs to the apartment he shared with his mother, passing two persons coming downstairs along the way. He said, "It took meticulous work . . . about four hours . . . dismembering it, getting rid of the blood, the gore, completely cleaning the bathroom."

Other methods for disposing of a murder victim's body may be less elaborate. In one case, the victim's partially decomposed body was found unburied in the desert. Police later determined that she had been killed elsewhere and her body transported to the desert area. Another killer merely dragged his victim's body a short distance to a wooded area, where it would be less visible.

Rather than moving the body to another location, the murderer may solve the practical problem of what to do with a victim's corpse by disposing of it at the murder scene. He may hide the body where he killed the victim, as in the following case:

The murderer's victims were sexually assaulted and strangled in the offender's house. The bodies were buried underneath the house; only after the killer ran out of space did he begin disposing of the bodies in a nearby river.

Another murderer buried his victim in a shallow grave in the same spot where she was killed. The murderer described his practical reason for doing so: "I just wanted to cover her up so that if anybody would be walking by, at first sight, unless they were really looking for a body they wouldn't notice it."

Other murderers make no attempt to hide the bodies of their victims and leave them visible at the murder scene. The man who murdered eight women killed them in various rooms of their townhouse and left them where they died. Alerted by the sole surviving victim, police found the bodies the next morning.

Body disposal methods are sometimes perfected by the offender through his incorporation of them into his fantasy of murder. While the offender who "freaked out" after his first murders and gave himself up was in prison, he spent an enormous amount of psychic energy mentally rehearsing and mastering body disposal. After his release, he murdered eight women.

I got rid of that icky feeling of messing with the dead. Only one guy that gets more casual around a body than me, a mortician or pathologist. But some of my fantasies were so bizarre that [they] would turn the stomach of a pathologist.

Body State

Additional clues to the murderer's behavioral characteristics can be found by examining the manner in which he leaves the body of his victim. The body's visibility, state of dress, and positioning all result from the murderer's making certain choices.

Visibility.   As was previously pointed out, the visibility of a victim's body is often the result of the killer's practical considerations. The body may be hidden to avoid detection, as in the case of the murderer who shot his victims in the woods and then covered them with snow. In this study, 58 percent of the bodies were concealed and 42 percent were exposed. The body may be left in the open because the circumstances do not allow the murderer to hide it, as in the case of the man who in blitz-style attacks shot young women from a distance at relatively public locations. The victims' bodies were left where they fell.

Other reasons for the visibility or lack of visibility of the dead body include the killer's desire to make a statement with the victim's body, which, one might speculate, was the reason for one man's depositing the body of one of his six female victims on the doorstep of his brother's house. In contrast, murderers seeking to maintain control over their act of murder may hide the bodies of their victims.

State of Dress.   Many victims' bodies are left in what might be termed sexual disarray. In one hundred cases with data, bodies were noted to be completely nude (47 percent); to have genitals exposed (5 percent), breasts exposed (9 percent), or buttocks exposed (11 percent); or to have clothing partly removed to expose various body parts. The victim's clothing may be used to bind or cover him or her, it may be left nearby, or it may even be folded neatly. Only twenty-eight (28 percent) of the victims were found clothed.

Occasionally the victim's state of dress is unusually bizarre. Many of the victims buried underneath one murderer's house were found with articles of clothing stuffed into their mouths and in varying stages of undress. In another case, the killer washed his dead victim, bandaged her wounds, dressed her in a clean nightgown, and placed her in her bed.

Positioning.   Although many murder victims are buried, hidden, or simply left at the crime scene, some may be arranged in a certain way for specific reasons. In thirty cases (28 percent), the body was specifically positioned, and in eighteen cases (17 percent) it was unclear. These reasons may include the murderer's need to obscure certain facts about the crime. In one case, the two murderers decided to position the murdered woman's body in a certain way so she would appear to have been raped.

The day after the murder, the two men and a girlfriend returned to the crime scene, where the body had been left, to move it to a location where it would be more easily found. They undressed the body, washed it with water from a nearby spring, and drove it to a nearby dumping area. There the girlfriend heard one of the men say, "We're going to make this look like a rape." After removing the body from the car, the men stabbed the body, attempted to decapitate it, and mutilated various body parts with a knife. One man then attempted to have intercourse with the corpse.

Some victims are positioned after death in ways that have meaning only to the killer and are based on his sexually violent fantasies. Not all positioning is as elaborate as in the above case. One killer merely draped the body of his victim face down over a log. Nevertheless, it appears that this positioning of the body had a certain meaning for the offender. By choosing to pose his victim, he revealed a distinct behavioral characteristic relating to his fantasies and premeditation of the crime.

Final Location

For the sexual killer, the final location chosen for the victim's body is important and the reason for this importance varies. Where the killer leaves the body may be important because it determines how soon it is found. The two men who positioned their victim's body in a manner suggestive of rape chose a frequented dumping area because they wanted the body to be found easily. In contrast, the man who weighted body parts and threw them in a river did not wish the bodies to be discovered.

The final location of the victim's body may be important because of what it represents to the murderer. It may contribute to the offender's overall fantasy of murder, as in the following case:

The murderer, who worked as a hospital ambulance driver, kidnapped his victims from the parking lot of a restaurant and took them to another location, where he raped and murdered them. He then anonymously telephoned police to report seeing a body, returned to the hospital to receive the ambulance call and then drive the ambulance with the body back to the hospital.

By leaving the body somewhere along the route where he would be responding through his job as an ambulance driver, the murderer was able to experience the realization of his fantasy through to its conclusion. One might speculate that the killer who buried his victims underneath his house not only wanted them hidden, but also wanted them nearby to fuel his fantasy, particularly in view of the fact that he slept with some of the corpses before burying them.

Another reason that the final location is important is that it expresses the murderers' relationship with or feeling toward another person. The man who left his victim's body near his brother's doorstep reportedly had a love/hate relationship with both his mother and his adopted brother. In another case, the killer buried the heads of two of his victims outside his mother's bedroom with their heads facing up toward her window. As was described earlier, the man had deep-rooted conflicts with his mother and murdered women his mother said would never date him. The murderer related that the buried heads fueled his fantasies. "People look up to you," he would tell his mother. The statement had meaning only to him.

In some instances, the final location of specific body parts is with the murderer himself. This presence provides the killer with further excitement. A murderer with a fetish for women's feet in high-heeled shoes cut off his victims' feet and saved then in his freezer. Another man saved the breasts of his victims and made molds of them. This murderer also described the heightened arousal state generated in disposing of the body as follows:

> I'm really rushed. My heart's beating ninety miles a minute. My blood pressure is so heavy it sounded like somebody crunching behind me. I jumped around and grabbed my gun and freaked out, but it was my blood pressure pounding in my ears. It was driving me. I thought I was going to croak while I was getting rid of the bodies or evidence.

The psychosis of some murderers is revealed through their choice of a final location for their victims. This is particularly true in one case. The murderer, a diagnosed paranoid schizophrenic, kept various internal organs of his victims. He drank their blood and their ground-up brains, claiming that flying saucers had ordered him to drink blood because his own was "drying up." The offender had a history of psychiatric hospitalizations, and he killed and mutilated animals in much the same way as he eventually killed his human victims.

Phase Four: Postcrime Behavior

During the final phase of murder, the reactions of the killer may range from a sense of relief or release of tension to a sense of purpose in avoiding apprehension. The crime has been committed; the body disposal has been completed. Nevertheless, the murderers' postcrime behavior often illustrates that for them, the murder fantasy continues.

Immediate Response

Immediately after leaving the crime scene, the murderer may feel a strong sense of relief. Some offenders have described returning home and falling into a deep sleep.

Other killers, when faced with the reality of their actions, respond in a more active manner. One man went to a tavern and ordered some food, which he was unable to eat. He later visited a prostitute, precipitated a fight, slashed his wrists, and was taken to a hospital. The physician recognized him from a police report and telephoned the authorities.

Flight may be an immediate postcrime response in some instances. The murderer may flee in a conscious attempt to avoid apprehension, in response to a lack of a plan of action, or even as a way to continue the excitement generated by the murder. Which of these rationales is operative may be difficult to ascertain. Sometimes the victim's car provides the murderer with the means for his flight.

> While traveling in her car to visit her boyfriend, the eighteen-year-old victim picked up the murderer, a stranger, in a restaurant parking lot where he was hitchhiking on his way across country. The man forced her to drive to a park, where he sexually assaulted, beat, and strangled her. After hiding her body in a nearby stream, the murderer continued his trip in the victim's car.

Nevertheless, it is unclear whether he fled as a reaction to the crime itself, as a way to escape, or as a means of sustaining his fantasy. The man kept the victim's car and her belongings, selling her possessions en route. If indeed he fled to avoid apprehension, he probably would not have left a trail of the victim's belongings behind him. Instead, it appears that his immediate post-crime response was fueled by a need to sustain the exhilaration of committing murder.

Subsequent Responses

The murderer's reactions after his initial response to his crime are generally tempered by the need for self-protection. He may dispose of evidence; he may keep a low profile; he may fabricate an alibi. However, his behaviors during this period often run counter to the need to avoid attention. These behaviors fall into four categories: (1) returning to the crime scene, (2) observing the discovery of the victim's body, (3) keeping souvenirs of the murder, and (4) participating in the investigation. Such responses illustrate that the need to sustain the excitement of murder often is so strong that it prevails over self-protective instincts.

Returning to the Crime Scene.   Detective fiction often describes a murderer's stealthy, midnight return to the scene of a crime. This depiction was accurate in 32 of 118 cases, or 27 percent.

Why do they return? Some of the multiple reasons in this sample of murderers were to relive the fantasy (31 of 118 cases, or 26 percent); to determine the progress of the police (22 of 118 cases, or 19 percent); to repeat a killing of another victim (9, or 8 percent); and to have sex with the corpse (7 of the 118 cases, or 6 percent).

One man returned to the crime scene fourteen hours after the murder and cut off the victim's breasts; another murderer returned as late as several weeks after the murder to involve the victim's body in various sexual activities. Even in the case of the two men who returned to simulate a rape murder, the extreme nature of the mutilations suggests that their return was not only to obscure evidence, but also to involve themselves further with the victim's body.

Observing the Body's Discovery. Participating in the discovery of the victim's body may also sustain the murderer's level of excitement by prolonging his involvement with the victim and his act of murder. He may telephone or write to police, or he may be in a crowd of people at the scene after the body has been discovered. The murderer may even confess to the crime in order to accompany police to the location of the victim's body. The case of the ambulance driver who orchestrated his own recovery of the corpse shows how the need to sustain the fantasy influences the killer's postcrime behavior. Another murderer telephoned police, informed them he had discovered the victim's body, and led them to it. Although this postcrime behavior placed him at great risk of apprehension, his need to be present during the discovery of the body outweighed the risk involved.

In contrast, other murderers maintain a feeling of control over events, and hence over the fantasy, by not becoming involved with the victim's body after its disposal. The murder is secret; these men generally have hidden the victim's body carefully. The killer's knowledge that he alone knows this secret gives him the sense of power and control that his fantasy requires.

Keeping Souvenirs. Many murderers' postcrime behavior involves the keeping of various items, generally associated with the victim, as "souvenirs" of the murder (this was the case in 32 of 118 murders, or 27 percent). The value to the killer of these items as reminders of the murder outweighs the risk of being identified through the possession of such incriminating evidence. The souvenirs provide the killer with tangible proof that he was able to activate his fantasy, as well as with a catalyst for further fantasizing.

Souvenirs kept by the murderer range from the ordinary to the bizarre. They may include the victim's belongings, such as clothing and jewelry; rings, watches, and underwear are often saved. As was described earlier, one man kept his victim's suitcase and car, which led to his eventual apprehension. The murderer may keep photographs of his victims: one man saved the photo identification cards his victims carried with them, while another offender took his own photographs of his nude victims before killing them. Body parts are also kept; feet, breasts, and blood have been kept by the various murderers.

Often the items retained by the murderer are those for which he has a particular fetish. These souvenirs have a special, sexual meaning; various articles of underwear are common fetish items saved by the killer, although other souvenirs may be less recognizable as fetish items. In the case of the man who kept the feet of his victims in the freezer, the women's feet in high-heeled shoes provided him with sexual excitement.

Not all souvenirs belong to or are directly associated with the murdered victim. The murder weapon itself may be of such importance to the killer that despite a seemingly commonsense need to discard evidence it is kept as a souvenir. In one case, the murderer refused to reveal to authorities where the gun and knife he used as murder weapons were hidden. Saying that they were "special" to him, the man stated that he was considering bronzing them if or when he was released from prison.

What the murderer ultimately does with the souvenirs is closely connected with the significance of both the items and the murder. The souvenirs may be cherished and repeatedly examined; fetish items in particular provide sexual stimulation. The souvenirs are sometimes given away, however. Again, it appears that in so doing the murderer faces a high risk of casting suspicion on himself. One murderer gave his victim's jewelry to his girlfriend and told her not to ask questions about it. In another case, the killer gave his wife the bag of groceries his victim had loaded into her car before she was killed. The wife's suspicions were aroused by the unfamiliar items in the grocery bag; her husband later confessed to her.

In this research project, personal items belonging to the victim that the offender kept were called souvenirs. In actual practice, FBI profilers distinguish between souvenirs and "trophies." The distinction lies in the meaning of the item to the offender. On one hand, it is found that the disorganized offender keeps items belonging to the victim as a remembrance of the event (the murder) and perhaps as fuel for fantasies of such acts. On the other hand, an organized offender tends to keep personal items belonging to the victim as a type of trophy or prize commemorating a successful endeavor. For him, the item is much like a mounted animal head is to the big game hunter—proof of his skill.

Participating in the Investigation The murderer's postcrime behavior may involve some form of participation in the police investigation of the murder (in twenty-four of 118 murder cases, or 20 percent). This participation may be an avid following of news accounts of the case or an active injection of the self into the police inquiry. Whichever form the murderer's involvement takes, it is clear from his behavior that this participation sustains the high level of excitement generated by the act of murder.

For those men who follow the investigation in the news media (54 of 118 murder cases, or 46 percent), it appears that they derive pleasure seeing how they have eluded police as well as how their acts have generated attention.

Their power to shape events have been, in a sense, validated through the news media's coverage of the murder. These men may seek out television, radio, and newspaper reports of the crime, they may save newspaper clippings, and they may even keep a written diary about the postcrime events.

The murderer who injects himself into the police investigation indicates his need to demonstrate his power and control as well as to maintain an active involvement in the murder, the source of his excitement. He believes he can fool investigators, and he may write or call police, or even leave clues for them to find. He taunts investigators to catch him. He is actively engaged in trying to show his superiority; thus, he may have made the body easy to find. As one murderer commented, "You wouldn't get any credit if it wasn't."

Evidence in at least one case suggests that the aftermath of the murder may be as or even more exciting than the act of killing. Although the murderer recalled feeling sexually excited as he shot his female victims from afar, it was the investigation of these murders that provided him with the full expression of his fantasies. After each of the six murders, the man saved news articles and photos concerning the murders and kept a detailed scrapbook of events. He repeatedly masturbated while looking at photographs of the victims; he wrote letters about the crimes to police and to the press throughout the investigation. One might speculate that for this man, the aftermath of the murders eclipsed the killings themselves in providing a sense of excitement and power.

Relation between Postcrime Behavior and
Method of Killing

Do these behaviors have any relation to the method of killing? The relation between the type of weapon used to murder in sixty-four cases with data and twelve postcrime behaviors was examined. Two categories of weapons were used for the analyses: (1) only a firearm (n = thirty-six of the sixty-four cases), and (2) only a blunt or sharp instrument (n = twenty-eight of the sixty-four cases). The results indicate that in murders in which only a firearm was used, the offender was more likely to have kept a diary (56 percent versus 26 percent), kept newspaper clippings (64 percent versus 26 percent), followed the case in the newspaper or other media (82 percent versus 50 percent), and to have confided in someone or hinted about his crime (21 percent versus 6 percent). The offender who used a firearm only was also somewhat more likely to have taken photos of the victim (21 percent versus 11 percent) and to have revisited the scene of the crime (44 percent versus 34 percent).

The offender who used a blunt or sharp instrument only was somewhat more likely to have interjected himself into the investigation in some manner. Little or no relation was found between the type of weapon used and keeping souvenirs of victims, communicating with police/media, changing residence or job, or leaving town.

The completion of this phase initiates the feedback filter whereby the offender reflects on his crime, justifies his actions, and learns from his experience in preparation to repeat another crime, if not apprehended.

Apprehension

Ultimately, police apprehension of the murderer brings his behavioral participation in the various phases of his act of killing to a conclusion. Apprehension occurred in a variety of ways. Some murderers were identified by a surviving victim (six out of thirty-six) or by a partner or spouse (two out of thirty-six). Some murderers turned themselves in (four out of thirty-six). Six were identified when apprehended for a crime other than the homicide. And eighteen or 50 percent were identified through police investigation. Two of the eighteen cases were profiled by the Behavioral Science Unit at the FBI Academy.

The murderers' fantasy-fueled postcrime responses may provide important information to investigators. The saving of souvenirs linked several murderers with their crimes, and in other instances police suspicions about the murderers' identities were confirmed by the evidence of the souvenirs.

Apprehension does not end the fantasy of murder. The level of excitement may drop; the physical stimulation may subside. Yet the fantasy continues; the murderer relives one murder and plans another. One of the murderers interviewed for the study became enraged when the agents wanted to see his cell. The walls were covered with pornographic (especially bondage) materials.

Legal Aspect

In reviewing the legal records of the thirty murderers, it was revealing to note that seven of the murderers (20 percent or seven out of thirty-five cases with data) had committed the murder while on bail. In thirty-two cases with data, nine (28 percent) of the murderers plea-bargained their current sentence (one to a nonsexual offense and seven to less time).

Prior Sexual Assaults

A review of previous offenses indicated that only two (6 percent or two out of thirty-four cases with data) had no prior sexual assault conviction and thirteen (38 percent) had four or more such convictions. Fourteen men answered the questions of the number of sexual assaults for which they were not apprehended and of that number three (21 percent) claimed no such assaults while eight (57 percent) reported between one and six sexual assaults for which they were not apprehended and three (21 percent) reported more than twenty-five such unapprehended assaults. When asked for the number of sexual assaults for which they were acquitted yet actually had committed, out of twenty men responding, thirteen (65 percent) reported none, four (20 percent) reported one and three (15 percent) reported two or more. In contrast, out of nineteen men responding to the question of the number of sexual assaults for which they were wrongly found guilty, sixteen (84 percent) reported none, two (11 percent) reported one, and one (5 percent) reported two. Out of twenty men reporting on the number of previous offenses plea-bargained, thirteen (65 percent) said none while seven (35 percent) reported that between one and three such sexual assault offenses were plea-bargained (two criminals bargained to a lesser sexual offense, three criminals bargained five offenses to nonsexual offenses, and three criminals bargained six offenses to less time).

The question of undetected sexual offenses occurring while in the military was asked of those who served in the military. Out of thirteen cases, eight (62 percent) were either yes (self-report) or suspected (from military record).

The age of first conviction for homicide indicated that ten (28 percent) of the murderers were juveniles when they first murdered. This early violent behavior is emphasized in chapter 6.

6
A Motivational Model for Sexual Homicide

The conceptual framework for understanding sexual homicide has five interacting components that were described in chapters 2–5: (1) the murderer's social environment, (2) child and adolescent formative events, (3) patterned responses to these events, (4) resultant actions toward others, and (5) the killer's reactions, via a mental "feedback filter," to his murderous acts (see figure 6–1). It is important to note that the model deals primarily with psychosocial and cognitive factors and does not address the influence of neurobiology or genetic factors that may be present under certain conditions. We also present a case example to illustrate the components of the model.*

The Model

Social Environment

Child and family theorists often suggest that the structure and quality of family and social interaction, especially in the way the child perceives family members and their interaction with him and with each other, are important factors in a child's development. For children growing up, the quality of their attachments to parents and to other members of the family is most important in how these children later as adults relate to and value other members of society. Essentially, these early life attachments (sometimes called "bonding") translate into a blueprint of how the child will perceive situations outside the family.

In our population of murderers, this social bonding fails or becomes narrow and selective. Caretakers either ignore, rationalize, or normalize various behaviors in the developing boy or, through their own problems (such as criminal behavior or substance abuse), support the child's developing distortions and projections ("I was framed."). People who are significant to the boy do not provide nurturing and protection; rather, they impose adult

---

*Caroline Montan, J.D., provided the legal analysis of official records for the case illustration and Carol R. Hartman, D.N.Sc., provided the psychological case analysis.

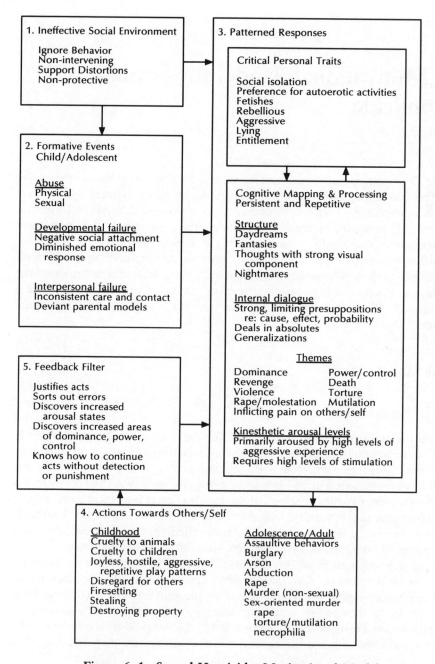

Figure 6–1. Sexual Homicide: Motivational Model

Source: A.W. Burgess, C.R. Hartman, R.K. Ressler, et al., 1986.

expectations on the boy ("Boys should be strong and take care of themselves."). Adults are nonprotective and nonintervening on behalf of the boy. The boy may be punished for a specific antisocial act, but the social restriction does not register in an experiential and cognitive way; that is, the boy is reprimanded or brought to court, but he normalizes the behavior as "all boys get into trouble." The ineffective social environment expands from caretakers to individuals in a community whose work brings them into contact with the young person (for example, teachers, counselors, ministers, police, attorneys, judges).

Formative Events

Three factors contribute to the formative events component of our model. The first of these is trauma, in the form of physical or sexual abuse. The developing child encounters a variety of life events, some normative and others beyond the range of normal, usually extraordinarily negative. In our second chapter, we describe some of the nonnormative events, which include direct trauma (physical and/or sexual abuse) and indirect trauma (witnessing family violence). Within the context of the child's ineffective social environment, the child's distress caused by the trauma is neglected. The child is neither protected nor assisted in recovery from trauma; his external environment does not address the negative consequences of the events.

One assumption regarding early traumatic events is that the child's memories of frightening and upsetting life experiences shape his developing thought patterns. The type of thinking that emerges develops structured, patterned behaviors that in turn help generate daydreams and fantasies. The literature on children traumatized by sexual and physical abuse and by witnessing violence reports the occurrence of dreams, nightmares, and disturbing memories of the trauma (Burgess and Holmstrom 1974, 1979; Conte 1984; Pynoos and Eth 1985). Other studies have documented these children's engaging in painful, repetitive acting-out of the traumas (Axline 1969; Gardner 1971; Terr 1979, 1981, 1983). Play of emotionally disturbed and troubled children often contains conflicted and obsessive themes, contrasting with the creative and flexible themes noted in nondisturbed children. We believe the traumatized child's play remains fixed on thoughts associated with the traumatic event (Hartman and Burgess 1986) rather than becoming integrated in play activities or in art expression through drawings (Howe, Burgess, and McCormack 1987). Successful resolution of traumatic events results in an adaptive integrated patterned response. Unsuccessful resolution of trauma underscores the victim's helplessness; and aggressive fantasies, aimed at achieving the dominance and control missing from reality, emerge (Burgess et al. 1984; Pynoos and Eth 1985; MacCulloch et al. 1983).

A second assumption regarding early traumatic events is that manifestations of the impact of distressing events, such as direct sexual and physical abuse, are influential in the child's social development (Burgess et al. 1984; Conte 1984; Pynoos and Eth 1985). Concurrent with the abusive event, the child may experience a sustained emotional/physiological arousal level. When this sustained arousal level interacts with repetitive thoughts about the trauma, the child's perceptions and patterns of interpersonal relationships may be altered.

The second factor contributing to the formative events component of our model is developmental failure. For some reason the child does not readily attach to his adult caretaker. As a result of this negative social attachment, the caretaker has no influence over the child and later over the adolescent. If the child has been psychologically deprived or neglected, he may feel a diminished emotional response.

Interpersonal failure, the third factor in this model component, is the failure of the caretaking adult to serve as a role model for the developing child. There are various reasons for this failure, including the caretaker's being absent or serving as an inadequate role model (for example, a parent with problems of substance abuse or an abusive parent). The child may experience a violent home environment where he sees aggression (such as drunken fights) associated with the sexual behavior of adult caretakers.

Patterned Responses

The patterned responses component (the manner in which the person operates) of our motivational model includes two subcategories: (1) critical personal traits, and (2) cognitive mapping and processing. These subcategories interact with each other to generate fantasies. ·

Critical Personality Traits. In the positive growth and development of a child, positive personality traits of trust, security, and autonomy help establish the child's relationships with others. These critical traits, in combination with the effective social environment, allow the child to develop competency and confidence.

There was a propensity for the thirty-six men in the murderer group to develop negative rather than positive personal traits. These negative traits interfere with the formation of social relationships and with the development of an emotional capacity within the context of adaptive human encounters. Increased social isolation encourages a reliance on fantasy as a substitute for human encounter. In turn, individual personality development becomes dependent on the fantasy life and and its dominant themes, rather than on social interaction. Without human encounters and negotiations, the individual fails to develop the corresponding social values.

The personal traits critical to the development of the murderers in our study include a sense of social isolation, preferences for autoerotic activities and fetishes, rebelliousness, aggression, chronic lying, and a sense of privilege or entitlement. The murderers' sense of social isolation is profound, as are their thoughts of being different from others. Very few indicate that they had close friends during school. What emerges is a disregard for human relationships or a well-fixed anger at a society that rejects them. This isolation is also revealed through the men's preferences for autoerotic activities. The murderers' chronic lying underscores their lack of trust and commitment to a world of rules and negotiation. Rather, distrust and a sense of entitlement to whatever they can get dominate their perceptions. Their social isolation and aggression interact, restricting sexual development based on caring, pleasure, and companionship. Because they are so isolated, the men have little opportunity for interpersonal experiences that might modify their misconceptions about themselves and others. They relate to other people only through fantasy. In turn, fantasy rather than real experience becomes the primary source of emotional arousal and that emotion is a confused mixture of sex and aggression.

Cognitive Mapping and Processing. Cognitive mapping refers to the structure and development of thinking patterns that both give control and development to one's internal life and link the individual to the social environment. The process of cognitive mapping generates the meaning of events for an individual. Cognitive mapping and processing are aimed at self-preservation through the reduction of helplessness, terror, and pervasive anxiety. They are introduced and sustained by our first two model components, ineffective social environment and unresolved traumatic formative events, and become established in the patterned responses.

In the murderers, cognitive mapping is fixed, negative, and repetitive, moving the individual to an antisocial position and view of the world. The individual does not interact positively with his social environment because his fantasies and thinking patterns are designed to stimulate only himself and to reduce tension. The stimulation enhances a primitive self-image terrifying to the individual himself and to imagined others. The reduction of tension reinforces his feeling of alienation.

The process continues and takes on a primary role in the psychological life of the individual. Themes of control and dominance over others become a substitute for a sense of mastery of internal and external experience. Consequently, personal motivations, goals, and objectives are shaped by the structure and themes of the cognitive mapping and processing.

Manifestations of cognitive mapping and processing include daydreams, nightmares, fantasies, and thoughts with strong visual components. Internal dialogue generally occurs and is focused on strong, limiting presuppositions regarding cause, effect, and probability. The murderers deal in absolutes and generalizations. They are aroused primarily by high levels of aggressive experience and require high levels of stimulation. The themes of their fantasies include dominance, revenge, violence, rape, molestation, power, control, torture, mutilation, inflicting pain on self/others, and death.

Actions Toward Others

Childhood actions are based on the child's regard and caring for others as well as on self-respect and flexibility. In other words, behavior patterns reflect the private, internal world of the child.

Interviews with the murderers in our study revealed that their internal world is filled with troublesome, joyless thoughts of dominance over others. These thoughts are expressed through a wide range of actions toward others. In childhood, these include cruelty to animals, abuse of other children, destructive play patterns, disregard for others, fire setting, stealing, and destroying property. In adolescence and adulthood, the murderers' actions become more violent: assaultive behaviors, burglary, arson, abduction, rape, nonsexual murder, and finally sexual murder, involving rape, torture, mutilation, and necrophilia.

The early expression of cruelty toward both animals and humans, we believe, sets the stage for future abusive behavior in two ways. First, the early violent acts are reinforced, since the murderers either are able to express rage without experiencing negative consequences or are impervious to any prohibitions against these actions. Second, impulsive and erratic behavior discourages friendships. The failure to make friends compounds earlier isolation from family members and interferes with the ability to resolve conflicts, to develop positive empathy, and to control impulses. Furthermore, there is no challenge to the offenders' beliefs that they are entitled to act the way they do. While this does not mean that superficially they cannot relate to people, it does indicate that in terms of socially effective learning, they have major deficits. They are loners, they are self-preoccupied. Either by daydreaming (loose thoughts) or fantasizing (structured and organized thoughts) they become absorbed in their own thoughts.

Feedback Filter

The murderer reacts to and evaluates his actions toward others and toward himself, and these reactions and evaluations influence his future actions. We term this reacting the feedback filter, because it both feeds back into the killer's patterned responses and filters his earlier actions into a certain way of thinking. All learning has a feedback system; in murderers it is negative and destructive.

Through the feedback filter, the murderer's earlier actions are justified, errors are sorted out, and corrections are made to preserve and protect the internal fantasy world and to avoid restrictions from the external environment. The murderer experiences increased arousal states through fantasy variations on the violent actions. Feelings of dominance, power, and control are increased. The murderer develops increased knowledge of how to avoid punishment and detection. All this feeds back into his patterned responses and enhances the details of his fantasy life.

Warren: A Case Example

The theme for this case is "getting away with murder." It describes the ease with which Warren (a pseudonym), all through his life, manipulated his family and social system (school, juvenile authorities, psychiatric evaluators, court officials) while seriously or fatally injuring many women. It underscores the great difficulty people who came into contact with Warren had in holding him accountable for his behavior.

The case illustrates that some people are highly involved in patterns of planned homicidal behavior and commit murder, not once, but many times. The application of the motivational model will highlight Warren's strong sense of entitlement and identification with his mother; the early development of sexual and aggressive fantasies expressed first through family violence, then extended to neighborhood acquaintances, and then to strangers. As an adolescent, juvenile delinquent acts escalated into his first murder at age fourteen, which was condoned and not revealed by his parents. Soon after his first separation from his family into the military, he attempted a second murder; the victim miraculously survived, and a jury convicted him. His violent fantasies and behavior continued in prison, but he succeeded in manipulating his evaluators, and his sentence was reduced by thirteen years. He was released, married, and attempted to murder his wife before committing three additional murders.

Social Environment

The social environmental circumstances of Warren's case were particularly supportive of family role confusion and deviant, sexually aggressive thoughts and behavior.

Warren was the fourth and last child of Mr. and Mrs. T. Born prematurely; he grew up believing he had died and was brought back to life. Over the years, his mother conveyed, in a dramatic way, other events such as his having seizures because of his specialness in being fragile and premature (even when his physician had said the seizures were due to high fever from tonsillitis). (See table 6–1 for Chronology of Events.)

Table 6–1
Chronology of Events in Warren's Life

Event	Observation
1947 Warren's birth	Nine days in incubator until weight five pounds.
Summer 1947	Tonsillitis with high fever causing "seizure." Warren believes he "died and was revived; it was fate."
1947–1953	Sleeps in same bed with mother.
1948–1952	In care of grandmother while mother works as a clerk in a store.
1953–1965	Mother and Warren sleep in separate twin beds.
1953	Elementary school.
1958	Warren slender.
1959	Warren gains 30 pounds. (In 1976 Warren reports a rape memory of two females using a knife and threatening castration.)
1960	Warren slender.
1961–1962	Involved in purse-snatchings and gang fights.
April 1963	Charged with assault and intent to ravish a fourteen-year-old girl. Charged with robbery (purse-snatching of elderly blind woman). Charges dismissed on a technicality.
May 1963	Interrogated for murder of elderly woman but not charged because of lack of evidence (admits to murder in 1976).
June 1965	Graduates high school.
September 1965	Enlists in the military.
October 1965	Charged with assault with intent to commit murder (convicted in 1966).
1966	Sentenced to twenty years in federal penitentiary.
April 1968	In penitentiary, threatens classroom instructor with bodily harm. Is disciplined.
June 1971	Writes a letter containing lewd comments and threatening to a female teacher. Was transferred to a maximum security prison. Teacher took threats seriously enough to request that she be notified upon his parole.
July 1971	Disciplined for fighting. A knife is found in his cell. Claims an inmate made a homosexual advance.
November 1973	After serving seven and one-half years, Warren is paroled.
September 1974	Marries a woman with four children.
1975	Wife claims Warren had her write a suicide note and had tried to strangle her with a rope.
March 1975	Terminates psychiatric counseling.
November 1975	Shoots and kills a clerk in a convenience store (admits the murder in 1976).

Table 6–1 *continued*

Event	Observation
April 1976	Rapes, murders, and mutilates a forty-four-year-old convenience store clerk.
October 1976	Rapes, murders, and mutilates twenty-four-year-old convenience store clerk. Charged with murder.
1977	Convicted of three murders and sentenced to die.
	Granted new trial. Convicted.
1985	Case under review for sentence.

After his birth, his mother took him into her bed (she claims because of crowded living conditions in the house) and relegated her alcoholic husband to the bedroom of Warren's older sister. This bedroom arrangement continued until Warren was fifteen although after age seven, Warren slept in a twin bed. Any efforts he or his sister made to question this arrangement were met by vague comments from both parents. In addition, Warren, his sister, his mother, and a reportedly domineering maternal grandmother were in a tight union against the father. Two older brothers left after high school and were unavailable as male role models. As Warren became older he was used as a foil to ward off approaches of his father toward his mother. He was encouraged by the women, including his sister, to hit his father. The father was said to be verbally abusive toward Warren when drunk.

In contrast to that closeness, the mother was a strict disciplinarian, described as hitting the children with an electrical cord and demanding obedience. The children were often left in the care of the maternal grandmother, who beat the children with impunity. A peculiar combination of being special and being used by the mother characterized Warren's primary relationship with her.

Early school experiences suggest his isolation from peers and a reliance on his mother, sister, and grandmother. As Warren approached puberty, his underlying anger toward females began to emerge. His school performance was inconsistent. Some teachers considered him very obedient, but a school principal noted in a report that Warren was frequently "lost in fantasy." This observation is paralleled in a report by his sister that at times Warren would sit on the couch, his eyes appearing wild and sunk into his head; he would seem totally absorbed. Although not violent toward his mother as a child, he later became assaultive toward her when he was angry. He would get violent over trivial things such as wanting two hot dogs or wanting chocolate syrup on his ice cream.

Some quotes from Warren's autobiography include the following: "I died when a few months old and [was] revived as if it were fate . . . I was a freak in others' eyes . . . I chose to swallow the insults." He made the analogy, "I was a dog who got petted when I used the paper."

Formative Events

The critical formative events are the overstimulating physical contact between Warren and his mother, the conflictual parental relationship, the physical and verbal abuse of the children, and the family-condoned aggression toward his parents that began around adolescence. These factors support Warren's failure at interpersonal attachment to people outside the family and to males within the family. The home environment denied or minimized the aggressive acts external to the family.

Patterned Responses

One critical personal trait of Warren's, entitlement, developed from the preferential treatment of Warren by his mother. Also important was the indication that Warren became lost in aggressive fantasy early in his development. Subsequent information revealed that this fantasy was sexually linked to masturbatory activity. He admits to compulsive masturbation, a fetish for female underwear, and spying on his sister in the bathroom. This clustering of sexualized interests, acknowledged by Warren, is his conscious awareness of his developing fantasies that are first passive (for example, masturbating under bed covers, peeking through keyholes, and stealing underwear) and confirms his reliance on fantasy to generate excitement and states of pleasure (in contrast to normal peer interaction).

The second part of the patterned responses is Warren's thinking. There was an early reliance on aggressive fantasies as the domain of primary emotional expression as noted in family violence. The sexualized fantasies began to merge with the aggressive behaviors, derived, in part, from anger and retaliation from childhood experiences. It is important to note the ease with which Warren can be violent. There are no thoughts blocking him or challenging his behavior either externally or internally. He knows how to be polite and superficially engaging but there is little that inhibits his expression of aggression first toward family members, then to neighborhood acquaintances, and later to strangers.

Action Toward Others

Although Warren had no juvenile convictions, there was delinquent gang behavior in his early teens. He and two peers snatched purses on a rather regular basis. He alone was accused of striking an elderly blind woman and taking her purse. The blind woman had a fourteen-year-old niece who accompanied her in the morning to the bus and who would bring her home after work when she got off the bus. One afternoon, Warren cursed at them and snatched the woman's purse. The niece picked Warren out of a lineup.

While the robbery was being investigated, an elderly woman who lived in the community and had reportedly been talking to Warren about his "wrong-doing" was found shot in the head in the same vicinity where the purse-snatching took place. Tracking dogs were brought to the scene, and the dogs led the police to the Warren's house. The father said Warren had been home all evening. Warren was taken to the police station for interrogation on the murder and the robbery. He was considered a prime suspect since he was present when neighbors noted their .38-caliber revolver missing. Warren and the boys belonging to this family had been playing with the revolver a day or two before its disappearance.

Warren refused to talk with police until his mother came to the police station. She reinforced that he not talk. Realizing Warren was not going to talk, the police suggested that he be given some psychiatric help. The parents were angry at this suggestion and retained a lawyer. Subsequently all charges were dropped—the robbery indictment because of a technicality, and the murder charge because of a lack of witnesses.

At no point during his childhood or adolescence did Warren show much interest in girls. His only girlfriend during high school was a thirteen-year-old he was unable to date. He would visit her at her home and maintained contact with her, asking her to wait for him until he returned from the service.

Warren completed his high school education and enlisted in the military. One month later he was charged with attempted murder of a young woman who was found unconscious and badly beaten. Prompt emergency attention was critical in saving her life. Physical evidence linked him to the crime.

Feedback Filter I

The dominant aspect of the first feedback filter (that operates until his arrest) is that all Warren's aggressive acts were somehow mitigated by the family system. The mother did not acknowledge or report the family violence but rather constantly protected and defended her son. The father was absent, unavailable and passive as a protector. At this point, we can see a strong environmental system of support for violence by the adolescent and degradation of the father. The family social system fails and the outside social system (police) is unable to intervene. Warren learned the system is basically weak as was his father, and he had complete reign and freedom; this added to an increased preoccupation and realization of very sadistic fantasies. He literally gets away with murder.

He completed high school and separated from the family for the first time when he entered the military. Within one month, he was again in serious trouble. Without parental protection and intervention, Warren was charged with the attempted murder.

Psychiatric Evaluation

In November 1965, Warren was psychiatrically evaluated as part of the pretrial investigation to ascertain whether the insanity defense could be raised before the court-martial. The legal standard at the time asked this question: Was the offender so far free from mental disease or defect at the time the crime was committed that he was able to distinguish right from wrong and adhere to the right?

During the examination period at a hospital, Warren made no attempt either to affirm or deny the charges against him. He did relate that he remembered securing the building in question except for one door, and then remembered seeing the woman working at her desk. At five-fifteen he took the bus home, arriving about six. He then went to the mess hall to eat dinner and after dinner went to play pool. At no time did he claim there was a period of time he could not remember. The panel of psychiatrists found him alert and oriented; however, there seemed to be less than the expected amount of anxiety present, considering the nature of the circumstances and the charges against him. Later he denied knowledge of the incident, saying that if he did do it he didn't remember it. The only time he seemed to express some feelings was when he mentioned his mother and how he thought she would be upset by all that had happened. When the victim was mentioned, his face seemed to cloud up a bit, and he seemed more anxious. If anything, his outward demeanor was calm and relaxed. When questioned about this, he said, "There is no reason to be concerned until I find out what they've got against me."

The psychiatric diagnosis given was: Aggressive reaction, chronic, severe. The report also noted that Warren had intense resentment toward authority figures and toward anyone he felt would be likely to push him around. He had a history of having been involved in gang fights during his teenage years, with aggressive, belligerent attitudes, and admitted fantasies of destructive behavior toward anyone he felt was crossing him. He also exhibited marked dependency needs, which he tended to deny but which were apparent in his intense and close relationship with his mother. The panel further found that at the time of the commission of the alleged offense, Warren was so far free from mental defect, disease, or derangement as to be able to distinguish right from wrong; that he possessed sufficient mental capacity both to understand the nature of the charges against him and to cooperate on his own behalf; and that he was not suffering from a chronic, disabling psychosis.

This testimony was accepted without further analysis, and it effectively ruled out Warren's chance of raising the insanity defense before the court-martial.

Warren pleaded not guilty at trial. The following, abstracted from the trial testimony of the victim, weighed heavily in the evidence.

> A nineteen-year-old enlisted woman, performing duties as an accountant, decided at quitting time to work late. Another department in the building was responsible for securing the building. Normally three doors were padlocked from the inside, and the only exit was through the southeast door. Fifteen minutes after quitting time, a young man came to the door and spoke to the woman. She had not seen the man before and did not recognize him. He was large and wore a uniform. He asked her to be sure to lock the windows and turn off the lights when she finished. She then heard him go to the northwest door, put the padlock on and then walk down through the middle section of the building. She remained ten or fifteen minutes and decided to go home. She picked up her coffee cup and a soda pop bottle and started toward the section containing the coatroom. The next thing she remembered was lying on the floor with her head over the stairs and someone on top of her choking her. This was a large white man. She kicked him away and turned over and started trying to crawl away, and he moved toward the corner and was holding a long object, which she thought to be one of the metal ashtrays. He said, "If you scream, I'll hit you." She doesn't remember him hitting her, and the next thing she remembered was someone pulling her hair. She asked why and the doctor said it was all right, that they were sponging her head.

Subsequently, she received medical treatment and was found to have multiple lacerations to the scalp, forehead, face, right ear, and nose. She had a fractured skull. Three teeth were broken. She was hospitalized for seven weeks. After release she continued to have frequent and severe headaches, memory loss, palpitations, and pounding heart.

Warren was convicted of assault with intent to murder and sentenced to twenty years at hard labor.

Internal and External Pressure on the System

The curtailment of freedom is difficult for an individual accustomed to getting what he wants. It is no surprise that once Warren was sentenced to prison, he and his mother exerted two types of pressure on the justice and psychiatric systems. At the legal level, letters for appeal began to build in Warren's file. When that endeavor failed, a change in Warren's behavior (from negative to positive) was noted in the psychiatric summaries. Suddenly there was a recommendation for clemency ("good behavioral progress") and a reduction in sentence.

Legal Summary of Appeals

The details of the appeal process are presented to illustrate the persistence of Warren and his mother as well as the time and energy provided by the justice system to ensure Warren's legal rights were protected.

Following approval of the sentence by the convening authorities in April 1966, letters began accumulating—first from Warren, regarding an appeal to the court of military appeals (CMA). The two legal issues on appeal were: (1) whether the testimony given by a nurse concerning the victim's words when she regained consciousness was hearsay, and (2) whether bloodstained clothing belonging to Warren had been seized illegally, and therefore had been erroneously admitted at trial.

Both of these issues were resolved against Warren, and the CMA affirmed the conviction in June 1967. The hearsay issue was dismissed because the victim had given the same testimony as the nurse. Therefore, the court held, whether the nurse's testimony was hearsay was immaterial, since it merely repeated the victim's testimony. The seizure of the clothing was held to be legal, since it was the result of a search incident to arrest, one of the major exceptions to the rule that a warrant is required before a search can take place.

A July 18 letter informing Warren of the decision of the CMA was received on July 25. He then wrote on October 9 to the director of military justice, Office of the Judge Advocate General, to request a new trial. On October 16, the judge advocate general replied that Warren was no longer eligible to petition for a new trial since the one-year period had expired (the convening authority had approved the conviction and sentencing on 28 April 1967).

In a November 1967 letter to a senator, Warren's mother protested the denial of a new trial, pointing out that Warren did not get the final opinion of the CMA until after the one-year period had expired, and that no one had advised him of the necessary petition for a new trial during that period. She also expressed concern about irregularities in the first trial and about her son's mental condition.

The senator referred the matter to the Air Force Office of Legislative Liaison, Congressional Enquiry Division. That office informed him that all procedures had been followed correctly, and that psychiatric testing at the time of trial had shown Warren to be competent and sane, although suffering from a character and behavior disorder. Thus, Warren had exhausted all his appellate remedies and was not entitled to petition for a new trial after the one-year period had expired. The only avenue left open to Warren, according to this office, was for him to apply to the Air Force Board for Correction of Military Records.

Correction of military records takes place only in extraordinary circumstances. To qualify for this remedy, Warren would have to prove that he had been a victim of injustice, in which event the board would review his case and make recommendations to the Secretary of the Air Force.

Warren's mother also wrote to another senator and congressman because the same information regarding the reason for not granting a new trial was sent to them.

In November 1967, Warren's request for clemency and restoration to duty was rejected.

In December 1967, Warren wrote to a second congressman, the chairman of the House Committee on Armed Services and to the Constitutional Rights Subcommittee of the Senate Committee on the Judiciary. In both of these letters he explained that he had delayed his petition for a new trial until he received the decision of the CMA, and that at no time had anyone told him about the one-year restriction. Again, these letters were referred to the Office of Legislative Liaison.

In replying to these letters, the Office of Legislative Liaison discussed the then-pending legislation that would extend the period for request for a new trial from one to two years after appeal of sentencing by the convening body. That legislation, if enacted, would make the extension retroactive for two years from the date of enactment. Thus, if the legislation were enacted on or before 27 April 1968, Warren *would* be able to petition for a new trial.

The office again suggested that Warren apply for a correction of military records, or that he apply for a writ of error *coram nobis*. That is, Warren would petition the original court-martial and would bring to the court's attention errors of fact in the original trial.

The new legislation was not enacted until October 1968. Therefore, Warren did not qualify to petition for a new trial, and he did not petition for *coram nobis*. However, in May 1968 he petitioned the CMA for relief. The basis of that petition was that even though the statute only allowed for the one-year period, the judge advocate general has discretionary power to ignore the statute, make a decision to set aside the original conviction, and grant a new trial after considering the subtance of a particular case. This, according to the petition, was particularly important in light of the fact that the one-year period was so short as to amount to an unconstitutional denial of due process.

On 14 June 1968, this petition was denied. Warren tried again in January 1971, writing the staff judge advocate and designating his letter a notice of appeal. This letter resulted in a reply informing Warren that he had exhausted all appellate remedies and that his only recourse was to apply to the Air Force Board for Correction of Military Records.

This application was made in September 1971 and claimed that error and/or injustice has occurred in his case because (1) he was not given his

Miranda warnings when he was arrested, and (2) evidence admitted at trial was insufficient to support the guilty verdict, and certain evidence that had been admitted at trial had prejudiced his case (presumably the bloodstained clothes).

Both issues were resolved against Warren and the request for correction of military records was denied. *Miranda* warnings are only required for arrests taking place after 13 June 1966, and Warren's arrest was March 1966, and the evidence questions had already been fully addressed and resolved by the board of review and the CMA.

Psychiatric Evaluation Summaries

Concurrent with the legal appeals, Warren was periodically evaluated by psychiatric evaluators at the first correctional facility for young federal offenders. It was recorded that he refused to participate in the vocational and educational training courses available. He did not cooperate with the staff and refused any mental health treatment offered. Because he was described as being disruptive to the program, he was transferred to an adult facility.

At his second facility, in March 1968, Warren was examined by a psychologist and found to be of normal intelligence, alert, irritable, nervous, resentful, and hostile. He was described as being impulsive, locked in an idiosyncratic view of the world, easily provoked, and suffering from a severe personality disorder. He was recommended for maximum security.

In September 1969, there was an annual review of his case, and the psychiatric staff did not recommend for clemency at that time. They found Warren had progressed very little in behavior modification and self-improvement since his previous review. He was described as continuing to show resentment and hostility in regard to his military confinement.

In October 1969, Warren was examined by a psychologist and diagnosed as a paranoid schizophrenic in partial remission. He was described as withdrawn, at times preoccupied, and even seemed to be listening to some inner voice (as though he were experiencing auditory hallucinations, which he denied). At intervals he grimaced, grinned for no apparent reason, laughed inappropriately, and frequently engaged in childish talk that was regressive and not pertinent to the examination. He was able to achieve 115 IQ on testing in spite of his air of detachment and seeming inattention. He was described as revealing an immature personality with considerable difficulties in his psychosexual development. He was described as having a self-concept more feminine than masculine and that his relationship patterns and feeling for adults were chaotic. This evaluator was the only one throughout Warren's history who indicated that there might be a possibility of Warren's experiencing auditory hallucinations, and he admitted it was a guess on his part.

In September 1970, Warren was evaluated by a psychologist who described him as being a very immature personality and prone to act inappropriately. He recommended that Warren learn to control and contain himself.

A change from negative to positive evaluations began in October 1970. At that time, the treatment team reviewed Warren's case and wrote that an affirmative action could be recommended in terms of clemency. They felt a reward was in order because Warren had shown constructive behavior patterns and was showing a marked change in his attitude and behavioral characteristics. The team suggested that consideration be given to granting clemency and reducing his sentence to ten years rather than the prescribed twenty. It was the team's belief that a reduction in sentence would allow further latitude in dealing with his repressed hostilities and further strengthen the controls he was exerting over his thought and behavior processes. The staff did not believe that parole at that time was appropriate and would recommend against it, but would suggest that a review of possible parole be given within a reasonable period of time.

In January 1972, however, a psychiatrist remarked on Warren's continued avoidance and denial of the crime. His report urged the parole board to reread the trial testimony, and if they believed Warren did commit the crime, then the parole should be denied. The evaluator did not believe Warren had been rehabilitated and felt he was a very definite threat to every female in the community where he resides. The psychiatrist assumed that he had committed the crime, adding that if he had not a great injustice had been done to the man. The evaluator continued to state that he would not release Warren until he sat down and talked about his feelings. Warren would not talk about his sexual feelings; he was evaluated as denying and repressing them. This psychiatrist believed Warren was manipulating the staff into thinking his behavior change was genuine. It is clear that staff who were recommending clemency did not believe Warren had committed the attempted murder. To this time, he had not admitted to the crime. This psychiatrist was far more convinced of the dangerousness and aware of the psychopathic quality of Warren. However, he held the minority opinion.

In September 1972, two evaluators examined Warren and their reports were a positive recommendation as to Warren's control of his behavior. They acknowledge that he was somewhat immature and self-centered yet believed he possessed sufficient self-control. It was felt he had grown sufficiently in self-control so that he might be recommended for release into society.

In November 1973, after serving seven and one-half years of a sixteen-year sentence (reduced from twenty years), Warren was given a favorable recommendation by the institutional board for parole to his mother. A job was found for him with a shipbuilding company and he was instructed to seek psychiatric treatment.

Warren's manipulation of the psychiatric evaluators is remarkable. No one recorded talking to him about his violent fantasies. In one example of Warren's self-control, they concluded that because he could work in a kitchen with knives (and not assault with them), he was safe to be released. However, they avoided commenting on two violent aggressions noted in a report toward a female teacher and an inmate.

Feedback Filter II

The second activation of the feedback filter for Warren began when he left prison. Prison provides time to reflect on past crimes and thoughts and fantasies that advance the criminal toward perfecting future crimes. We return to Warren's life chronicle and learn what happened after he left prison.

Released and Living in the Community

After his parole in November 1973, Warren lived with his mother and began working. He dated a thirty-year-old divorced woman with one child for several months. She stopped dating him because of his "weird" behavior. Two specific behaviors were described as "watching TV while wiggling his feet and giggling when there was nothing funny on the station," and "making me drive his car because I would have to wear the shoulder seat belt. He would just sit there and watch me drive and grin up a storm." This woman also said he never made any sexual advances toward her.

In March and June 1974, Warren received two moving traffic violations. Warren's mother called the probation officer to report this because Warren was at work. He was given a ticket for speeding and drinking and one for running a stop sign. He was fined $87.50 for driving eighty-five miles-an-hour in a fifty-five miles-an-hour zone. These tickets were not considered of a serious nature by either his probation officer or his counselor.

Warren met a woman, a divorced mother of four, at work and dated her about seven months before marrying her in September 1974. She described Warren as being very quiet and understanding of her and her problem with her ex-husband over visitation rights. She said he was nice and good and different from other men she had met. She did not feel he exhibited unusual behaviors.

By October, Warren reported to his probation officer that his wife had "run off" and he did not know where she was living. He did know she had been to the home of her ex-husband's girlfriend. At that time, she was arrested by local police on a complaint by the girlfriend and charged with aggravated assault and battery. She was taken to the county jail and booked and released on bond. Following her release she did not return to her husband but went to the home of her parents. As of the November parole report, the couple were separated.

Warren's wife described some upsetting incidents that illustrate a repetitious pattern of family violence. Shortly after their marriage she was depressed over the visitation rights of her ex-husband and remarked that she should just commit suicide. She said she wasn't really serious, but he seemed to take it so and told her that if she really wanted to die, he would just kill her. At first they were just "playing around" and he picked up a pillow and pretended to smother her with it. She became very frightened when she realized he seemed to be losing control of himself. She lost consciousness and reported the incident to the police. She said he had forced her to write a suicide note.

In a second incident, she referred to a time when Warren had been drinking. She asked him to help her. He became enraged and threatened to "crush her skull in" if she didn't leave him alone.

A third incident involved a pet rabbit that killed a baby rabbit. Warren, in turn, killed the rabbit by knocking its head up against a post and then he cleaned it for dinner. His wife was shocked by the amount of blood on Warren.

Warren's wife said they had an active and satisfying sex life until the birth of their daughter, at which point Warren lost all interest in sex and helping her around the house. Initially they both worked the day shift but changed to the night shift when Warren said he did not like getting up so early.

Warren's personality and behavior changed so drastically after the birth of the baby that his wife suspected he was seeing another woman. When she questioned him, he would either tell her she didn't know what she was talking about or he didn't remember. He was sleeping poorly. Previously he would go to bed with her at night, but now he would stay up after she went to bed and sit by himself in the living room and watch TV. One night she found him sitting in the dark living room. The television was on without a picture. He claimed he was concerned that something would happen to the baby or to her. The wife described him as just not being himself.

In December 1974, Warren wrote a letter to his probation officer asking to terminate psychiatric counseling. He related talking to his counselor: "I told him I might be able to get a bonus [at work] if I had no absences. My counselor said he couldn't see any difference in seeing me fifteen minutes a month than not at all. He said he was satisfied that I had been on my own long enough and had no problems other than my traffic tickets, which he said he also had. He was agreeable to discontinue my visits. I told him I saw no problems that I could not handle and that I would leave it up to him. So if it's all right with you, I will no longer have to visit the clinic. If I have a problem arise I will call my counselor for advice and the help I might need." By March 1975, Warren's psychiatric counseling was terminated after one year.

In October 1975, Warren's probation officer wrote in support of a reduction in sentence. He reported that Warren was reunited with his wife and that he had maintained his job. In November 1975, Warren's sentence was reduced thirteen years and he was due to complete parole supervision March 1979.

Charged with Murder

On October 1976 Warren was charged with murder, robbery, and rape after police apprehended him leaving a crime scene. The following include a description of the crime scene and Warren's confession.

A twenty-four-year-old, five-feet-four-inch tall, 170-pound mother of two children was reported missing from her job as a clerk in a convenience store by a customer who found the store empty at 10:00 P.M. The woman was last seen sweeping the steps of the convenience store at 9:45 P.M. by a man living across the street. Another witness stated that about 10:00 P.M. he had heard a vehicle "spin out" and leave the store at a high rate of speed. The following day a massive search party failed to reveal any leads or clues.

Two days later a landowner observed a man acting suspicious in his woods. He reported a description of the man and his truck and then went to the site. He found a nonmutilated body and reported it to police. While waiting for the police, the landowner saw the man return to the site. When police arrived, the body was noted to be mutilated.

The body was located in a wooded area adjacent to an old corn field. Approximately thirty yards off the main road appeared to be the initial crime scene. The grass in this area was smashed down, approximately eighteen inches high, and bloody. There were drag marks in this area to where the body was located. Postmortem lividity indicated that the body, found laying face up, had spent some time, probably at least eight hours, on its back after death. Grass found clutched in the victim's hand was growing at the scene where the initial attack was believed to have taken place. The left breast had been cut off and was missing. There was an incision in the right breast at the rib cage approximately three inches long and an incision four inches long in the victim's abdomen. All of the cuts were made postmortem. The body was partially covered in the lower area by a couple of old boards that appeared to have been in the area. Wounds were noted to the back of the head area.

Police set up a roadblock to apprehend the suspect seen leaving the area. Before reaching the roadblock, Warren turned off the road onto a narrow trail that led to an open field. After wrecking his truck, he jumped out of the vehicle and into some bushes. The police helicopter observed this, and began circling the area; there was no way for him to escape out of the small wooded area as it was soon surrounded with deputies and their cars.

Approximately one hour after the area had been sealed off and secured, Warren's wife was brought to the scene. She was put on the public address system and begged her husband to give himself up. Warren yelled to his wife that he did everything the police said he did. He also said, "I'm going to make you [the police] kill me." Then he walked out and the police handcuffed him.

After informing Warren of his rights, the officers asked some questions and obtained the following information regarding the crime. Warren said there had been a birthday party for his baby that night and his wife's sister, her husband, and Warren's mother stayed for dinner. He took his mother home and stopped to get gas at the convenience store. He then went to the dog track. He left there and went back to the convenience store, forced the clerk into his vehicle at gunpoint, and drove to a dirt road where he parked the vehicle and raped the woman. He then took her into the woods, forced her to sit down, and shot her.

He went home and lay down, but he couldn't sleep, so he got up and made some chocolate. The next day he went back to the crime scene. He saw some boys walking in the woods and thought they would find the body. He left.

He came back to the crime scene the following day, moved the body to a wooded area, and cut on the victim's breast and stomach with his knife. He then left for a short time, returning to see people and vehicles at the location.

New Information Following Arrest

In further interviewing after arrest, Warren confessed to additional murders. On 11 November 1975, a white, twenty-seven-year-old female was found beaten and shot one time over the eye in the convenience store where she worked. Warren reported that he and his wife had bought gas at the convenience store. He later returned, saw boys in the store, drove on, and returned when the boys were gone. He went into the store and shot the clerk in the forehead. He did not take any money.

On 16 April 1976, a white forty-four-year-old, blue-eyed, blond-haired, 170-pound woman clerk at a convenience store was reported missing at 2:50 A.M. by the man delivering the morning papers. The store was empty. The woman's purse, containing $85, cigarettes, lighter, and glasses case, was in the store. There was no sign of a struggle, nothing was disturbed, and nothing was out of place.

Three days later, the woman's naked body was found near an old abandoned farmhouse. The body was lying face upward; her underclothes were around her ankle. Both breasts had been removed and were lying between the legs. There was a midline incision on the body as well as incised wounds on both legs. There was a bloodstained pathway leading away from the house. A detective magazine was lying near the body and clutched in her right hand were dying kudzu vines. It appeared the killer returned to the scene to make cuts to the inner and outer thigh. The coroner listed the cause of death as a hammer blow to the head.

Warren confessed he abducted the woman at gunpoint, taking her to the abandoned house. He forced her to lay down on the ground after making her take her slacks and underpants off. He then shot her in the face. He returned the next day, moving her closer to the house where he cut her in the stomach, cut off her breasts, and cut her legs.

Trial Preparation

In preparing for trial, Warren's attorneys continually impressed upon him the seriousness of the charges against him and the need for him to search his background for anything out of the ordinary and to tell, if possible, when he began to act or feel abnormal. After a pretrial hearing, Warren indicated his intent to talk. As he talked he began to sweat profusely. His body tensed and his eyes bulged out to about twice their normal size. He began to shake violently and told his attorneys that two female teenagers raped him when he was twelve years old. He did not know them and they did not go to his school. He said he was walking along a road (the same small suburb where he was living at the time of the murders and where he grew up and where all the victims lived) late in the afternoon from school with a baseball glove in his hand. He said the two women began walking beside him and started talking to him about having sex with him. He said he resisted and they took him by the hand and led him into a grassy field near the road where they opened their shirts and one of them took her shorts off. He said they tried to make him have an erection and he said that he "couldn't get it up." He said they kicked him in his testicles and really hurt him. He said they threw him on the ground, one woman sat on him and the other one took off her shorts and placed her vagina over his mouth and, with a knife to his neck, made him "eat her out" (something he says he had never done before or since). He said that after they let him go, he walked home in great pain and was forced by his parents to return to look for his ball glove, which he found near the area where he was attacked. When asked why he did not tell his parents, he said that his dad was always drunk and that "you never mentioned sex or anything like that" around his mother.

He told his attorneys that, on another occasion, he beat up a woman because she tried to get friendly with him and he was deathly afraid. He also said he shot one woman because she looked just like the woman who sat on top of him. He said he returned to his crime scenes and cut on the women because he wanted them to feel pain, "pain like [the females] made me feel."

The attorneys learned about Warren's assault upon a fourteen-year-old girl before his entry into the military service. His version was that he was about to have sexual relations with the girl when she became frightened and refused to cooperate. He said he had intercourse with her on previous occasions and that she was promiscuous around the neighborhood.

Warren also confessed to murdering the elderly woman when he was an adolescent, a crime he had previously denied. The murder gun, subsequently determined to have killed the elderly woman, was found several years later when his family house was torn down.

Pretrial Psychiatric Examination: The Question of Sanity

A pretrial psychiatric examination of Warren was conducted and he was diagnosed as a severe schizoid personality with marked paranoid traits. Also found were necrosadistic traits and episodic discontrol. Warren, it was concluded, was presently sane and competent to stand trial. He knew the difference between right and wrong, he generally had the capacity to adhere to the right, and he could assist in his own defense. However, it was also considered possible that at the time the murders took place, he had not been able to exercise sufficient control over himself to prevent himself from committing the offenses.

Because Warren had already confessed to the murders, his guilt or innocence in a literal sense was not at issue. The question before the jury at trial was whether he was sane at the time the murders were committed. If the jury were to find that he had been sane at that time, there was a strong possibility that the death penalty would be imposed. If the jury were to find he had been insane at that time, he could not be held criminally responsible for his acts. Defense counsel therefore stressed that although Warren was presently sane and could differentiate between right and wrong, at the time the murders took place he had been unable to control his behavior. This inability, they claimed, was solely the result of mental illness and Warren was therefore not criminally responsible for his actions.

For the defense, one psychiatrist diagnosed Warren as being a schizoid personality with paranoid and necrosadistic features and episodic discontrol. He found Warren competent to stand trial. He described Warren as operating at a level of relative detachment from interpersonal relationships, with an outward appearance of being calm and stable; however, at all times Warren was under massive intrapsychic conflicts and immense anxiety. He possessed projective tendencies and erupted in violent behavior. The psychiatrist believed Warren departed from reality at the times of the murders and stated that the murders were so gruesome that they must be considered acts of a psychotic person. This psychiatrist testified that Warren's personality had always been poor in function and, at times, became so further disrupted that Warren became psychotic. It was at those times that the murders occurred and Warren was unable to prevent himself from killing the women.

In attempting to explain why Warren committed the murders, the psychiatrist pointed to his background, making the following observations:

1. Warren grew up in a home where women were in control and men were denigrated.
2. Warren's traumatic victimization at age twelve by two older girls served to confirm his picture of the world.
3. Warren's marriage to a woman with four children demonstrates his tendency to empathize more with children than adults and his feelings about mother figures.
4. The timing of the murders indicated a rekindling of Warren's own childhood fears as a result of the events of pregnancy and childbirth; thus, he perceived it necessary to destroy these women in order to prevent his own destruction.
5. The mutilation of his victims was an attempt to remove gender identification from his victims and render them nonfemale.

During an intense cross-examination, the prosecution established:

1. Warren's choice of female victims with a particular physical appearance demonstrated he could exert some control over his behavior.
2. Had another person discovered Warren during the course of one of the murders, he probably would have been able to attempt to leave the scene and escape detection.
3. Warren was sane between his periods of loss of control and that no known psychiatric program could reasonably be expected to be successful in treating Warren; consequently, he would, in all probability, continue his former pattern of behavior, and might even become more violent over time.

For the prosecution, a psychologist found Warren to be overcontrolled in emotional life, and his contact with reality adequate. Warren used defense mechanisms of denial, repression, projection, and rationalization. Warren was found to be highly ambivalent, emotionally immature, demanding, and threatened by adult role relationships and close ties. Warren was found to have control sufficiently intact to plan and execute the murders without endangering himself. The diagnosis was mixed personality disorder characterized by paranoid and schizoid ideation.

Warren was found guilty on 9 August 1977 and sentenced to death on 7 September 1977. The death penalty was imposed because the aggravating circumstances (the murders were especially heinous, atrocious, or cruel) outweighed mitigating circumstances (no mitigating circumstances such as, offender acting under duress, a consenting victim, or insane).

The conviction was appealed on several grounds. First, it was claimed that Warren had committed the murders under the influence of extreme mental or emotional disturbance, and this should have been taken into account as a mitigating factor in making the decision to impose the death penalty. The court of criminal appeals rejected this argument and concluded that the trial court in this case had applied the aggravating/mitigating circumstances test appropriately, and then correctly imposed the death penalty.

However, two other arguments made on appeal convinced the court of criminal appeals that the conviction should be reversed and the case remanded to the trial court for a new trial. First, the remarks made by the prosecuting attorney were prejudicial. The remarks in question related to the consequences that would result if the jury found Warren had been insane at the time he committed the murders. A pretrial motion precluded the prosecutor from referring at trial to the fact that an insanity finding might allow Warren's immediate release since he was evaluated as presently sane. It was further ruled that no reference was to be made to the fact that Warren had been released before and had subsequently committed these murders. The reason for this ruling was that such references would have no value in providing whether Warren was insane when he committed the murders, concededly the only question before the jury. In closing remarks, the prosecutor stressed testimony that referred to Warren's current sanity. The second ground for reversal concerned a problem with the wording of the verdict form. Warren had been indicted for rape and intentional killing. The trial judge, however, instructed the jurors that if they found Warren guilty, the verdict form should read, "We, the jury, find the defendant guilty of murder as charged in the indictment and fix the punishment at death." This instruction, by itself, was considered improper because it theoretically asked the jury to find Warren guilty of a crime for which he had not been indicted. To complicate things even further, the jury then returned a guilty verdict that read, "We, the jury, find the defendant guilty of capital murder as charged in the indictment and fix his punishment at death by electrocution."

If a jury found a defendant guilty of an offense not charged in the indictment, there was, under state law at the time, said to be a "fatal variance" between indictment and judgment. The legal principle was that a defendant may never be convicted of a crime for which he has not been indicted. Under those circumstances the judgment had to be reversed and the case remanded for a new trial.

There were concurring and dissenting opinions written by judges in the court of criminal appeals and the state supreme court. One of the dissenters from the supreme court decision not to hear the case expressed the opinion that the wording of the jury's verdict was adequate to allow the trial judge to enter judgment, the only real requirement. This is in contrast to the judge who wrote a special opinion concurring with the court of criminal appeals decision. That judge would have rejected the prosecuting attorney's remarks as a ground for reversal, but he considered the "fatal variance" problem to have been enough in itself to justify the court's decision to reverse.

The prosecution petitioned the court of criminal appeals for a rehearing, but the petition was denied. They then appealed to the state supreme court, which refused to hear the case. Thus, the reversal and remand order stood and Warren was entitled to a new trial.

Warren was retried and found guilty in August 1981 and the death sentence was again imposed in September 1981. The case was again appealed; the appeals court affirmed the guilty finding and the case then went to the state supreme court. The case was again remanded to the trial court, this time for a review of the death sentence. The certificate for remand was received in the circuit court in July 1984. Also pending is a civil lawsuit brought by one of the victim's husband against the United States Board of Parole and the United States Bureau of Prisons. In that lawsuit, the husband and children claim money damages for injury to them (i.e., being deprived of their wife/mother) caused by the negligence of government employees in releasing Warren when they were in possession of medical reports confirming him as a homicidal psychotic.

The second feedback filter was in operation during Warren's prison time and was activated upon his release from prison for the attempted murder conviction. Our confidence that Warren's patterned responses had not been challenged and our understanding of the escalation of the sadistic violence was information as to his total resistance and refusal to any kind of psychotherapeutic intervention during his prison or parole time. There were no reports of anyone talking to him about his preoccupation with murderous fantasies. These fantasies had not pushed him to where he thought he was abnormal or crazy; rather they continued to be a primary source of pleasure with which he identified. They remained cognitively implanted at the time of his release.

Three aspects of his second set of murders deserve comment: (1) the escalation of the violent fantasies, (2) his identification with his mother, and (3) the report of his adolescent rape victimization by two females.

Without psychiatric treatment to confront his fantasies, they persisted, intensified, and escalated during his prison time. He had time to become more organized in planning the sequence of his crimes. After release he committed three mutilation murders before being apprehended, indicating an escalation of violent bloody fantasies. His planning and fantasy are noted in his revisiting of the crime scenes with every suggestion of sexual encounters with the dead body indicating his rational rather than irrational behavior.

Warren's marriage occurred after release from prison and represented complex dynamics related to his identification with his mother and his selection of wife and victims. Warren's wife symbolically resembled his mother (a woman with four children). His fantasies toward her led to an attempted murder that was missed by the systems (psychiatric and probation). In the second series of crimes, there is the birth of his own child, followed by his sexual rejection of his wife (recall mother's behavior with father following Warren's birth).

Warren then selected victims outside of the family, repeating the behavior noted in the first feedback filter loop. He knew the three victims in an oblique manner such as purchasing items from the store where they work. As with the first murder victims, he then used his fantasy to build up a dialogue that ended in a justification for murder. That the victims were not total strangers in his mind was the connection and identification with the mother. She is there and she isn't there. He knows them but he doesn't.

With the first crimes, one significant event is his rape at adolescence by the two females. The intriguing question is how to treat this rape memory. One reaction is to disbelieve the account on the basis that deviant female sexuality does not usually manifest itself in such a manner. One could argue that it was a projection of Warren's own sadistic sexual inclinations. Or it might be argued, if the account of rape were believed, that rather than two females, Warren was raped by two males but was unable to admit this fact. If he believed as he reported, another question would be whether a psychic trauma at age twelve had the power to account for the destructive behavior evidenced by Warren. His symptoms suggest it was a reality: the weight fluctuation (e.g., pregnancy fantasy) and the outburst of aggression through the rape and murder include his rage at being sexually inadequate.

Model Summary

When adolescent and adult criminals are studied in terms of the contribution of past events to their criminality, the emphasis in earlier studies has been on the event itself, rather than on the subject's response and reaction to the event. Our motivational model suggests that unaddressed traumatic and early damaging experiences to the murderers as children set into motion certain thinking patterns. Although there may be initial attempts to work through the trouble-some effects of the experience, these attempts become patterns for limiting choices. In addition, a structure of thinking begins to emerge that motivates and sustains deviant behavior through developmental and interpersonal failure and through the alliance of distorted perceptions. Of particular importance is the activation of aggression and its link to sexual expression. The lack of attachment to others gives a randomness to the sexual crimes; however, scrutiny of the thinking patterns of the offenders indicates that there is planning in these crimes, whether the men rely on chance encounters with any victim or whether they plan to snare victims. Although the crimes themselves are premeditated, the choice of victim is generally impersonal and a result of chance selection. If lacking in evidence of sexual assault, the crime appears random and motiveless; the killer's internal fantasy motivating his actions remains unknown.

To summarize these points to the case of Warren, his sense of entitlement, derived from his family environment (demanding whatever he wanted), combined with a role reversal (relegating father ineffective with mother) and narcissistic rage at any infringment in this area (family violence).

We next hear of his teenage activities with his neighborhood peers, an involvement not to be confused with friendships. Teenagers with gang membership often have empty relationships, feeling different or separate because of their preoccupations and fantasy interests and juvenile delinquency is an outlet (for example, Warren's autobiography quotes). Warren advances to major crimes of rape and murder in frustration over being identified for the purse-snatching. He is furious when betrayed by the elderly lady and the fourteen-year-old girl. The entitlement surfaces and he justifies the rape by projecting the girl to be consenting and/or promiscuous. For the murder, he thinks to himself: She criticizes me; she is berating me; therefore, I am justified in killing her. There is also a linkage to the peer group: He proved he could rape and kill. Neither peers nor parents betrayed him; both provided protection and alibis. The childhood indulgence by the parents is the psychopathy; he learns he can get away with murder. He becomes bolder in his violence.

Separated from parental protection, his next known violent act catches him. Physical evidence links him to the crime and he is convicted.

Once inside prison, pressure is applied for his release. He claims innocence and begins the appeal process. The justice system responds fairly to Warren and his mother's letters to high-placed persons and the conviction holds. In prison, he is not held accountable for his actions; he maintains his innocence, which divides and confuses the psychiatric evaluators. Only one evaluator fully appreciates his dangerousness; the majority voted for clemency and he is released after finishing one-third of his sentence. There is no evidence that psychiatric intervention has touched his patterned responses and violent fantasies.

In the community, both the mental health counselor and probation officer are totally unaware of the sexually violent thoughts and behaviors and permit all external controls to be terminated, at which time his third murder is discovered and he is again apprehended and convicted. The justice system is tested a second time; a retrial held; and the appeal to the death sentence is still pending.

Notes

Axline, V.M. *Playtherapy*. New York: Ballantine Books, Inc., 1969.

Burgess, A.W. and Holmstrom, L.L. Rape trauma syndrome. *American Journal of Psychiatry*, 1974, *131*:981–986.

Burgess, A.W. and Holmstrom, L.L. *Rape: Crisis and Recovery.* Bowie, MD: Brady, 1979

Burgess, A.W. and Hartman, C.R., McCausland, M.P., and Powers, P. Response patterns in children and adolescents exploited through sex rings and pornography. *American Journal of Psychiatry*, 1984, *141* (5), 656–662.

Burgess, A.W., Hartman, C.R., Ressler, R.K., Douglas, J.E. and McCormack, A. Sexual homicide: A motivational model. *Journal of Interpersonal Violence*, 1986, *1*:251–72.

Conte, J.R. Progress in treating the sexual abuse in children. *Social Work*, 1984, 258–263.

Gardner, R.A. *Therapeutic communication with children.* New York: Science House Books, 1971.

Hartman, C.R. and Burgess, A.W. The genetic roots of child sexual abuse. *Journal of Psychotherapy and the Family*, 1986, *2* (2), 83–92.

Howe, J.W., Burgess, A.W., and McCormack, A. Adolescent Runaways and their Drawings. *Arts and Psychotherapy 14*, 1987: 35–40.

MacCulloch, M.J., Snowden, P.R., Wood, P.J.W., and Mills, H.E. Sadistic fantasy, sadistic behaviors and offending. *British Journal of Psychiatry*, 1983, *143*:20–29.

Pynoos, R.S., and Eth, S. Developmental perspective on psychic trauma in childhood. In C.R. Figley (Ed.), *Trauma and its wake.* New York: Brunner/Mazel Psychological Stress Series, 1985.

Pynoos, R.S., and Eth, S. Witness to violence: The child interview. *Journal of American Academy of Child Psychiatry*, forthcoming.

Terr, L. Children of Chowchilla: A study of psychic trauma. *Psychoanalytic Study of the Child.* 1979, *34*:547–623.

Forbidden games: Post-traumatic child's play. *Journal of the American Academy of Child Psychiatry*, 1981a, *20*:741–760.

Psychic trauma in children. *American Journal of Psychiatry*, 1981b, *138*:14–19.

Life attitudes, dreams and psychic trauma in a group of "normal" children, *Journal of the American Academy of Child Psychiatry*, 1983, 22: 221–230.

7

The National Center for the Analysis of Violent Crime

The year 1980 marked the beginning of a new decade. It was a time for looking back at the record and evaluating America's progress toward the good life on the one hand and for looking ahead toward the best possible future on the other. Despite many significant accomplishments made during the previous decade, one glaring societal failure stood out. Violent crime had steadily increased in American society and it was continuing to increase at an alarming rate.[1] In fact, the violent crime wave which had begun in 1963 was showing no signs of abatement well into 1980.[2] One of the more reliable indexes, the homicide rate had more than doubled since 1962. More than twenty thousand people were being murdered per year as we entered the new decade. The year 1980 itself became a record year with more than twenty-three thousand people becoming victims of homicide.[3] It was unprecedented mayhem. The rates for other serious violent crimes, such as aggravated assault, forcible rape, and robbery, were equally disturbing. Predatory stranger-to-stranger violent crime was increasing steadily, while the number of cases cleared by arrest were decreasing.[4] Lois Haight Herrington, chairperson of the President's Task Force on Victims of Crime, summarized the national situation like this:

> "Something insidious has happened in America: crime has made victims of us all. Awareness of its danger affects the way we think, where we live, where we go, what we buy, how we raise our children, and the quality of our lives as we age. The specter of violent crime and the knowledge that, without warning, any person can be attacked or crippled, robbed, or killed, lurks at the fringes of consciousness. Every citizen of this country is more impoverished, less free, more fearful, and less safe, because of the ever present threat of the criminal. Rather than alter a system that has proven itself incapable of dealing with crime, society has altered itself."[5]

It was a downward spiral. Something had to be done.

By Roger L. Depue, Ph.D., Special Agent/Unit Chief, Behavioral Science Instruction and Research Unit and Administrator, National Center for the Analysis of Violent Crime, FBI Academy, Quantico, VA. Sections reprinted from the *FBI Law Enforcement Bulletin*, 1986, 55, 2–30.

In 1981, the attorney general of the United States, William French Smith, established the Attorney General's Task Force on Violent Crime. It was his intention to assemble a group of knowledgeable individuals who were highly recognized for their expertise in a variety of pertinent professions and academic disciplines to study the problem of violent crime in America. The task force was to make recommendations regarding what might be done to curb the rapid growth of violent crime and to reduce its adverse impact on the quality of American life.[6]

In addition to establishing the task force, Smith required each agency of the Department of Justice to submit a report outlining what the agency might do to assist in a national effort to reduce the level of violent crime. The Federal Bureau of Investigation (FBI) received its mandate, and Director William H. Webster began a systematic survey of Bureau resources to determine those which could be applied to this national cause. The FBI's Training Division, located at the FBI Academy at Quantico, VA, was immediately considered to be a major resource to draw upon for ideas. It was often used as a think tank to address issues of this nature. After submitting its initial report, the Training Division was designated the lead division in formulating the FBI's role in combating violent crime in America, and within it, the Behavioral Science Unit (BSU) became the center of activity.

Over the years, the BSU had established an impressive record of furnishing assistance to federal, state, and local law enforcement agencies. During training on violent criminal behavior, police officers would frequently discuss unsolved cases and ask for the instructor's opinion about the type of person they might be seeking. They were also interested in obtaining innovative investigative ideas, and the instructors helped them plan case strategies. Soon, the BSU was consulting on unsolved cases on a regular basis through a formalized Crime Analysis and Criminal Personality Profiling Program.

In addition to their training, research, and consultation functions specifically designed to help law enforcement officers deal more effectively with violent crime, members of the Behavioral Science Unit traveling throughout the country had occasion to observe a variety of state and local programs designed to deal with violent crime problems and to identify the best. Ideas such as former Los Angeles Police Department Commander Pierce R. Brooks' Violent Criminal Apprehension Program (VICAP) and the Arson Information Management System (AIMS), codeveloped by Dr. David Icove, were identified, and their founders invited to the FBI Academy for consultation. Such a meeting was held with the Criminal Personality Research Project Advisory Board in November 1982, and resulted in the concept of a National Center for the Analysis of Violent Crime (NCAVC). The main idea of this center was to bring together the fragmented efforts from around the country so that they could be consolidated into one national resource center available to the entire law enforcement community.

In addition to the attorney general's emphasis on the problem of violent crime, the 98th Congress of the United States had shown interest in specific violent crime issues, such as "missing and murdered children," the "sexual exploitation of children," "unidentified dead bodies," and "serial killers."[7,8] For instance, in 1983, Senator Arlen Specter, chairperson of the Subcommittee on Juvenile Justice, Committee on the Judiciary, U.S. Senate, with the strong support of Senator Paula Hawkins, held hearings as a means of gaining information from violent crime "experts" upon which to base new legislative initiatives and funding decisions. The goal was to strengthen the criminal justice system's capabilities to deal more effectively with a breed of human predator that often seemed to travel throughout the country with relative impunity, coldly murdering vulnerable women and children for no apparent motive.

Since 1982, the Office of Juvenile Justice and Delinquency Prevention (OJJDP) had been investigating the possibility of awarding a grant to a diversified group of individuals made up of criminal justice professionals, academicians, writers, and other interested persons in order to establish a pilot VICAP program. Together with the National Institute of Justice, OJJDP funded a meeting of interested parties which was held in the summer of 1983 at Sam Houston State University's Center for Criminal Justice located in Huntsville, Tex. At the conclusion of the two-day meeting, and after several presentations on violent crime topics, the participants unanimously agreed that a National Center for the Analysis of Violent Crime should be established. Furthermore, they agreed that it should be administered by the FBI's Behavioral Science Unit and physically located at the FBI Academy. It was to be a law-enforcement-oriented behavioral science and data processing resource center to consolidate functions for the purpose of providing assistance to federal, state, and local law enforcement agencies who were confronted with unusual, bizarre, and/or particularly vicious or repetitive violent crime.

Speaking at the National Sheriff's Association Annual Conference in Hartford, Conn., on 21 June 1984, President Ronald Reagan announced the establishment of the NCAVC with the primary mission of identifying and tracking repeat killers.[9] It was described as a joint project of the Department of Justice and the FBI.

In June 1984, the NCAVC was given life as a pilot project supported with NIJ funds furnished by way of an interagency agreement between the NIJ and the FBI. In October 1985, the total cost of funding the center was absorbed in the annual budget of the FBI.

As it was originally conceived, the NCAVC consisted of four programs—

Research and Development, Training, Profiling and Consultation, and VICAP. These four basic programs constituted the backbone of the NCAVC and continue to exist today; however, the FBI has found it administratively feasible to divide the programs within *two* Behavioral Science Units.

In January 1986, the original Behavioral Science Unit which administered the NCAVC was split into two units, with each unit responsible for the administration of two of the four NCAVC programs. The Behavioral Science Instruction and Research (BSIR) Unit continues the traditional training functions of the original Behavioral Science Unit, as well as administers the Research and Development and the Training Programs of the NCAVC. The Behavioral Science Investigative Support (BSIS) Unit administers the Profiling and Consultation and the Violent Criminal Apprehension Programs of the NCAVC. The chief of the BSIR is the administrator and the chief of the BSIS is the deputy administrator. The organizational chart of the NCAVC is set out in figure 7–1.

The overall goal has been to reduce the amount of violent crime in American society. The NCAVC's role in this regard is to serve as a law enforcement clearinghouse and resource center for the most baffling and fearful of the unsolved violent crimes, such as homicide, forcible rape, child molestation/abduction, and arson. The NCAVC collects and analyzes violent crime data and provides assistance to law enforcement agencies in their attempts to identify, locate, apprehend, prosecute, and incarcerate the persons responsible for these and other violent crimes and to develop new programs for the prevention of violent crime victimization.

The NCAVC represents a new and powerful weapon in the law enforcement arsenal to combat violent crime. Its research efforts are bringing forth new insights into violent criminal behavior and personality. Its training programs are disseminating the latest violent crime information and investigative techniques. More and more cases are being successfully analyzed, and criminal profiles are being constructed with remarkable accuracy. Imaginative investigative and prosecutive strategies are being developed, resulting in earlier detection and arrest and more-certain conviction and confinement. VICAP is operating to link unsolved violent crimes to one another from throughout the country and to provide assistance in the coordination of complex interagency investigations. The latest advancements in computer engineering are being applied to violent crime problems with promising results.

The concerned efforts of the U.S. Congress, the Department of Justice, and federal, state, and local criminal justice agencies to bring violent crime under control have made a difference in America. They have contributed to slowing the downward spiral and increasing the risk for the violent offender. The National Center for the Analysis of Violent Crime was born out of these national efforts and represents the new feeling in America. We are not only going to fight back—we are going to win.

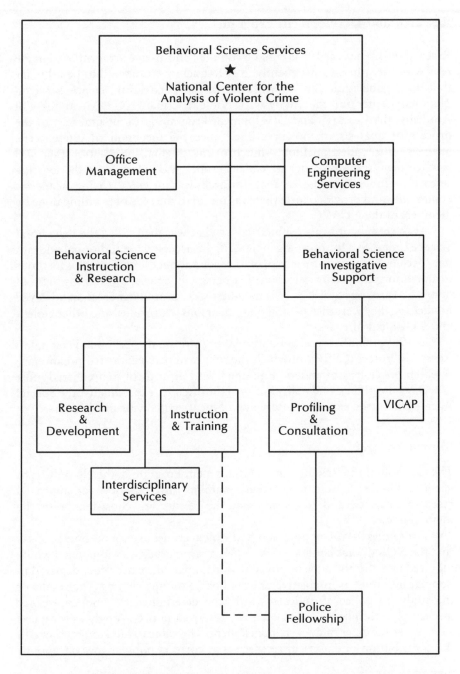

Figure 7–1. Organizational Chart for the National Center for the Analysis of Violent Crime

Research and Development Program*

Research is often regarded as either a complex and arcane art form or a simple review of literature. Consequently, it is frequently considered to be a luxury that an organization can do without. In the Behavioral Science Services/ National Center for the Analysis of Violent Crime (NCAVC) at the FBI Academy, the Research and Development Program is an integral part of the process of analysis of violent crime. Since the inception of crime scene analysis—also called profiling—much of the original information that was used to profile the offender of violent crimes was taken from the existing research. However, most of that research was oriented to the academic community and provided little that was useful to the type of profiling done by members of the NCAVC.

As the number of cases submitted to what was then called the Behavioral Science Unit (BSU) for profiling increased, the necessity for additional relevant data became obvious. Information was needed about the offender, his methods of operation, his victim selection, his personality makeup, and his view of himself. Moreover, by 1978, BSU members were profiling more than unsolved homicides; they were also profiling rapes, arsons, extortions, and other violent and nonviolent offenses.

In 1979, the BSU received approval to institute the Criminal Personality Research Project (CPRP), in which the unit members conducted preliminary research on violent offenders. Equipped with a protocol that covered most aspects of the offense and many facets of the offender's personality, the Special Agents conducted extensive interviews of incarcerated violent offenders.

Current Research

The function of the Research and Development Program in the NCAVC is to generate interest in research, provide administrative support for approved research projects, and to assure that the results are consistent with the methodology.

The studies of violent offenders and violent crimes are not the only projects that the NCAVC has conducted. In 1985, a rape survey was completed which inquired into the attitudes of police toward rape. Police are often depicted in popular literature as insensitive or even hostile to rape victims. The results of the study on police attitudes toward rape determined that police are *not* insensitive to the plight of rape victims. Moreover, police strongly view rape as a serious crime deserving severe punishment. The value of this study is found in the contribution of empirical research that corrects popular misconceptions

*By Richard L. Ault, Jr., Ph.D., Special Agent/Program Manager, Research and Development Program, Behavioral Science Instruction and Research Unit, National Center for the Analysis of Violent Crime, FBI Academy, Quantico, VA.

and reveals what the police themselves think about other aspects of the criminal justice system which prosecutes the offenders.

Another research project accomplished by the NCAVC involved an inquiry into risk-taking and life-experience stress by police officers. The purpose of the study was to ascertain the relationship of recent life experiences—such as divorce, marriage, change of environment—and load stress to risk-taking. Among the results, the researcher found that even though police officers with greater negative life experiences (divorce, death in the family, etc.) took more risks, they did not necessarily fail to achieve their goal more. That is, they may take more risks to achieve a goal, but those risks will not necessarily result in failure.

Still other important research includes studies on arson. The capability exists in the NCAVC to analyze multiple arsons. One NCAVC member developed a computer-assisted system to collect, organize, and analyze information that is important in the evaluation of multiple arson cases. Called the Arson Information Management System (AIMS), it provides computer assistance to fire departments and police to help them develop strategies to predict and prevent multiple incendiary crimes. The latest application of computer analysis of arson is set out in a study based on information received from the Prince Georges County, Md., Fire Department. The results of the study provide significant information on profiles of offenders and their motives for the offenses. Providing the law enforcement community accurate information about motives of perpetrators enables investigators to conduct logical, motive-based investigations. The importance of this type of accurate information cannot be overstated, and the results of these studies will be published in future issues of the *FBI Law Enforcement Bulletin.*

Research is also currently conducted in other topics such as the history of psychological services in policing and the administrative goals of the NCAVC. These projects will be finished in the near future, and their conclusions published as they are completed.

Yet another important area for research is terrorism. An NCAVC member will soon be publishing the results of several years of research into training programs that are designed to enable individuals who may be held as hostages in terrorist—or other—situations to cope more effectively with the stress of their captivity. This research emphasizes hostage survival.

The future itself is a study for the NCAVC. The anticipation of future problems in law enforcement is not being neglected. Using Delphi methodology, a member of the NCAVC is now completing a serious study that attempts to determine the directions of law enforcement in the next twenty years.

Future Research

The future also holds promise for other research topics. Using unique—yet valid—methods for research, members of the NCAVC can address such areas as public corruption, fugitives from justice, jury selection, child molestation, terrorism, and extortion. In fact, areas in the criminal justice system still needing research are limitless.

The changing image and mission of the FBI in the past ten years have provided the National Center for the Analysis of Violent Crime with an unparalleled opportunity to dig into the foundations of violent and nonviolent crimes with the hope of discovering clues about the behavior of offenders that can be applied in a practical fashion to investigations. Members of the NCAVC hope to continue searching to support investigations into violent crime.

The NCAVC Training Program*

The training program of the National Center for the Analysis of Violent Crime (NCAVC) is responsible for all education and training associated with the NCAVC. This responsibility includes providing guest speakers, conducting specialized training for police and FBI Special Agents, and administering the NCAVC Police Fellowship in criminal personality profiling.

NCAVC educational and training efforts are directed primarily toward the law enforcement community. However, we are also interested in sharing whatever knowledge and expertise we may possess with other members of the criminal justice system and those disciplines which have historically provided invaluable assistance to law enforcement (mental health, victim advocates, and various academic fields).

A Training Commitment

The NCAVC was established to provide the law enforcement community with a clearinghouse and resource center for unsolved violent crimes. It does so by collecting and analyzing violent crime data and providing innovative investigative assistance, such as criminal personality profiling and the Violent Criminal Apprehension Program (VICAP). A natural extension of this assistance is to train law enforcement officers in, or at least acquaint them with, the application of behavioral science techniques to the investigation of violent crime. The NCAVC training program accomplishes this task in four ways: (1) Field police schools, (2) FBI Academy courses, (3) speaking engagements, and (4) NCAVC police fellowships.

Field Police Schools

Members of the NCAVC and specially trained Agents assigned to FBI field offices provide cost-free training in violent crime investigative methodology

---

*By Robert R. Hazelwood, M.S., Special Agent/Program Manager, Training Program, Behavioral Science Instruction and Research Unit, National Center for the Analysis of Violent Crime, FBI Academy, Quantico, VA.

for law enforcement agencies throughout the United States. Such courses are one and five days in length and are conducted at sites selected by the requesting agency.

FBI Academy Courses

Courses three to fourteen days in length are conducted at the FBI Academy and include speakers from a variety of disciplines. Officers invited to attend the courses do so at no expense to themselves or their departments.

Speaking Engagements

The NCAVC provides speakers for law enforcement and other professional organizational meetings or conferences. Since June 1985, NCAVC speakers have participated in national meetings of the International Association of Chiefs of Police, the National Sheriffs Association, the Harvard Associates in Police Science, and the FBI National Academy Associates, to name a few. The NCAVC training program has also provided guest lecturers for courses offered at the Southern Police Institute, the Delinquency Control Institute, the Armed Forces Institute of Pathology, and the Federal Law Enforcement Training Center.

Police Fellowship Program

The NCAVC offers a one-year fellowship in criminal personality profiling at the FBI Academy to selected officers. All expenses except salary and benefits are borne by the FBI.

Profiling*

Quickly apprehending a perpetrator of a violent crime—rape, homicide, child abduction—is a major goal of all law enforcement agencies. Unlike other disciplines concerned with human violence, law enforcement does not, as a primary objective, seek to explain the actions of a violent offender. Instead, its task is to ascertain the identity of the offender based on what is known of his actions. Described by one author as an emitter of signals during commission of

---

*By John E. Douglas, M.S., Special Agent/Program Manager, Profiling and Consultation Program, Behavioral Science Investigative Support Unit, National Center for the Analysis of Violent Crime, FBI Academy, Quantico, VA and Alan E. Burgess, M.Ed., Special Agent/Unit Chief, Behavioral Science Investigative Support Unit and Deputy Administrator, National Center for the Analysis of Violent Crime, FBI Academy, Quantico, VA.

a crime,[10] the criminal must be identified as quickly as possible to prevent further violence. While studies explaining why certain individuals commit violent crimes may aid them in their search, law enforcement investigators must adapt the study findings to suit their own particular needs. Criminal profiling is a tool law enforcement may use to combine the results of studies in other disciplines with more traditional techniques in an effort to combat violent crime. It is described in depth in this book.

Case in Point

Criminal profiling uses the behavioral characteristics of the offender as its basis. Sexual homicides, for example, yield much information about the mind and motivation of the killer. A new dimension is provided to the investigator via the profiling technique, particularly in cases where the underlying motivation for the crime may be suddenly hidden from even the more-experienced detective. The following case will illustrate this point.

During the fall of 1982, an urban Midwest police department detective telephonically contacted the FBI's Behavioral Science Unit at the FBI Academy asking for some assistance. The detective described in detail the rape/murder of a twenty-five-year-old white married woman. The detective advised that the apartment where the victim was killed had been ransacked, but they were unable to determine at that time if anything was taken by the killer. In view of the fact that many leads were still outstanding and information concerning the autopsy, laboratory examinations, background of the victim, previously reported neighborhood crimes, etc., was still pending, the detective was advised that a profile could not be provided at that time. After approximately one week, the detective forwarded the necessary information to the local FBI field office criminal profile coordinator. After reviewing the case for completeness, the profile coordinator forwarded the materials to the Behavioral Science Investigative Support Unit at the FBI Academy for analysis.

Color eight-by-ten-inch crime scene photographs re-created the crime and revealed that the victim was killed in her living room, with no evidence of any struggle or defense attempts by her. The victim was lying face up on the living room floor. Her dress was raised up over her hips exposing her genital area, and her panties were pulled down to her knees. The murder weapon (hammer) belonging to the victim was found in kitchen sink, and it appeared that the victim's blood had been washed off the hammer by the subject. Crime scene photographs further revealed that the subject opened dresser drawers and closet doors. Investigative reports indicated the victim's husband advised that jewelry belonging to victim was missing.

The victim and her husband lived in the apartment for approximately six months, and neighbors and associates reported they were friendly and quiet and kept to themselves. The medical examiner concluded in his protocol that there was no apparent indication that the victim was sexually assaulted. Laboratory reports indicated that the victim had been drinking at the time of the assault, and there was no evidence of semen present in or on the victim or her clothing.

From the above information, the criminal profiler advised the detective that he had already interviewed the killer. The surprised detective was presented with the following probable crime scenario.

The victim was drinking with the offender prior to her death. An argument ensued, reaching a threshold where the offender could not take it any longer. Angered, he obtained a "weapon of opportunity" from a kitchen cabinet and returned to the living room where he confronted the victim face to face and repeatedly struck victim about her head and face. After killing her, the offender realized that the police would surely implicate him as the obvious murderer. He then washed blood from his hands in the kitchen sink and also cleaned blood and fingerprints from the hammer. He rolled the victim over in a face-up position and "staged" the crime to appear the way he felt a sexually motivated crime should look. He conducted the staging by making it appear that the offender searched for money or personal property in the apartment.

Upon hearing this analysis of the crime, the detective exclaimed, "You just told me the husband did it."

The detective was coached regarding suggested reinterview techniques of the victim's husband. In addition, the detective was further advised that if the victim's husband were given a polygraph examination, he in all probability would react more strongly to the known fact that he was "soiled" by his wife's blood than to questions concerning his wife's murder. The detective was told to have the polygraph examiner direct questions at the husband, acknowledging the fact that he got blood on his hands and washed them off along with the hammer in the kitchen sink.

About five days later, the detective called the criminal profiler to advise that the victim's husband failed the polygraph and subsequently admitted his guilt to the polygraph examiner.

The Profiling and Consultation Program

The FBI's profiling program has grown considerably since the late 1970s from "informal" analysis and profiling during criminal psychology classes at the FBI Academy to the present formalized program. Currently, the program consists of one program manager and seven criminal profilers and crime analysts. These Agents were selected primarily for their investigative experience, expertise, and educational backgrounds. The Behavioral Science Investigative Support Unit has found that anyone seeking transfer into this highly specialized program must possess above all other attributes and accomplishments a strong investigative background that includes participating in, supervising, and managing major case assignments.

During 1985, the Criminal Profiling and Consultation Program received over six hundred requests for profiling assistance. It is anticipated that once the FBI's Violent Criminal Apprehension Program (VICAP) is fully operational, the number of profiling requests will nearly double annually.

One key link to the success of the FBI's Criminal Profiling Program is its criminal profile coordinators who are located at every one of the FBI's fifty-nine field offices. These highly trained and selected Agents are responsible for screening cases and for providing preliminary investigative suggestions to investigators. While the field coordinators do not have the authority to provide profiles to requesting law enforcement agencies, they are authorized to prepare preliminary "rough draft" profiles which are reviewed by the profiling staff at the FBI Academy prior to being disseminated to the requesting agency.

Criminal profiling is available to local, state, federal, and foreign law enforcement agencies or departments. It should be noted that not every violent crime matter lends itself to the profiling process. The criminal profile coordinators in the FBI field offices determine during review of the case whether it can be profiled. However, while a case may not be suitable for profiling, the coordinator may still submit it to the Behavioral Science Unit for other types of services. Criminal profilers at the FBI Academy may assist the law enforcement community by providing interview/interrogation techniques, investigative suggestions and techniques, establish probable cause for search warrants as a result of National Center for the Analysis of Violent Crime violent offender research findings, assist prosecutors relative to prosecutive strategies, and possibly provide testimony as a witness for the prosecution or as an expert witness during the sentence phase of the trial. All cases must be submitted to the local FBI field office for review and administrative handling by that criminal profile coordinator.

Lt. Vernon J. Geberth, commander of homicide for the New York City Police Department wrote in his book, *Practical Homicide Investigation: Tactics, Procedures and Forensic Techniques*, "This program has proven to be beneficial to law enforcement and has provided homicide detectives with a viable investigative tool . . . . "

Criminal profiling will never take the place of a thorough and well-planned investigation nor will it ever eliminate the seasoned, highly trained, and skilled detective. Criminal profiling has, however, developed itself to a level where the detective has another investigative weapon available to him in solving a violent crime. The offender, on the other hand, has an added worry that in time he will be identified, indicted, successfully prosecuted, and sentenced for his crime.

Automated Crime Profiling*

In the fall of 1983, Special Agents from the FBI's Behavioral Science Unit constructed a criminal personality profile describing an individual who could have been responsible for a series of fires at religious homes and houses of worship that summer in a posh New England community. The profile was prepared at the request of the community's police department, which later discovered that the FBI's profile not only accurately described the suspect in detail but also pinpointed his residence, based upon a series of intricate computer calculations using artificial intelligence technology. The suspect later confessed to the crimes.

This pioneering use of artificial intelligence technology in crime analysis and criminal personality profiling provided the groundwork for the present automation efforts at the FBI's National Center for the Analysis of Violent Crime (NCAVC)[12] In an active project at the NCAVC, experts in criminal personality profiling are taking advantage of the existing technology of artificial intelligence, or AI as it is known to its users, to capture the elusive decisionmaking rules associated with the profiling of serial violent criminals.

This section is an overview of the ongoing research and development efforts by the NCAVC to automate the criminal personality profiling process. Future articles are planned to advise law enforcement researchers and investigators as to the success of this exciting and thought-provoking technology.

Violent Crime Model

The relationship of AI to the profiling process is best described using the "Violent Crime Systems Analysis Model." (See figure 7–2.) This model was developed during the conceptualization and development of the NCAVC computer systems and traces the philosophical activities involved with the detection, prediction, and prevention of violent crime.

The model is divided into *reactive* and *proactive* investigative strategies. Reactive strategies include crime scene investigative support during immediate response to incidents, while proactive strategies explore effective anti-crime programs to both deter and apprehend offenders.

Briefly, the model emphasizes the reporting of violent crimes (step 1) to the NCAVC for crime pattern analysis and classification. This information may come from written media accounts (step 2), crime scene processing (step 3), VICAP crime reports (step 4), or violent crime research findings (step 5). Crime

---

*By David J. Icove, Ph.D., P.E., Senior Systems Analyst, Behavioral Science Investigative Support Unit, National Center for the Analysis of Violent Crime, FBI Academy, Quantico, VA.

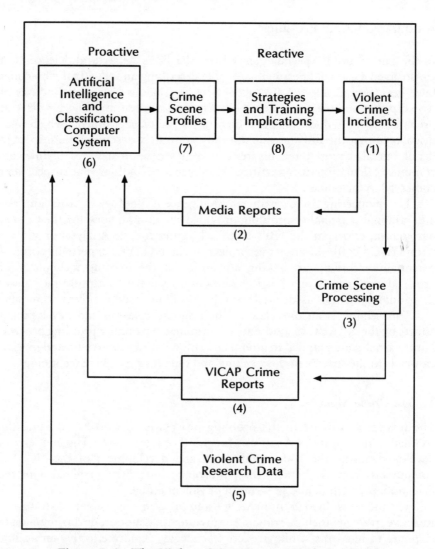

Figure 7–2. The Violent Crime System Analysis Model

pattern analysis (step 6) can determine if any case trends are detected in the profiled incident that have existed in the past, predict the probability of the occurrence of future incidents, and check for the possible identification of prior known/unknown criminal offenders based upon their past methods of operation.

Crime pattern recognition analysis can also classify incidents into naturally occurring groups, such as the type of crime, motive, or temporal conditions. Furthermore, pattern analysis can reveal multidimensional trends and profiles in the crime data which in the past have gone undetected.

Based upon prior profiling experiences in combating violent crimes (step 7), effective prevention strategies are documented for future operational and training use (step 8). Using historical information, actual probabilities of success can be assigned to the suggestions of specific, proven prevention strategies.

The use of effective crime prevention strategies will minimize the risk of future violent crime incidents. Many strategies include operational, personnel, and physical security programs. However, once an incident occurs, the effective case management of the investigation must be carried out. The violent crime investigator at the scene summarizes the incident and submits a VICAP report. The feedback loop is then completed with an inquiry into the model of the encoded case data.

Several computer systems presently serve the needs of the NCAVC in support of the VICAP, profiling and consultation, and research programs. The computers are located at both Quantico, Va., and Washington, D.C.

VICAP

The Violent Criminal Apprehension Program (VICAP) computer system is located at FBI Headquarters in Washington, D.C., and stores information on unsolved homicide-related violent crimes reported to the NCAVC. VICAP crime reports are entered on-line from the NCAVC at Quantico, using a secure telecommunications network.

When a new case is entered, the VICAP computer system simultaneously compares and contrasts over one hundred selected modus operandi (MO) categories of that case with all other cases stored in the data base. After overnight processing, a printed computer report is returned to the VICAP crime analyst handling the case. This report lists, in rank order, the top ten "matches" in the violent crime databank; that is, the ten cases that were most similar to the new case. This crime pattern analysis technique, called template pattern matching, was specifically designed for VICAP and programmed by the FBI's Technical Services Division. The VICAP computer system also produces selected management information system reports which monitor case activity geographically, with hope that it will eventually trace the travels of serial violent criminals across the United States.

Profiling

The profiling and consultation program uses a collection of crime pattern recognition computer programs on mini- and microcomputers at the NCAVC's offices to detect and predict the behavior of violent criminals. The Arson Information Management System (AIMS) is a crime pattern analysis computer program used at the NCAVC which has enabled staff members to predict accurately the times, dates, and locations of future incidents, as well as the most probable residence of suspects.[13]

Computer technology is also necessary to support ongoing behavior science research efforts. NCAVC staff members are encouraged to perform and publish research studies on all aspects of violent crime and rely upon computers at Quantico for their support. Some research projects include the use of portable computers carried into the field.

Artificial Intelligence Project

Using the insight and experience gained with VICAP and AIMS computer technology, the NCAVC staff is now developing a comprehensive AI knowledge-based expert system which will assist users of the NCAVC computer system in tracking and predicting violent crimes. Knowledge-based expert systems have proven effective in applying knowledge to solve problems that ordinarily require human intelligence.[14] Figure 7–3 illustrates this system and the relationships of the various individuals in its design and use. It is anticipated the project will be completed in two years.

Following the diagram in figure 7–3, the *knowledge engineer* transforms prior experiences of the *crime profiler* and the results of *violent crime research* into a *knowledge base*. Using artificial-intelligence computer software, the knowledge base is transformed into *decision rules* defining an *inference engine*. The NCAVC investigators input new cases and receive consultation via a *user interface*.

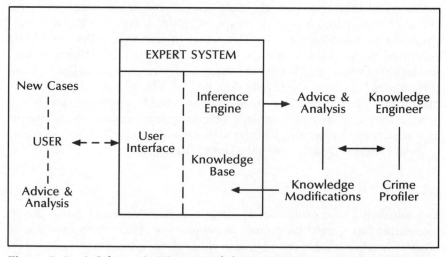

Figure 7–3. A Schematic Diagram of the NCAVC's Artificial Intellligence Knowledge-Based Expert System

The expert-based computer system under development will allow the NCAVC to:

1. Eliminate useless investigative paths which historically have proven fruitless in profiling and identifying the offender.

2. Preserve and recall knowledge of similar cases, criminal personality profiles, and research studies;

3. Display the hierarchy of complex criminal network problems from the general to specific level;

4. Develop and use decision rules which accelerate computation time, as well as allow the investigator to understand the problem better;

5. Receive advice and consultation from the expert system on new and existing cases based upon prior knowledge captured by the system;

6. Preserve information in an active form as a knowledge base, rather than a mere passive listing of facts and figures;

7. Train novices to think as an experienced crime profiler would; and

8. Create and preserve in an active environment a system that is not subject to human failings, will respond to constant streams of data; and can generalize large bodies of knowledge.

AI applications show greater potential for solving complicated crime profiling and assessment problems. Research is currently being conducted in two such uses which will be integrated into the NCAVCs AI computer project.

Social network analysis is a behavioral-science-oriented approach that describes the interaction patterns between people.[15] This analysis can be used to identify possible courses of action an individual or group might take, as well as to surmise as to the hierarchical structure of an organization or group. Examples of the application of social network analyses include structures of organized crime syndicates, motorcycle gangs, and terrorist groups. NCAVC staff members are developing AI procedures to manipulate data and compute the probable hierarchies and interactions of complex organizations.

The behavioral analysis of threatening oral and written communications in extortions, bombings, and terrorist incidents is another viable application of artificial intelligence technology to real-world law enforcement problems.[16]

The NCAVC is actively researching and experimenting with computer-assisted linguistic analysis techniques to evaluate the content of these communications in an effort to determine the authorship profile and assess the viability of the threat.

Summary

Presented in this section have been the systems approach to the management of violent crime data and the development of an artificial intelligence crime profiling computer system for the National Center for the Analysis of Violent Crime. The major benefit of this effort is an effective management information system which will track the activities of the program, assess the impact of law enforcement efforts against violent crime, and introduce automated computer-assisted profiling technology.

The Violent Criminal Apprehension Program*

Origin of the VICAP Concept

On the afternoon of 29 May 1985, Pierce R. Brooks sat down in front of a computer terminal at the FBI Academy and saw his idea, which was some twenty-seven years in the making, become a reality. On that afternoon, he watched as data from the first VICAP crime report were entered into the brand new VICAP computer system. Brooks, who had lived at the FBI Academy for approximately nine months while serving as the first program manager of the FBI's new Violent Criminal Apprehension Program, was just two days from returning to his wife and home in Vida, Oreg.

In 1958, Pierce Brooks, already a ten-year veteran with the Los Angeles Police Department, had been assigned two "different" homicides among his many cases. He believed that both killers had killed before and decided to attempt to find out if similar murders had occurred elsewhere in the country. His available resources were sparse. There was no national information center which collected information on the modi operandi (MOs) of transient killers. There was a teletype system, but teletypes were easily lost and many were not even read. Brooks employed a new tact in the investigations; he began going to the city library and reviewing major city newspapers looking for stories describing similar cases.

The use of the library to search for similar cases during a homicide investigation in the late 1950s was a primitive forerunner of VICAP. It was that effort which spawned the idea that grew into today's reality.

VICAP and the FBI

During the 1970s, Brooks spoke with officials of the U.S. Department of Justice about his concept. Eventually, LEAA funds were approved to finance a

---

*By James B. Howlett, M.A., Senior Crime Analyst VICAP, Kenneth A. Hanfland, Crime Analyst VICAP, and Robert K. Ressler, M.S., Special Agent/Program Manager VICAP, Behavioral Science Investigative Support Unit, National Center for the Analysis of Violent Crime, FBI Academy Quantico, VA.

task force to study the idea. Homicide investigators, crime analysts, and other criminal justice experts from over twenty state and local law enforcement agencies participated.

Coincidental with the activities of the VICAP Task Force were discussions by members of the FBI's Behavioral Science Unit (BSU) at the FBI Academy regarding the development of a National Center for the Analysis of Violent Crime (NCAVC). The NCAVC was seen as a formalization and extension of the existing programs within the unit, as well as an attempt to identify other innovative concepts being developed around the country. The BSU programs had resulted from the work in the development of criminal personality profiling and the supporting research done by members of the unit in the area of violent crime.

A BSU staff member joined the VICAP Task Force, and the Behavioral Science Unit programs merged conceptually with VICAP. In 1984, the National Center for the Analysis of Violent Crime was formally established by an interagency transfer of funds from the National Institute of Justice to the FBI.

VICAP had until then been only a concept, and it was decided that the first year of operation would be considered a field test of all aspects of the program, including the VICAP Crime Report form, the computer support system, and internal procedures. VICAP officially became operational on 29 May 1985, two days before the self-imposed deadline of 1 June 1985.

What is VICAP?

As envisioned by Brooks and implemented by the FBI with his assistance, VICAP is a nationwide data information center designed to collect, collate, and analyze specific crimes of violence. Currently, cases which meet the following criteria are accepted by VICAP:

1. Solved or unsolved homicides or attempts, especially those that involve an abduction; are apparently random, motiveless, or sexually oriented; or are known or suspected to be part of a series;
2. Missing persons, where the circumstances indicate a strong possibility of foul play and the victim is still missing;
3. Unidentified dead bodies where the manner of death is known or suspected to be homicide.

It is important that cases in which the offender has been arrested or identified are still submitted so that unsolved cases in the VICAP system can be evaluated for possible linkage to known offenders. Also, it is anticipated that the VICAP system will be expanded to include rape, child sexual abuse, and arson cases within the next twelve to twenty-four months.

By analyzing the case-related information submitted by law enforcement agencies, the VICAP staff determines if similar pattern characteristics exist among the individual cases in the VICAP system. The identification of similar patterns is made by analyzing MO, victimology, physical evidence, suspect description, and suspect behavior exhibited before, during, and after the crime.

The goal of VICAP is to provide all law enforcement agencies reporting similar pattern violent crimes with the information necessary to initiate a coordinated multiagency investigation which will lead to the expeditious identification and apprehension of the offender responsible for the crimes.

VICAP's First Year

The attainment of the first objective, becoming "operational" by 1 June 1985, and the entry of the first data into the computer were, of course, only the beginning. A very comprehensive three-part VICAP Crime Report form had been developed to collect the information necessary to support the operations of VICAP.* The Bureau's profile coordinators from each of the fifty-nine field divisions received in-depth training regarding the VICAP Program itself, as well as the use and completion of the report form. It then became the job of these individuals to provide training to state and local law enforcement personnel, especially homicide investigators, regarding VICAP and the submission of information using the form.

Perhaps the largest task was that of continuing the development of the computer programs necessary to allow the analysts to manipulate the vast amounts of data in a meaningful way.

The level of detail collected by the report form dictated that large and complex programs be developed. And the type of case matching demanded by VICAP had never been accomplished before on such a large scale. All of these factors combined to make the entire development process slow and occasionally frustrating.

A Major Revision

Approximately six months after VICAP began to receive cases for entry into the system, two things became evident. First, the number of cases being received by VICAP was fewer than originally anticipated. Second, developing a good understanding or overview of individual cases from information contained in the VICAP reports was difficult for the VICAP staff. The VICAP Crime Report form was collecting information that was too detailed for its intended purpose of providing crime analysts with the information necessary to establish linkages among cases.

---

*This form is reproduced in the Appendix.

VICAP's purpose was not to investigate cases but to analyze them. In order to do so effectively, general patterns have to be discernible, and that is better done by establishing the general parameters of events rather than extremely specific reconstructions. Crime scenes are seldom exactly replicated, but general MOs are. Crime analysis and criminal investigation require different levels of specificity.

In addition, feedback regarding the report form was being received from the investigators who were completing the form. A vast majority commented that it was "just too time consuming." The value of VICAP and the benefits to be derived from completing the form were not the issues. It was, however, becoming apparent that the time had come to carefully review and reevaluate the VICAP Crime Report.

In early 1986, the report underwent an extensive review, revision, and validation process. The revision was tested during controlled tests by over thirty experienced investigators attending the 144th Session of the FBI National Academy and modified further based upon their input. Finally, it was reviewed by nationally known homicide investigators who had both an extensive knowledge of VICAP and extensive experience completing the existing form. The final product of these efforts is the VICAP Crime Analysis Report form.

Notes

1. Federal Bureau of Investigation, *Crime in the United States–1984* (Washington, D.C.: U.S. Department of Justice, 1985).

2. James Q. Wilson, *Thinking About Crime* (New York Basic Books, 1975), p. 5.

3. Supra note 1.

4. R. M. Holmes and J. E. DeBurger, "Profiles in Terror: The Serial Murderer," *Federal Probation*, vol. 49, 1985, pp. 29-34.

5. Final Report of the President's Task Force on Victims of Crime, by L. H. Herrington, Chairperson (Library of Congress Cataloging in Publication Data Report No. 82-24146) (Washington, DC: The White House, 1982), p. vi.

6. Report of Attorney General's Task Force on Violent Crime, Washington, DC, 1981.

7. "Crime Scene and Profile Characteristics of Organized and Disorganized Murderers," *FBI Law Enforcement Bulletin*, vol. 54, No. 8, August 1985, pp. 18-25.

8. U.S. Congress, Senate, Committee on the Judiciary, *Patterns of Murders Committed by One Person, in Large Numbers with No Apparent Rhyme, Reason, or Motivation*. Hearings before the Subcommittee on Juvenile Justice of the Committee on the Judiciary, 98th Congress, 1st sess., June 1983, (Serial No. J-98-52) (Washington, DC: U.S. Government Printing Office).

9. B. T. Roessner, "President Extols 'War on Crime,' " *The Hartford Courant*, June 21, 1984, pp. A1, A14.

10. M. Willmer, *Crime and Information Theory* (Edinburgh, England: The University of Edinburgh, 1970).

11. Vernon J. Geberth, *Practical Homicide Investigation: Tactics, Procedures and Forensic Techniques* (New York: Elsevier, 1983), p. 399.

12. D. J. Icove, et al., *Incendiary Fire Analysis and Investigation*. Open Fire Service Learning Program (Lexington, MA: Ginn Publishing Co., 1984); D. J. Icove, V. B. Wherry, and J. D. Schroeder, *Combating Arson-For-Profit: Advanced Techniques for Investigators* (Columbus OH: Battelle Press, 1980).

13. J. L. Bryan and D. J. Icove, "Recent Advances in Computer-Assisted Arson Investigation," *Fire Journal,* National Fire Protection Association, vol. 71, No. 1, January 1977; D. J. Icove and H. L. Crisman, "Application of Pattern Recognition to Arson Investigation," *Fire Technology,* National Fire Protection Association, February 1975; "Arson, the Prevention Chain," National Clearinghouse for Criminal Justice Systems, U.S. Department of Justice, May 1980.

14. B. G. Buchanan and E. H. Shortliffe, *Rule-Based Expert Systems* (Reading, MA: Addison-Wesley Publishing Co., Inc., 1984).

15. R. H. Davis, "Social Network Analysis: An Aid in Conspiracy Investigations," *FBI Law Enforcement Bulletin,* vol. 50, No. 12, December 1981.

16. M. S. Miron and J. E. Douglas, "Threat Analysis: The Psycholinguistic Approach," *FBI Law Enforcement Bulletin,* vol. 48, No. 9, September 1979; U. Perret, "Computer Assisted Forensic Linguistic System 'TEXTOR,' " IEEE International Conference: Security through Science and Technology, September 1980.

8
Crime Scene and Profile Characteristics of Organized and Disorganized Murderers

When requested by a law enforcement agency to assist in a crime scene investigation, the agents at the Behavioral Science Unit (BSU) of the FBI Academy provide a behaviorally based suspect profile. Using information received from law enforcement about the crime and the crime scene, the agents have developed a technique for classifying offenders as organized or disorganized. They arrived at this classification method through years of experience. This chapter provides examples of the two types of murderers and represents one of the first research endeavors by the FBI's National Center for the Analysis of Violent Crime. The case examples illustrate the rich interview material gained regarding the thinking and actions of killers.

The Organized Offender

Profile Characteristics

Organized offenders tend to have a high birth order, often being the firstborn son in a family. The father's work history is generally stable. Parental discipline is perceived as inconsistent (see table 8–1).

The organized offender has an average or better-than-average IQ but often works at occupations below his abilities. The organized offender has a history of working at a skilled occupation, although his work history is uneven. He also prefers a skilled occupation.

Precipitating situational stress prior to the murder is often present and includes such stresses as financial, marital, relationships with females, and employment problems. The organized offender is socially adept and usually is living with a partner.

Sections reprinted with permission from Sage Publications: Ressler, R.K., Burgess, A.W., Douglas, J.F., Hartman, C.R., and D'Agostino, R.B. Sexual Killers and their victims. *Journal of Interpersonal Violence*, 1 1986:288–308.

Table 8–1
Profile Characteristics of Organized and Disorganized Murderers

Organized	Disorganized
Good intelligence	Average intelligence
Socially competent	Socially immature
Skilled work preferred	Poor work history
Sexually competent	Sexually incompetent
High birth order status	Minimal birth order status
Father's work stable	Father's work unstable
Inconsistent childhood discipline	Harsh discipline in childhood
Controlled mood during crime	Anxious mood during crime
Use of alcohol with crime	Minimal use of alcohol
Precipitating situational stress	Minimal situational stress
Living with partner	Living alone
Mobility, with car in good condition	Lives/works near crime scene
Follows crime in news media	Minimal interest in news media
May change jobs or leave town	Minimal change in life-style

The organized offender may report an angry frame of mind at the time of the murder or state that he was depressed. However, he reports himself as calm and relaxed during the commission of the crimes. Alcohol may be used prior to the crime.

The organized offender is likely to have a car that is in good condition. Evidence of continued fantasy can be seen in his taking souvenirs from the victim or crime scene. Newspaper clippings of the crimes are often found during searches of the subject's residence, indicating that the offender followed the crime investigation in the newspaper.

Crime Scene Characteristics

The crime scene of an organized offender suggests that a semblance of order existed prior to, during, and after the offense. This sense of methodical organization suggests a carefully planned crime that is aimed at deterring detection (see table 8–2).

Although the crime may be planned, the victim is frequently a stranger and is targeted because he or she is in a particular location staked out by the offender. In this sense, the victim becomes a victim of opportunity. Victims of serial murderers have been noted to share common characteristics. The offender often has a preference for a particular type of victim and thus may spend considerable time searching for the "right" victim. As one offender said, "I'm a night person. Plenty of times that I went out looking, but never came across nothing and just went back home. I'd sit waiting and as I was waiting, I was reliving all the others." Common characteristics of victims selected by an individual murderer may include age, appearance, occupation, hairstyle, and life-style. Targeted victims in this sample included adolescent male youths,

Table 8–2
Crime Scene Differences between Organized and Disorganized Murderers

Organized	Disorganized
Offense planned	Spontaneous offense
Victim a targeted stranger	Victim or location known
Personalizes victim	Depersonalizes victim
Controlled conversation	Minimal conversation
Crime scene reflects overall control	Crime scene random and sloppy
Demands submissive victim	Sudden violence to victim
Restraints used	Minimal use of restraints
Aggressive acts prior to death	Sexual acts after death
Body hidden	Body left in view
Weapon/evidence absent	Evidence/weapon often present
Transports victim or body	Body left at death scene

hitchhiking female college students, nurses, women frequenting bars, women sitting in automobiles with a male companion, and solitary women driving two-door cars.

The organized offender is socially adept and may strike up a conversation or a pseudorelationship with the victim as a prelude to the attack. Offenders may impersonate another person's role as a method of gaining access to a victim. The offender's demeanor is not usually suspicious. He may be average or above average in appearance, height, and weight; he may be dressed in a business suit, a uniform, or in neat, casual attire. In the organized style of attack, aimed at gaining the confidence of the victim, there is first the effort to strike up a conversation and to use verbal means to capture the victim rather than physical force. The organized offender frequently uses his or the victim's vehicle in committing the offense.

Rape as well as murder may be the planned crime. Murder is always a possibility following rape; the assailant threatens the victim's life and shows a weapon. Sexual control is continued past conversation to demands for specific types of reactions (fear, passivity) during the sexual assault. When the victim's behavior counters being passive and compliant, the offender may increase the aggression.

Control over the victim is also noted in the use of restraints. Some of the restraints include ropes, chains, tape, belts, clothing, chemicals, handcuffs, gags, and blindfolds. The way weapons or restraints are used may suggest a sadistic element in the offender's plan. The killing is eroticized, as in torture where death comes in a slow, deliberate manner. The power over another person's life is seen in one example in which a murderer described tightening and loosening the rope around the victim's neck as he watched the victim slip in and out of a conscious state.

Fantasy and ritual dominate in the organized offender. Obsessive, compulsive traits surface in the behavior and/or crime scene patterns. The offender often brings a weapon with him to the crime, taking it with him upon departure. He carefully avoids leaving evidence behind and often moves the body from the death scene.

Although sexual acts are part of the fantasy planning of the crime, murder may not be a conscious intent until a triggering cue occurs. This is illustrated by the following murderer's statement:

> I had thought about killing her . . . saying what am I going to do when this is over. Am I going to let her go so she can call the cops and get me busted again? So when she took off running—that decided it in my mind that killing her was what I was going to do.

A Case Example of an Organized Offender

Jeff (a pseudonym) was the youngest of three children, having an older adopted brother and natural sister. The parents separated and divorced when Jeff was seven years old, with both parents remarrying shortly thereafter. Jeff continued to live with his mother even though the second marriage dissolved. He completed age-level work until his senior year in high school when he was involuntarily withdrawn from school because of excessive absenteeism and lack of progress. He was of average intelligence and had aspired to attend college. He was athletically inclined and played league baseball. He was outgoing, often attending social events, and had a close circle of friends, both male and female. He saw himself as a leader, not a follower. At birth, it is reported that he was an Rh baby and required a complete blood transfusion. He has reportedly suffered no major health problems.

Jeff was sent out of state to a psychiatric residential facility following his first felony of rape and burglary at age fourteen. During his nineteen-month stay he received psychotherapy, and the discharge recommendation was that he live at home, attend public school, and continue psychotherapy on a weekly outpatient basis, with his mother actively involved in his treatment. He readily admitted to the use of alcohol and drugs of all types from his early teen years. He worked sporadically throughout his high school years as part of a program in which he attended school in the morning and worked in the afternoon.

His antisocial behavior is recorded at age nine when he and three other boys were caught by the school principal writing "cuss" words on the sidewalk. The boys were required to wash the sidewalks until the words were removed. Starting at age twelve the criminal behavior record begins with the assaultive and disruptive behavior of breaking into an apartment and stealing property valued at one hundred dollars. At age thirteen he was charged with driving without an operator's license; at age fourteen he was charged with burglary and rape, and he committed two other minor acts of petty larceny and stealing a car before being sent to the residential facility.

Three weeks after returning home from the residential facility, he was charged with attempted armed robbery—an act intended to be rape. This charge took one year to come before the judge for sentencing, and in that time the first rape and murder had been committed but not charged to the offender. The disposition on the attempted armed robbery was probation and outpatient psychotherapy, until his apprehension for the five murders. His psychiatric diagnoses have included adolescent adjustment reaction, character disorder without psychosis, and multiple personality. At the time of his arrest for the murders the young man was nineteen years old, weighed 144 pounds and was five feet, seven inches tall. He was given five life sentences for the five rape murders. After two years of incarceration, he admitted to six additional rapes for which he was never charged. (See table 8–3.)

Victim Profiles.   Of the thirteen victims, eight were white, four were black, and one was hispanic. All were female with an age range of seventeen to thirty-four, and all were older than the offender by as much as nine years. Several victims were taller and heavier. Ten victims were total strangers; three were known by sight. Two of the ten stranger-victims recognized him after capture. All of the victims were of middle-income status, and the majority lived in the apartment complex where the offender also lived with his mother. All of the victims except one high school student were employed full-time, working in such positions as teacher, postal supervisor, store buyer, airline stewardess, and administrative assistant. Some victims, in addition, held part-time jobs as well, and/or were continuing their college education. The majority of victims were not married; several were divorced. Two victims were known to have children. Five of the women were raped and murdered; five were raped; two were gang raped; and one escaped from the offender prior to the completion of a criminal act. Most of the victims were approached at knife point as they entered the elevator to their apartment building. All the rape murder victims were abducted from the same location, killed in different areas, and found fully clothed. The time elapsed in locating their bodies ranged from one day to six weeks.

The Offender's Behavior.   The offender's criminal behavior changed in two major ways: (1) the level of sexual aggression escalated from rape to rape and murder, and (2) the offenses increased in frequency, as noted by the decrease in time between offenses. Of special note are the facts that (1) all rape and murder offenses except the first were committed while the offender was under psychiatric supervision and probationary regulation; (2) the six rapes that were not charged to the offender were also committed while he was under psychiatric supervision and probationary regulation; and (3) the five homicides were neither linked to one offender nor indicated to include rape until the offender was apprehended and described the offenses.

Table 8–3
Escalation of Criminal Behavior

Date	Offender's Age	Offense	Victim's Age/Race	Disposition
9/1971	12	Petty larceny		Probation: 11/71–6/72
9/1971	12	Disrupting school		Probation: 11/71–6/72
10/1972	13	No operator's license		Continued until eighteenth birthday
4/1973	14	Burglary and rape	25/white	State Dept. Welfare Inst. (Psychiatr. Center 2/74–8/75)
6/1973	14	Petty larceny		SDWI
7/1973	14	Breaking and entering		SDWI
12/1974	16	Rape	25/black	Never charged
2/1975	16	Rape	25/Cuban	Never charged
3/1975	16	Burglary and rape (Co-offender)	17/white	Never charged
6/1975	16	Rape (Co-offender)	25/white	Never charged
9/1975	17	Attempted armed robbery	22/white	Probation and outpatient treatment under probation 9/1 5/30
4/1976	18	Rape	25/white	Never charged
8/1976	18	Rape and murder	24/white	Life in prison
3/1977	19	Rape and murder	22/white	Life in prison
4/1977	19	Rape and murder	34/black	Life in prison
4/1977	19	Rape	25/white	Never charged
4/1977	19	Rape and murder	27/black	Life in prison
5/1977	19	Rape and murder	24/white	Life in prison

Rape: The First Seven Offenses. The first charged rape (when Jeff was fourteen) involved a twenty-five-year-old neighbor woman. He broke into her apartment, woke her up, and raped her several times, left through her front door, returned to his own apartment and went to sleep. He was apprehended three weeks later.

The second rape (first never-charged rape) occurred when Jeff, age 16, was home for Christmas vacation. The evening before returning to the residential facility, he approached a woman in the elevator to the apartment complex and at knife point took her to another location and raped her. The second never-charged rape (the third in sequence) occurred three months later when he approached a woman in the school parking lot where he was attending a local school for the residential facility. He forced the woman at knife point to drive to her apartment, where he raped her. The third and fourth never-charged rapes included co-offenders. While on a weekend pass, the offender and two patients stole a car, traveled out of state, broke into a house, stole two guns and money, and each raped a seventeen-year-old female who was in the house. Jeff then returned home; however, his mother immediately sent him back to the residential facility, and he was counseled on his runaway behavior. Three months after returning to the facility, Jeff and another patient went to a local swimming pool. They broke into a women's locker room and raped a young woman, covering her head with a towel.

The fifth offense took place three weeks after Jeff's release from the residential treatment facility, when he was arrested for attempted armed robbery. He had targeted a woman entering the elevator of the apartment complex, wore a ski mask, and held a knife to the victim. She was successful in escaping:

> She broke . . . pushed me out of the way and started going to the front of the elevator, pushed the button to open the door, started to run, and stumbled. I started to run after her and stumbled over her and at that point the knife fell, and she was on the ground hollering and I was on the ground next to her, scared to death. My mind went blank. I ran out of the building.

The sixth rape (the fifth never-charged rape) took place prior to Jeff's first rape and murder, and involved a woman he had seen in his own apartment building. He obtained an air pistol, captured her in the apartment elevator, took her to a storage room, and raped her twice, covering her face with her jacket.

During all the rapes, Jeff was concerned about being identified. During the rapes, he either covered the victim's face, wore a mask, or left town immediately following. However, in the seven offenses, he was caught twice and both times he had worn the mask. Although the first rape victim was not able to identify him positively, the sixth victim did make a positive identification.

Murder: The Last Six Offenses.   The last six victims were selected at random as Jeff watched cars drive into the apartment complex where he lived. Once he had targeted someone, Jeff would then walk behind the victim, follow her into the apartment elevator, pull his knife, and tell her it was a stickup. Then they would leave the building, either for the victim's car or for an area near the apartment complex. In one case the pattern was reversed. Jeff was hitchhiking and was given a ride by a woman who was going to a party in his apartment complex. She left him off at his building; he then watched her park her car and then ran across the complex, entered the elevator, and captured her. All the abductions and murders occurred within his own territory. Thus, known territory was a distinct advantage: "Going somewhere that I didn't know or where the cops patrolled might get me caught. I knew what time the cops came by in the morning because I'd be sitting there." Indeed he was right. One of the reasons he was not caught until after the fifth murder was that the police were looking for strangers and suspicious characters—not a teenager living in the area.

Jeff's use of either verbal and/or physical strategies to assert control over the victim depended on the initial response of the victim. The victim who was compliant with the show of a weapon received no additional threats or orders. Victims who screamed received verbal threats, and those who refused to cooperate were physically struck, as in the following case.

> She faints and falls down on the floor. I pat her face. She wakes up, has a real frightened look on her face and she starts to scream. I stick the gun to her head and tell her if she screams I'm going to blow her head off. She asks what I want and I tell her I want money and to rape her. She balked on that and said, "No white man doing that to me." I'm thinking she's one of those prejudiced types. I backhanded her. She whimpered. I told her to take off her clothes. She refuses. I cocked the trigger back and she started hurrying up. And this time I'm feeling good because I'm domineering over her and forcing her to do something and I'm thinking this prejudiced bitch is going to do what I want her to do.

Interaction between Victim and Offender. Reconstruction of the victims' talk and actions as viewed from the offender's perspective reveals that conversation and behavior serve either to neutralize or escalate the affective state of the offender.

Rape murder victim one, rape victim eight: After the rape had taken place and both were dressing, Jeff states that he had not decided what to do with the victim and that her attempt to escape angered him, which resulted in an increase in aggression.

> She took off running down the ravine. That's when I grabbed her. I had her in an arm lock—she was bigger than me. I started choking her and she started spitting up on my arm. She started stumbling; lost consciousness. We rolled down the hill into the water. I banged her head against the side of a rock and held her head under water.

Death in this case was caused by strangulation.

Rape murder victim two, rape victim nine: The victim's talk consisted of many questions that served to annoy Jeff: "She asked all kinds of questions: why I wanted to do this; why did I pick her; didn't I have a girlfriend; what was my problem? I am resenting this all the time, telling her to shut up." As Jeff was driving after the rape, he says that he was uncertain as to his actions. The victim questions his next move and then acts to counter his control of the car.

She asked what I was going to do: kill her or tie her up and leave her. I told her I hadn't decided. I felt I had decided to let her go but would knock her out and tie her up or shoot her—not killing her—but hurt her to where she would know that if she did say anything that someone would be after her to scare the hell out of her. So she started going down the road, stomps on the gas and says, "If you don't throw that gun out of the car right now I'm going to run into this tree down here." She's going about 70 miles per hour. I turned the ignition off and stepped my foot on the brakes and the car slides sideways. Then she gets out and runs across the road to the barbed wire fence. She is screaming. It's just getting light out. I get the knife. She's run into the woods. I go into the woods after her. I see her run from behind a tree and that's when I go after her. From then on I knew I had to kill her. She trips and falls over a log and that's when I catch up to her and I just start stabbing her.

The victim was stabbed fourteen times in the chest.

Rape murder victim three, rape victim ten: Jeff claimed he had not decided whether he would kill this victim. He would not let her talk as they drove in the car because "the more I got to know about women the softer I got." He ordered the victim to be quiet and to turn the car radio on. He said he decided to kill her when he heard her moving from the place where he left her: "I was thinking . . . I've killed two. I might as well kill this one too . . . because something in me was wanting to kill. I said to myself that I had to preserve and protect myself." Jeff stabbed the victim, and the cause of death was twenty-one stab wounds to the left thorax and upper abdomen.

Rape victim eleven: Jeff had decided to kill this victim but her talking saved her life. She told him that her father was dying of cancer and that she was very depressed over that fact. This talk evidently neutralized Jeff's aggression ("She had it bad already"), and he decided to let her live.

I thought of my own brother who had cancer. I couldn't kill her . . . I took the car keys and threw them out in the woods and told her not to move for ten minutes, that I was going to be in the woods watching, but during that time I was running.

Rape murder victim four, rape victim twelve: Jeff had decided to kill this victim.

She put back on her clothes. We took a short cut. I decided to kill her then. Had to go up an embankment. I helped her, and as I started to climb up, she had ahold of my hand like she's trying to help. She let go of my hand and swings down with her hand and she scratched me across the side of the face with her long nails. I got mad and she started to run. I got up from falling down . . . she ran into a tree and I caught her. We wrestled, rolled over the embankment into the water . . . She was fighting and she was strong. But I put her head underneath the water and I just sat there with my hands on her neck.

I saw bubbles coming up and then the bubbles stopped. I sat there maybe a good forty-five minutes before I got out of the water.

The cause of death for this victim was forced drowning.

Rape murder five, rape victim thirteen: The victim's talk led Jeff to realize that she knew him. This knowledge escalated the fear of disclosure and, in turn, led to Jeff's confessing the four previous murders.

I realized I had known her younger brother until he was killed in an accident. I met her at a funeral and she had been really broken up about it. So she knew me and I knew I had to kill her. I told her I was the one who did the four murders in that area.

The cause of death was multiple (more than fifty) stab wounds.

Following the murders, Jeff would usually take some item of jewelry from the victim's body for a souvenir, go back to the victim's car and search through her purse for money, drive the victim's car for an extended time period, park the victim's car several blocks from his apartment, return to his apartment and go to bed, and watch the television and read the newspapers to see if the body was discovered.

The Disorganized Offender

Profile Characteristics

The disorganized offender is likely to be of below average intelligence or of low birth status in the family. Also, harsh parental discipline is sometimes reported in childhood. The father's work history is unstable, and the disorganized offender seems to mirror this pattern with his own inconsistent and poor work history (see table 8–1).

Typically, this offender is preoccupied with recurring obsessional and/or primitive thoughts and is in a confused and distressed frame of mind at the time of the crime.

The disorganized offender is socially inadequate. Often he has never married, lives alone or with a parental figure, and lives in close proximity to the crime scene. This offender is fearful of people and may have developed a well-defined delusional system. He acts impulsively under stress, finding a victim usually within his own geographic area.

The offender is also sexually incompetent, often never having achieved any level of sexual intimacy with a peer. Although the offenders in this sample claimed to be heterosexual, there is a clear suggestion that the disorganized offender is ignorant of sex and often may have sexual aversions.

Crime Scene Characteristics

The overall impression given by the disorganized crime scene is that the crime has been committed suddenly and with no set plan of action for deterring detection. The crime scene shows great disarray; it has a spontaneous, symbolic, unplanned quality. The victim may be known to the offender, but the age and sex of the victim do not necessarily matter (see table 8–2).

If the offender is selecting a victim by randomly knocking on doors in a neighborhood, the first person to open a door becomes the victim. The offender kills instantly to have control; he cannot take the risk that the victim will get the upper hand.

The offender uses a blitz style of attack for encountering the victim. He either approaches the victim from behind, suddenly overpowering her, or he kills suddenly, as with a gun. The attack is a violent surprise, occurring out of the blue and in a location where the victim is going about his or her usual activities. The victim is caught completely off guard.

The offender depersonalizes the victim. Specific areas of the body may be targeted for extreme brutality. Overkill or excessive assault to the face is often an attempt to dehumanize the victim. Destruction to the face may also indicate that the killer knows the victim or that the victim resembles or represents a person who has caused the offender psychological distress. The offender may wear a mask or gloves, cover the victim's face as he attacks, or blindfold her. There is minimal verbal interaction aside from orders and threats. Restraints are not necessary, as the victim is killed quickly.

Any sexually sadistic acts, often in the form of mutilation, are usually performed after death. Offenders have attempted a variety of sexual acts, including ejaculating into an open stab wound in the victim's abdomen. Evidence of urination, defecation, and masturbation in the victim's clothing and home has been found. Mutilation to the face, genitals, and breast, disembowelment, amputation, and vampirism may also be noted on the body.

Disorganized offenders might keep the dead body. One murderer killed two women and kept their body parts in his home for eight years. He made masks from their heads and drums and seat covers from their skins. Earlier he had exhumed the bodies of eight elderly women from their graves and performed similar mutilative acts to their bodies.

The death scene and crime scene are often the same for the disorganized offender, with the victim being left in the position in which she or he was killed. If the offender has mutilated the body, it may be positioned in a special way that has significance to the offender.

No attempt is made to conceal the body. Fingerprints and footprints may be found, and the police will have a great deal of evidence to use in their investigation. Usually, the murder weapon is one obtained at the scene and is left there, providing investigators with evidence.

A Case Example of a Disorganized Offender

Murder 1: A husband returning from work at 6:00 P.M. discovered his wife's dead body in the bedroom of their home. The autopsy revealed that she had been murdered sometime in the morning after being confronted by the assailant as she took garbage outside. The victim was shot in the head four times and thereafter disemboweled with a knife obtained in her home. No evidence of sexual assault or molestation was found, other than slash wounds to breasts and mutilation to internal reproductive organs. The victim was first slashed in the abdomen, and the assailant pulled her intestines out of the body cavity. The victim had what was later determined to be animal feces in her mouth. Garbage was strewn about the house. A yogurt cup was found, and indications were that the murderer used the cup to collect blood from the victim, which he then drank.

Crime 2: On the same date, a house burglary occurred within a quarter mile of the victim's residence. Garbage was strewn throughout the home. Evidence indicated that the burglar urinated on female clothing and also defecated in the house. No one was home at the time.

Crime 3: Two days later the carcass of a dog was found in the same neighborhood. The dog had been shot in the head, and the bullet was determined to have come from the gun used in the first murder. The dog was also disemboweled.

Murder 2: Four days after the first slaying, a woman, who was waiting for a male friend to pick her up for a day's outing with her next-door neighbor, noticed that the man's car had pulled into her neighbor's driveway. She telephoned to say she would be right over; receiving no answer, however, she looked out her window again, only to see that the man's car had gone. Becoming suspicious, she went over to the house and discovered the bodies of her male friend, her female neighbor, and the neighbor's child. A twenty-two-month-old infant was also missing from the home; however, a bullet hole was found in the pillow of the crib where the child had been, with what appeared to be brain and skull matter. This was also found in the half-filled bathtub, indicating that the child had been killed and the body washed and removed from the scene. The woman victim had been severely slashed and mutilated. She had been murdered in the bedroom, where she was also disemboweled from the breastbone to the pelvic area. Internal organs, including spleen, kidneys, and reproductive organs, had been removed and mutilated. No attack was noted to external genitals. The murderer had attempted to remove an eye and had also inserted a knife in the anal canal, cutting the victim severely in this area. Definite fingerprints with blood were found on the abdomen, shoulders, and legs of this victim. Additionally, a ring of blood was found on the floor, indicating that a bucket-type container was used for collecting blood.

The following information was extracted from a profile developed by the BSU.

> Suspect description: white male aged twenty-five to twenty-seven; thin, undernourished appearance; single; living alone in a location within one mile of abandoned station wagon owned by one of the victims. Residence will be extremely slovenly and unkempt, and evidence of the crimes will be found at the residence. Suspect will have a history of mental illness and use of drugs. Suspect will be an unemployed loner who does not associate with either males or females and will probably spend a great deal of time in his own residence. If he resides with anyone, it will be with his parents. However, this is unlikely. Suspect will have no prior military history; will be a high school or college dropout; probably suffers from one or more forms of paranoid psychosis.

The police narrowed their search to a one-mile radius of the stolen vehicle, seeking a man of the suspect's description. A twenty-seven-year-old white male, five feet, eleven inches tall, and weighing 149 pounds, was located in an apartment complex within the same block as the abandoned car. The man was in possession of a gun that matched the murder weapon in the slayings. Also found in the apartment were numerous body parts thought to be animal and possibly human. The man had previously been diagnosed as a paranoid schizophrenic and had been committed to a mental facility after he was found sucking blood from a dead bird. After being released, he was found blood-stained and wearing a loincloth in the desert. He told police he was sacrificing to flying saucers. He was released by police; however, a child's body was later found in the same vicinity. In his apartment evidence was found indicating his obsession with blood, mutilation, and possible cannibalism and devouring of animals.

Summary

This research study of differences between organized and disorganized sexual murderers in regard to profile characteristics and crime scene indicators provides an important foundation for the investigative technique of criminal profiling. We have established that variables do exist that may be useful in drawing up a criminal profile and that differentiate between organized and disorganized sexual murderers. It is important to be aware of the limitations of this study. We do not mean to imply that all unsolved cases can be profiled successfully. We wish to emphasize that this study was exploratory and indicates that we have identified significant variables in crime scene analysis.

9
Criminal Profiling from Crime Scene Analysis

"You wanted to mock yourself at me! . . . You did not know your Hercule Poirot." He thrust out his chest and twirled his moustache.

I looked at him and grinned . . . . "All right then," I said. "Give us the answer to the problem—if you know it."

"But of course I know it."

Hardcastle stared at him incredulously . . . "Excuse me, Monsieur Poirot, you claim that you know who killed three people. And why? . . . All you mean is that you have a hunch."

"I will not quarrel with you over a word. . . . . Come now, Inspector. I know—really know . . . I perceive you are still sceptic. But first let me say this: To be sure means that when the right solution is reached, everything falls into place. You perceive that in no other way could things have happened."

Agatha Christie, *The Clocks*
(New York: Pocket Books, 1963), 227–28

The ability of Hercule Poirot to solve a crime by describing the perpetrator is shared by the expert investigative profiler. Evidence speaks its own language of patterns and sequences that can reveal the offender's behavioral characteristics. Like Poirot, the profiler can say, "I know who he must be."

This chapter focuses on the developing technique of criminal profiling by Special Agents at the FBI Academy who have demonstrated expertise in crime scene analysis of various violent crimes, particularly those involving sexual homicide.

The process used by an investigative profiler in developing a criminal profile is quite similar to that used by clinicians to make a diagnosis and treatment plan: data are collected and assessed, the situation is reconstructed, hypotheses are formulated, a profile is developed and tested, and the results are reported back. Investigators traditionally have learned profiling through brainstorming, intuition, and educated guesswork. Their expertise is the result of years of accumulated wisdom, extensive experience in the field, and

Sections reprinted with permission from John Wiley and Sons: Douglas, J.E., Ressler, R.K., Burgess, A.W., and Hartman, C.R. Criminal Profiling from Crime Scene Analysis. *Behavioral Sciences and the Law 4*, 1986: 401–21.

familiarity with a large number of cases.

A profiler brings to the investigation the ability to make hypothetical formulations based on his or her previous experience. A formulation is defined here as a concept that organizes, explains, or makes investigative sense out of information, and that influences the profile hypotheses. These formulations are based on clusters of information emerging from the crime scene data and from the investigator's experience in understanding criminal actions.

A basic premise of criminal profiling is that the way a person thinks (that is, the patterns of thinking) directs his or her behavior. Thus, when the investigative profiler analyzes a crime scene and notes certain critical factors, he or she may be able to determine the motive and type of person who committed the crime.

The Criminal Profile-Generating Process

Investigative profilers at the FBI's Behavioral Science Unit (now part of the National Center for the Analysis of Violent Crime [NCAVC]) have been analyzing crime scenes and generating criminal profiles since the 1970s. Our description of the construction of profiles represents the off-site procedure as it is conducted at the NCAVC, as contrasted with an on-site procedure (Ressler et al. 1985). The criminal profile generating process has five main stages, with a sixth stage or goal being the apprehension of a suspect (see figure 9–1).

Stage One: Profiling Inputs

The profiling inputs stage begins the criminal profile generating process. Comprehensive case materials are essential for accurate profiling. In homicide cases, the required information includes a complete synopsis of the crime and a description of the crime scene, including such factors affecting the area at the time of the incident as weather conditions and the political and social environment.

Complete background information on the victim is also vital in homicide profiles. The data should cover domestic setting, employment, reputation, habits, fears, physical condition, personality, criminal history, family relationships, hobbies, and social conduct.

Forensic information pertaining to the crime is also critical to the profiling process, including an autopsy report with toxicology/serology results, autopsy photographs, and photographs of the cleansed wounds. The report should also contain the medical examiner's findings and impressions regarding estimated time and cause of death, type of weapon used, and suspected sequence of delivery of wounds.

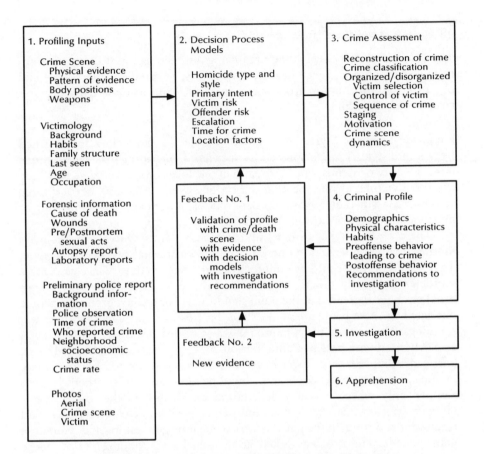

Figure 9–1. Criminal Profile Generating Process

In addition to autopsy photographs, aerial photographs (if available and appropriate) and eight-by-ten-inch color pictures of the crime scene are needed. Also useful are crime scene sketches showing distances, directions, and scale, as well as maps of the area (which may cross law enforcement jurisdiction boundaries).

The profiler studies all this background and evidence information, as well as all initial police reports. The data and photographs can reveal such significant elements as the level of risk of the victim, the degree of control exhibited by the offender, the offender's emotional state, and his criminal sophistication.

Information the profiler does *not* want included in the case materials is that dealing with possible suspects. Such information may subconsciously prejudice the profiler and cause him or her to prepare a profile matching the suspect.

Stage Two: Decision Process Models

The decision process begins the organizing and arranging of the inputs into meaningful patterns. Seven key decision points, or models, differentiate and organize the information from stage one and form an underlying decision structure for profiling.

Homicide Type and Style.   As is noted in table 9–1, homicides are classified by type and style. A *single* homicide is one victim, one homicidal event; *double* homicide is two victims, one event, and in one location; and a *triple* homicide has three victims in one location during one event. Anything beyond three victims is classified as a *mass* murder—that is, a homicide involving four or more victims in one location, and within one event.

There are two types of mass murder: *classic* and *family*. A classic mass murder involves one person operating in one location at one period of time. That period of time could be minutes or hours, or even days. The classic mass murderer is usually described as a mentally disordered individual whose problems have increased to the point that he acts out against groups of people unrelated to these problems; unleashing his hostility through shootings and stabbings. One classic mass murderer was Charles Whitman, who in 1966 armed himself with boxes of ammunition, weapons, ropes, a radio, and food; barricaded himself on a tower in Austin, Texas; and opened fire for ninety minutes, killing sixteen people and wounding more than thirty others. He was stopped only when he was killed during an assault on the tower. James Huberty was another classic mass murderer. In 1984, he entered a fast-food restaurant and fired on the patrons with a machine gun, killing and wounding many people. He also was killed at the site by responding police. More recently, Pennsylvania mass murderer Sylvia Seegrist (nicknamed "Ms. Rambo" for her military-style clothing) was sentenced to life imprisonment for opening fire with a rifle on shoppers in a mall in October 1985, killing three and wounding seven.

The second type of mass murder is family-member murder. If more than three family members are killed and the perpetrator takes his own life, it is

Table 9–1
Homicide Classification by Style and Type

	Style					
	Single	Double	Triple	Mass	Spree	Serial
Number of victims	1	2	3	4+	2+	3+
Number of events	1	1	1	1	1	3+
Number of locations	1	1	1	1	2+	3+
Cool-off period	N/A	N/A	N/A	N/A	No	Yes

classified as a mass murder/suicide. Without the suicide and with four or more victims, the murder is called a family killing. Examples include John List, an insurance salesman who killed his entire family on November 9, 1972, in Westfield, New Jersey. The bodies of List's wife and three children (ages sixteen, fifteen, and thirteen) were discovered in their front room, lying side by side on top of sleeping bags as if in a mortuary. Their faces were covered and their arms were folded across their bodies. Each had been shot once behind the left ear, except one son who had been shot several times. A further search of the residence discovered the body of List's mother in a third-floor closet. She had also been shot once behind the left ear. List disappeared after the crime, and his car was found at an airport parking lot.

In another family-killing case, William Bradford Bishop beat to death his wife, mother, and three children in the family's Bethesda, Maryland, residence in March 1976. He then transported them to North Carolina in the family station wagon where their bodies, along with the family dog's, were buried in a shallow grave. Bishop was under psychiatric care and had been prescribed antidepressant medication. No motive was determined. Bishop was a promising midlevel diplomat who had served in many overseas jobs and was scheduled for higher-level office in the U.S. Department of State. Bishop, like List, is a federal fugitive. There are strong indications that both crimes were carefully planned, and it is uncertain whether the men have committed suicide.

Two additional types of multiple murder are *spree* and *serial*. A spree murder involves killing at two or more locations with no emotional cooling-off period between murders. The killings are all the result of a single event, which can be of short or long duration. On September 6, 1949, spree murderer Howard Unruh of Camden, New Jersey, took a loaded German luger with extra ammunition and randomly fired the handgun while walking through his neighborhood, killing thirteen people and wounding three in about twenty minutes. Even though Unruh's killings took such a short length of time, they are not classified as a mass murder because he moved to different locations.

Serial murderers are involved in three or more separate events with an emotional cooling-off period between homicides. This type of killer usually premeditates his crimes, often fantasizing and planning the murder in every aspect, with the possible exception of the specific victim. Then, when the time is right for him and he has cooled off from his last homicide, he selects his next victim and proceeds with his plan. The cool-off period can be days, weeks, or months and is the main element that separates the serial killer from other multiple killers.

However, there are other differences between the types of murderers. The classic mass murderer and the spree murderer are not concerned with who their victims are; they will kill anyone who comes in contact with them. In contrast, a serial murderer usually selects a type of victim. He thinks he will never be caught, and sometimes he is right. A serial murderer controls the events, whereas a spree murderer, who oftentimes has been identified and is being closely pursued by law enforcement, may barely control what will happen next. The serial killer is planning, picking and choosing, and sometimes stopping the act of murder.

A serial murderer may go on a murdering spree. In 1984, Christopher Wilder, an Australian-born businessman and race car driver, traveled across the United States killing young women. He would target victims at shopping malls or would abduct them after meeting them through a beauty contest setting or dating service. While a fugitive as a serial murderer, Wilder was investigated, identified, and tracked by the FBI and by almost every police department in the country. He then went on a long-term killing spree throughout the country and eventually was killed during a shoot-out with police.

Wilder's classification changed from serial to spree because of the multiple murders and the lack of a cooling-off period during his prolonged murder event, which lasted nearly seven weeks. This transition has been noted in other serial/spree murder cases. The tension caused by his fugitive status and the high visibility of his crimes gives the murderer a sense of desperation. His acts are now open and public, and the increased pressure usually means no cooling-off period. He knows he will be caught, and the coming confrontation with police becomes an element in his crimes. He may place himself in a situation where he forces the police to kill him.

It is important to classify homicides correctly. For example, say a single homicide is committed in a city; a week later a second single homicide is committed; and the third week, a third single homicide. Three seemingly unrelated homicides are reported, but by the time a fourth occurs, there is a tie-in through forensic evidence and analysis of the crime scenes. These four single homicides now point to one serial offender. It is not mass murder because of the multiple locations and the cooling-off periods. The correct classification assists in profiling and directs the investigation as serial homicides. Similarly, profiling of a single murder may indicate that the offender had killed before or would repeat the crime in the future.

Primary Intent of the Murderer.   In some cases, murder may be an ancillary action and not itself the primary intent of the offender. The killer's primary intent could be (1) criminal enterprise, (2) emotional, selfish, or cause-specific, or (3) sexual. The killer may be acting on his own or as part of a group.

When the primary intent is criminal enterprise, the killer may be involved in the business of crime for his livelihood. Sometimes murder becomes part of this business, even though there is no personal malice toward the victim; the primary motive is money. In the 1950s, a young man placed a bomb in his mother's suitcase, which was loaded aboard a commercial aircraft. The aircraft exploded, killing forty-four people. The young man's motive had been to collect money from the travel insurance he had taken out on his mother prior to the flight. Criminal enterprise killings involving a group include contract murders, gang murders, competition murders, and political murders.

When the primary intent involves emotional, selfish, or cause-specific reasons, the murderer may kill in self-defense or in compassion (mercy killings in which life support systems are disconnected). Family disputes or violence may lie behind infanticide, matricide, patricide, and spouse and sibling killings. Paranoid reactions may also result in murder as in the previously described Whitman case. The mentally disordered murderer may commit a symbolic crime or have a psychotic outburst. Assassinations, such as those committed by Sirhan Sirhan and Mark Chapman, also fall into the emotional intent category. Murders in this category involving groups are committed for a variety of reasons: for example, religious groups (Jim Jones and the Jonestown, Guyana, case), cult groups (Charles Manson), and fanatical organizations such as the Ku Klux Klan and the Black Panther Party of the 1970s.

Finally, the murderer may have sexual reasons for killing. Individuals may kill to engage in sexual activity, dismemberment, mutilation, evisceration, or other activities that have sexual meaning only for the offender. Occasionally, two or more murderers commit these homicides together as in the 1984–85 case in Calaveras County, California, where Leonard Lake and Charles Ng are suspected of committing as many as twenty-five sex-torture slayings.

Victim Risk. The concept of the victim's risk is involved at several stages of the profiling process and provides information about the suspect in terms of how he or she operates. Risk is determined using such factors as age, occupation, life-style, and physical stature of the victim, and is classified as high, moderate, or low. High-risk victims are those targeted by the murderers who know where they can find victims. Killers seek high-risk victims at locations where people may be vulnerable, such as bus depots or isolated areas. The young and the elderly may be high-risk victims because of their lack of resistance abilities. Low-risk types include those whose occupations and daily life-styles do not lead them to being targeted as victims. The information on victim risk helps to generate an image of the type of perpetrator being sought.

Offender Risk. Data on victim risk is integrated with information on offender risk, or the risk the offender was taking to commit the crime. For example, abducting a victim at noon from a busy street is high risk. Thus, that a low-risk victim is snatched under high-risk circumstances generates ideas about the offender, such as personal stresses he is operating under, his belief that he will not be apprehended, the excitement he needs in the commission of the crime, or his emotional maturity.

Escalation. Information about escalation is derived from an analysis of facts and patterns from the prior decision process models. Investigative profilers are able to deduce the sequence of acts committed during the crime. From this deduction, they may be able to make determinations about the potential of the criminal not only to escalate his crimes (for example, from peeping to fondling to assault to rape to murder), but to repeat his crimes in serial fashion. One case example is David Berkowitz, the "Son of Sam" killer, who started his criminal acts with the nonfatal stabbing of a teenage girl and who escalated to the subsequent .44-caliber killings.

Time Factors. There are several time factors that need to be considered in generating a criminal profile. These factors include the length of time required (1) to kill the victim, (2) to commit additional acts with the body, and (3) to dispose of the body. The time of day or night that the crime was committed is also important, for it may provide information on the life-style and occupation of the suspect (and also relates to the offender risk factor). For example, the longer an offender stays with his victim, the more likely it is that he will be apprehended at the crime scene. In the case of the New York murder of Kitty Genovese, the killer carried on his murderous assault to the point where many people heard or witnessed the crime, which led to his eventual prosecution. A killer who intends to spend time with his victim therefore must select a location to preclude observation or one with which he is familiar.

Location Factors. Information about location—where the victim was first approached, where the crime occurred, and whether the crime and death scenes differ—provides yet additional data about the offender. For example, such information provides details about whether the murderer used a vehicle to transport the victim from the death scene or whether the victim died at her point of abduction.

Stage Three: Crime Assessment

The crime assessment stage in generating a criminal profile involves the reconstruction of the sequence of events and the behavior of both the offender and the victim. Based on the various decisions of the previous stage, this reconstruction of how things happened, how people behaved, and how they planned and organized the encounter provides information about specific characteristics to be generated for the criminal profile. Assessments are made about the classification of the crime, its organized/disorganized aspects, the offender's selection of a victim, strategies used to control the victim, the sequence of the crime, the staging (or not) of the crime, the offender's motivation for the crime, and crime scene dynamics.

The classification of the crime is determined through the decision process outlined in the first decision process model. The classification of a crime as organized or disorganized includes factors such as victim selection, strategies to control the victim, and sequence of the crime. An organized murderer is one who appears to plan his murders, target his victims, display control at the crime scene, and act out a violent fantasy against the victim (sex, dismemberment, torture). For example, Ted Bundy's planning was noted through his successful abduction of young women from highly visible areas (for example, beaches, campuses, a ski lodge). He selected victims who were young, attractive, and similar in appearance. His control of the victim was initially through clever manipulation and later physical force. These dynamics were important in the development of a desired fantasy victim.

In contrast, the disorganized murderer is less apt to plan his crime in detail; he obtains victims by chance and behaves haphazardly during the crime. For example, Herbert Mullin of Santa Cruz, California, who killed fourteen people of varying types (for example, an elderly man, a young girl, a priest) over a four-month period, did not display any specific planning or targeting of victims; rather, the victims were people who happened to cross his path, and their killings were based on psychotic impulses as well as on fantasy.

The determination of whether or not the crime was staged (that is, whether the subject was truly careless or disorganized, or whether he made the crime appear that way to distract or mislead the police) helps direct the investigative profiler to the killer's motivation. In one case, a sixteen-year-old high school junior living in a small town failed to return home from school. Responding to the father's report of his missing daughter, police began their investigation and located the victim's scattered clothing in a remote area outside of town. A crude map was also found at the scene which seemingly implied a premeditated plan of kidnapping. The police followed the map to a location that indicated a body might have been disposed of in a nearby river. Written and telephoned extortion demands were sent to the father, a bank executive, for the sum of eighty thousand dollars, indicating that a kidnap was the basis of the abduction. The demands warned police in detail not to use electronic monitoring devices during their investigative efforts.

Was this crime staged? The question was answered in two ways. The details in one aspect of the crime (scattered clothing and tire tracks) indicated that the subject was purposely staging a crime, while the details in the other (extortion) led the profilers to speculate who the subject was; specifically, that he had a law enforcement background and therefore had knowledge of police procedures concerning crimes of kidnapping and extortion. Thus, the crime was determined to be a staged kidnapping, hiding the primary intent of sexual assault and possible murder. With this information, the investigative profilers recommended that communication continue between the suspect and the police, with the hypothesis that the behavior would escalate and the subject become bolder.

While further communications with the family were being monitored, profilers from the FBI's Behavioral Science Unit theorized that the subject of the case was a white male who was single, in his late twenties to early thirties, unemployed, and had been employed as a law enforcement officer within the past year. He would be a macho outdoors type of person, who drove a late model, well-maintained vehicle with a CB radio. The car would have the overall appearance of a police vehicle.

As the profile was developed, the FBI continued to monitor the extortion telephone calls made to the family by the subject. The investigation, based on the profile, narrowed to two local men, both of whom were former police officers. One suspect was eliminated, but the FBI became very interested in the other since he fitted the general profile previously developed. This individual was placed under surveillance. He turned out to be a single, white male who was previously employed locally as a police officer. He was now unemployed and drove a car consistent with the FBI profile. He was observed making a call from a telephone booth, and after hanging up, he taped a note under the telephone. The call was traced to the residence of the victim's family. The caller had given instructions for the family to proceed to the phone booth the suspect had been observed in. "The instructions will be taped there," stated the caller.

The body of the victim was actually found a considerable distance from the "staged" crime scene, and the extortion calls were a diversion to lead the police investigation away from the sexually motivated crime of rape murder. The subject never intended to collect the ransom money, but he felt that the diversion would throw the police off and take him from the focus of the rape murder inquiry. The subject was subsequently arrested and convicted of this crime.

Motivation. Motivation is a difficult factor to judge because it requires dealing with the inner thoughts and behavior of the offender. Motivation is more easily determined in the organized offender, who premeditates, plans, and has the ability to carry out a plan of action that is logical and complete. On the other hand, the motivations of the disorganized offender frequently are derived from mental illnesses and accompanying distorted thinking (resulting from delusions and hallucinations). Drugs and alcohol, as well as panic and stress resulting from disruptions during the execution of the crime, are factors that must be considered in the overall assessment of the crime scene.

Crime Scene Dynamics. Crime scene dynamics are the numerous elements common to every crime scene that must be interpreted by investigating officers and are at times easily misunderstood. Examples include location of the crime scene, cause of death, method of killing, positioning of the body, excessive trauma, and location of wounds.

The investigative profiler reads the dynamics of a crime scene and interprets them, based on his experience with similar cases where the outcome is known. Extensive research by the Behavioral Science Unit at the FBI

Academy and in-depth interviews with incarcerated felons who have committed such crimes have provided a vast body of knowledge of common elements that link crime scene dynamics to specific criminal personality patterns. For example, a common error of some police investigators is to assess a particularly brutal lust-mutilation murder as the work of a sex fiend and to direct the investigation toward known sex offenders, when, in fact such crimes are commonly perpetrated by individuals with no criminal record.

Stage Four: The Criminal Profile

The fourth stage in generating a criminal profile deals with the type of person who committed the crime and that individual's behavioral organization with relation to the crime. Once this description is generated, the strategy of investigation can be formulated, as this strategy requires a basic understanding of how an individual will respond to a variety of investigative efforts.

Included in the criminal profile are background information (demographics), physical characteristics, habits, beliefs and values, preoffensive behavior leading to the crime, and postoffensive behavior. It may also include investigative recommendations for interrogating or interviewing, identifying, and apprehending the offender.

This fourth stage has an important means of validating the criminal profile—feedback number 1. The profile must fit with the earlier reconstruction of the crime, with the evidence, and with the key decision process models. In addition, the investigative procedure developed from the recommendations must make sense in terms of the expected response patterns of the offender. If there is a lack of congruence, the investigative profilers review all available data. As Hercule Poirot would suggest: To know is to have all of the evidence and facts fit into place.

Stage Five: The Investigation

Once the congruence of the criminal profile has been determined, a written report is provided to the requesting agency and added to its ongoing investigative efforts. The investigative recommendations generated in stage four are applied, and suspects matching the profile are evaluated. If identification, apprehension, and a confession result, the goal of the profile effort has been met. If new evidence is generated (for example, by another murder) and/or there is no identification of a suspect, reevaluation occurs via feedback number 2. The information is reexamined and the profile revalidated.

Stage Six: The Apprehension

Once a suspect has been apprehended, the agreement between the outcome and the various stages in the profile generating process are examined. When an apprehended suspect admits guilt, it is important to conduct a detailed interview to check the total profiling process for validity.

A Case Example

A young woman's nude body was discovered at 3:00 P.M. on the roof landing of the apartment building where she lived. She had been badly beaten about the face and strangled with the strap of her purse. Her nipples had been cut off after death and placed on her chest. Scrawled in ink on the inside of her thigh was, "You can't stop me." The words "Fuck you" were scrawled on her abdomen. A pendant in the form of a Jewish sign (Chai), which she usually wore as a good luck piece around her neck, was missing and presumed taken by the murderer. Her underpants had been pulled over her face; her nylons had been removed and very loosely tied around her wrists and ankles near a railing. The murderer had placed symmetrically on either side of the victim's head the pierced earrings she had been wearing. An umbrella and inkpen had been forced into the vagina, and a hair comb was placed in her pubic hair. The woman's jaw and nose had been broken and her molars loosened. She suffered multiple face fractures caused by a blunt force. Cause of death was asphyxia by ligature (pocketbook strap) strangulation. There were postmortem bite marks on the victim's thighs, as well as contusions, hemorrhages, and lacerations of the body. The killer also defecated on the roof landing and covered the excrement with the victim's clothing.

The following discussion of this case in the context of the six stages of the criminal profile generating process illustrates how the process works.

Profiling Inputs

In terms of *crime scene evidence*, everything the offender used at the crime scene belonged to the victim. Even the comb and the felt-tip pen used to write on her body came from her purse. The offender apparently did not plan this crime; he had no gun, or tape for the victim's mouth. He probably did not even plan to encounter her that morning at that location. The crime scene indicated a spontaneous event; in other words, the killer did not stalk or wait for the victim. The crime scene differs from the death scene. The initial abduction was on the stairwell; then the victim was taken to a more remote area.

Investigation of the *victim* revealed that the twenty-six-year-old, ninety-pound, four-foot, eleven-inch white female awoke around 6:30 A.M. She dressed, had a breakfast of coffee and juice, and left her apartment for work at a nearby day care center, where she was employed as a group teacher for handicapped children. She resided with her mother and father. When leaving for work in the morning, she would take the elevator or walk down the stairs, depending on her mood. The victim was a quiet young woman who had a slight curvature of the spine (kyphoscoliosis).

The *forensic information* in the medical examiner's report was important in determining the extent of the wounds, as well as how the victim was assaulted and whether evidence of sexual assault was present or absent. No semen was noted in the vagina, but semen was found on the body. It appeared that the murderer stood directly over the victim and masturbated. There were visible bite marks on the victim's thighs and knee area. He cut off her nipples with a knife after she was dead and wrote on the body. Cause of death was strangulation, first manual, then ligature, with the strap of her purse. The fact that the murderer used a weapon of opportunity indicated that he did not prepare to commit this crime. He probably used his fist to render her unconscious, which may be the reason no one heard any screams. There were no deep stab wounds, and the knife used to mutilate the victim's breasts apparently was not big, probably a penknife that the offender normally carried. The killer used the victim's belts to tie her right arm and right leg, but he apparently untied them in order to position the body before he left.

The *preliminary police report* revealed that another resident of the apartment building, a white male, aged fifteen, discovered the victim's wallet in a stairwell between the third and fourth floors at approximately 8:20 A.M. He retained the wallet until he returned home from school for lunch that afternoon. At that time, he gave the wallet to his father, a white male, aged forty. The father went to the victim's apartment at 2:50 P.M. and gave the wallet to the victim's mother.

When the mother called the day care center to inform her daughter about the wallet, she learned that her daughter had not appeared for work that morning. The mother, the victim's sister, and a neighbor began a search of the building and discovered the body. The neighbor called the police. Police at the scene found no witnesses who saw the victim after she left her apartment that morning.

Decision Process

This crime's *style* is a single homicide with the murderer's primary intent making it a sexually motivated *type* of crime. There was a degree of *planning* indicated by the organization and sophistication of the crime scene. The idea of murder had probably occupied the killer for a long period of time. The sexual fantasies may have started through the use and collecting of sadistic pornography depicting torture and violent sexual acts.

Victim risk assessment revealed that the victim was known to be very self-conscious about her physical handicap and size and that she was a plain-looking woman who did not date. She led a reclusive life and was not the type of victim who would or could fight an assailant or scream and yell. She would be easily dominated and controlled, particularly in view of her small stature.

Based upon the information on occupation and life-style, we have a low-risk victim living in an area that was at low risk for violent crimes. The apartment building was part of a twenty-three-building public housing project in which the racial mixture of residents was 50 percent black, 40 percent white, and 10 percent Hispanic. It was located in the confines of a major police precinct. There had been no other similar crimes reported in the victim's or nearby complexes.

The crime was considered very *high risk* for the offender. He committed the crime in broad daylight, and there was a possibility that other people who were up early might see him. There was no set pattern of the victim's taking the stairway or the elevator. It appeared that the victim happened to cross the path of the offender.

There was no *escalation* factor present in this crime scene.

The *time* for the crime was considerable. The amount of time the murderer spent with his victim increased his risk of being apprehended. All his activities with the victim—removing her earrings, cutting off her nipples, masturbating over her—took a substantial amount of time.

The *location* of the crime suggested that the offender felt comfortable in the area. He had been here before, and he felt that no one would interrupt the murder.

Crime Assessment

The crime scene indicated that the murder was one event, not one of a series of events. It also appeared to be a first-time killing, and the subject was not a typical organized offender. There were elements of both disorganization and organization; the offender might fall into a mixed category.

A reconstruction of the crime/death scene provides an overall picture of the crime. To begin with, the victim was not necessarily stalked but instead confronted. What was her reaction? Did she recognize her assailant, fight him off, or try to get away? The subject had to kill her to carry out his sexually violent fantasies. The murderer was in known territory and thus had a reason to be there at 6:30 in the morning: either he resided there or he was employed at this particular complex.

The killer's control of the victim was through the use of blunt force trauma, with the blow to her face the first indication of his intention. Because she didn't fight, run, or scream, it appears that she did not perceive her abductor as a threat. Either she knew him, had seen him before, or he looked nonthreatening (that is, he was dressed as a janitor, a postman, or a business-man) and therefore his presence in the apartment would not alarm his victim.

In the sequence of the crime, the killer first rendered the victim unconscious and possibly dead; he could easily pick her up because of her small size. He took her up to the roof landing and had time to manipulate her body while she was unconscious. He positioned the body, undressed her, and acted out certain fantasies that led to masturbation. The killer took his time at the scene, and he probably knew that no one would come to the roof and disturb him in the early morning since he was familiar with the area and had been there many times in the past.

The crime scene was not staged. Sadistic ritualistic fantasy generated the sexual motivation for murder. The murderer displayed total domination of the victim. In addition, he placed the victim in a degrading posture, which reflected his lack of remorse about the killing.

The crime scene dynamics of the covering of the killer's feces and his positioning of the body are incongruent and need to be interpreted. First, as previously described, the crime was opportunistic. The crime scene portrayed the intricacies of a long-standing murderous fantasy. Once the killer had a victim, he had a set plan about killing and abusing the body. However, within the context of the crime, the profilers note a puzzle: the covered feces. Defecation was not part of the ritual fantasy, and thus the excrement was covered. The presence of the feces also supports the length of time taken for the crime, the control the murderer had over the victim (her unconscious state), and the knowledge he would not be interrupted.

The positioning of the victim suggested that the offender was acting out something he had seen before, perhaps in a fantasy or in a sadomasochistic pornographic magazine. Because the victim was unconscious, the killer did not need to tie her hands. Yet he continued to tie her neck and strangle her. He positioned her earrings in a ritualistic manner, and he wrote on her body. This reflects some sort of imagery that he probably had repeated over and over in his mind. He took her necklace as a souvenir, perhaps to carry around in his pocket. The investigative profilers also noted that the body was positioned in the form of the woman's missing Jewish symbol.

Criminal Profile

Using the information gained during the previous stages, investigators generated a criminal profile of the murderer. First, a physical description of the suspect stated that he would be a white male, between twenty-five and thirty-five, or the same general age as the victim, and of average appearance. The murderer would not look out of context in the area. He would be of average intelligence and would be a high school or college dropout. He would not have a military history and might be unemployed. His occupation would be blue-collar or skilled. Alcohol or drugs would not assume a major role, as the crime occurred in the early morning.

The suspect would have difficulty maintaining any kind of personal relationships with women. If he dated, he would date women younger than himself, since he would have to be able to dominate and control in the relationships.

He would be sexually inexperienced, sexually inadequate, and never married. He would have a pornography collection. The subject would have sadistic tendencies; the umbrella and the masturbation act are clearly acts of sexual substitution. The sexual acts showed controlled aggression, but rage or hatred of women was obviously present. The murderer was not reacting to rejection from women as much as to morbid curiosity.

In addressing the habits of the murderer, the profile revealed there would be a reason for the killer to be at the crime scene at 6:30 in the morning. He could be employed in the apartment complex, in the complex on business, or he might reside in the complex.

Although the offender might have preferred his victim conscious, he had to render her unconscious because he did not want to get caught. He did not want the woman screaming for help.

The murderer's infliction of sexual, sadistic acts on an inanimate body suggests that he was disorganized. He probably would be a very confused person, possibly with previous mental problems. If he had carried out such acts on a living victim, he would have a different type of personality. The fact that he inflicted acts on a dead or unconscious person indicated his inability to function with a live or conscious person.

The crime scene reflected that the killer felt justified in his actions and that he felt no remorse. He was not subtle. He left the victim in a provocative, humiliating position, exactly the way he wanted her to be found. He challenged the police in the message he wrote on the victim; the messages also indicated that the subject might well kill again.

Investigation

The crime received intense coverage by the local media because it was such an extraordinary homicide. The local police responded to a radio call of a homicide. They in turn notified the detective bureau, which notified the forensic crime scene unit, medical examiner's office, and the county district attorney's office. A task force was immediately assembled of approximately twenty-six detectives and supervisors.

An intensive investigation resulted, which included speaking to and interviewing more than two thousand people. Records checks of known sex offenders in the area proved fruitless. Handwriting samples were taken of possible suspects to compare to the writing on the body. Mental hospitals in the area were checked for people who might fit the profile of this type of killer.

The FBI's Behavorial Science Unit was contacted in order to draw up a profile. In the profile, the investigation recommendation mentioned that the offender knew that the police sooner or later would contact him because he either worked or lived in the building. The killer would somehow inject himself into the investigation, and although he might appear cooperative to the extreme, he would really be seeking information. In addition, he might try to contact the victim's family.

Apprehension

The outcome of the investigation was the apprehension of a suspect thirteen months after the discovery of the victim's body. After receiving the criminal profile, the police reviewed their files of twenty-two suspects they had interviewed. One man stood out. This suspect's father lived down the hall in the same apartment building as the victim. Police originally had interviewed the father, who told them his son was a patient at the local psychiatric hospital. Police learned later that the son had been absent without permission from the hospital the day and evening prior to the murder.

They also learned that he was an unemployed actor who lived alone; his mother had died of a stroke when he was 19 years old (eleven years previously). He had had academic problems of repeating a grade and had dropped out of school. He was a white, thirty-year-old, never-married male who was an only child. His father was a blue-collar worker who also was an ex-prizefighter. The suspect reportedly had his arm in a cast at the time of the crime. A search of his room revealed a pornography collection. He had never been in the military, had no girlfriends, and was described as being insecure with women. The man suffered from depression and was receiving psychiatric treatment and hospitalization. He had a history of repeated suicidal attempts (hanging/asphyxiation) both before and after the offense.

The suspect was tried, found guilty, and is serving a sentence of twenty-five years to life for this mutilation murder. He denies committing the murder and states he did not know the victim. Police proved that security was lax at the psychiatric hospital in which the suspect was confined and that he could literally come and go as he pleased. However, the most conclusive evidence against him at his trial, was his teeth impressions. Three separate forensic dentists, prominent in the field, conducted independent tests and all agreed that the suspect's teeth impressions matched the bite marks found on the victim's body.

Conclusion

Criminal personality profiling has proved to be a useful tool to law enforcement in solving violent, apparently motiveless crimes. The process has aided significantly in the solution of many cases over the past decade. It is believed that through the research efforts of personnel in the FBI's National Center for the Analysis of Violent Crime and professionals in other fields, the profiling process will continue to be refined and be a viable investigative aid to law enforcement.

Notes

Christie, Agatha. *The clocks*. New York: Pocket Books, 1963.

Ressler, R.K., Burgess, A.W., Douglas, J.E., and Depue, R.L. Criminal profiling research on homicide. In A.W. Burgess (ed.), *Rape and sexual assault: a research handbook* (pp. 343–349). New York: Garland, 1985.

10

The Role of Forensic Pathology in Criminal Profiling

James L. Luke, M.D.

Thinking Through the Issues

Those of us who are privileged to serve as participants in the arena of medical-legal death investigation, whether as uniformed police officers, homicide detectives, or physicians, are trained to insulate ourselves from emotional involvement in the cases we investigate. In order to maintain perspective and objectivity, it is important to detach oneself from the pathos of the tragedy of sudden death. However, I doubt that there are many of us who don't, from time to time, fall into the habit of personalizing the case at hand. This is a natural, expected, and, I believe, positive human attribute. By personalizing, I mean identifying with the victim, and painful though it may be, imagining yourself or your spouse or your child in the victim's stead. The positive result of this level of emotional involvement is that is ensures, to some extent at least, that the case will be investigated with caring, with compassion, and with discretion. It guarantees that the humanity of the victim will not be obscured by the mayhem of the moment. Whether it also ensures that better investigative decisions will be made is not possible to know.

More to the point of this discussion, personalizing a case also forms the basis for pondering about the sort of person who could have committed the crime in the first place. There are few of us who will not have spent many hours over the course of our careers wondering who did it, how long it lasted, how it must have felt to the victim, and to be acutely aware, in spite of the spectacular advances that have been achieved in some areas of the forensic sciences, of the woeful lack of meaningful progress in others. Forensic pathology would fall into the latter category. It is all too easy with a difficult case at our doorstep to become frustrated at our inability to call up a simulated rewitnessing of the fatal event. Fanciful though that notion may seem to the uninitiated, the work products of the various disciplines that constitute the forensic sciences are directed toward precisely that end. Consequently, this is the mind-set that prompted in 1984 the active inclusion of forensic pathology in the criminal profiling activities of the Behavioral Science Unit at the FBI Academy in Quantico, Virginia.

The interface between the disciplines of criminal profiling and forensic pathology forms the basis upon which a substantial portion of the profiling exercise is established. Gaps in available knowledge about what happened to the victim are, proportionally, gaps in the final profiling product. In this context, the forensic pathologist reviews and evaluates the postmortem pathologic findings contained in the various materials submitted for profiling. He examines the diagrams, the photographs, and the narrative autopsy report. He familiarizes himself with the police reports pertaining to the particular circumstances of the case before him and reviews the reports of forensic scientific laboratory analyses performed.

At this point it might be useful to spend a moment or two describing the sorts of pathology-related information that should optimally be included in this type of exercise.

A comprehensive police report, which may or may not include a chronology of investigative events.

A scene diagram with a description of climatic conditions, body position, signs of death (including body temperature and postmortem rigidity and lividity, and appropriateness of each of the latter, in terms of the position of the body when found, for example), clothing worn by the deceased, drug paraphernalia found at the scene, if any, and other pertinent scene descriptors.

Photographs of the scene of death and of the pertinent autopsy findings, and a diagram of wound pattern distribution. If a picture is worth a thousand words, a diagram is worth at least five hundred. And, speaking of pictures, the autopsy photographs ideally should be eight-by-ten inch prints, in focus, and the wounds depicted should have been cleaned of dried blood and other extraneous material.

Reports of toxicological and other forensic scientific analyses.

The bottom line is that it is not possible to provide too much factual information.

After the review and synthesis of all available and pertinent information, an evaluation is made regarding both the completeness and the validity of the data provided. If additional information is necessary to determine the nature and type of postmortem findings (the size, shape, and extent of the wounds, for example), the submitting pathologist is contacted by telephone for clarification and/or elaboration. This personal interaction is extremely useful, not only regarding exposition of findings of fact, but also to elicit the pathologist's own interpretation of the findings relative to the circumstances of the case, and, depending on the level of his training and experience, on the degree of certainty he places on his interpretations. Bearing in mind that autopsy reports are narrative descriptions of fact and do not normally contain interpretive judgments, this sort of person-to-person contact is to be encouraged whenever possible and in many cases is a prerequisite to proper case understanding and analysis.

The relationship between forensic pathology and the criminal justice system is both subtle and complicated, and varies from one medical-legal jurisdiction to another. Let's start at the beginning. What is forensic pathology? It is a recognized medical subspecialty requiring supervised training and case-handling experience. Prior to being eligible to take the American Board of Pathology certifying examination, the candidate must have spent at least one year in an approved residency training program.

From the standpoint of forensic pathology, the two major parameters that form the basis of any case investigation are (1) identification and documentation of the postmortem findings present, and (2) interpretation of those findings within the context of the circumstances of death. Postmortem findings can be *positive*, in the sense of a demonstrated gunshot wound, or *negative*, in the sense of absence of an anatomic evidence of blunt force injury, for example, in a shooting homicide said to have been preceded by an altercation in which the victim is alleged to have been beaten with a pipe. The circumstances of death might usefully be extended to include the past medical history of the victim and/or review of his or her hospital records, when applicable. The root problem here, of course, is that identification of the postmortem findings and interpretation of their significance is a subjective, judgmental exercise. In that regard, there is no facet of the work of a forensic pathologist that does not require the use of training and experience to generate the subjective conclusions reached. I am reminded of a remark by the late Dr. Milton Helpern, former chief medical examiner of New York City, when he was asked to evaluate a case using only the pathologic findings enumerated at autopsy. "Forensic pathology is not a specialty," he said, "where you can ring up an itemized listing of findings on an autopsy room cash register and expect to total up the conclusion." That statement can be applied to the forensic sciences in general, and, for that matter, to any aspect of the art of death investigation. Without judgment and common sense, we all might be well advised to seek some other form of employment.

Training programs in forensic pathology vary widely regarding caseload volume and the extent of trainee supervision. Although somewhere between one hundred and two hundred board-certified forensic pathologists in this country practice their specialty on a full-time basis, significant variability exists in the skill level, motivation, time available per case, and other important factors that are brought to bear on the individual case. Similar variability exists in budget, equipment, and other administrative resources provided for death investigative efforts within and between medical-legal jurisdictions. In some jurisdictions, medical-legal postmortem examinations are performed by pathologists who have received little or no formal training in forensic pathology. Systems vary. People vary. When these two intangibles are combined and applied to a given victim of a major crime in a particular jurisdiction, it is surprising that so many cases are reasonably well handled. It is also not surprising that a number of cases fall through the procedural cracks.

It is important, therefore, to realize that the validity and competence of forensic pathologic information that is provided to the criminal profiler will not be uniform, and that further inquiry must be made to improve the quality and usefulness of these important data. At one extreme of the performance spectrum, the forensic pathology findings and conclusions may be inadequate to the extent that they invalidate even the certified cause and manner of death. At the other end of the spectrum, clarification of postmortem findings may provide valuable data pertaining to estimating bullet caliber (in an in-and-out skull wound, for example), sequence of injury, prior drug involvement, and a host of similar parameters that, in a given case, may be critically important in discovering what happened to the victim. And what happened to the victim is, in large part, determined by the motivation, character, and mind-set of the offender.

Once we have examined and analyzed the information provided and have made a rough determination concerning its validity, it is time to begin a sorting process that is part of the intellectual armamentarium of every medical-legal death investigator, including forensic pathologists: What credence can we place on the facts we have developed? What is the degree of certainty of the forensic pathology evidence?

Time of death

Postmortem interval

Range of gunfire

Type of blunt force weapon

Identification of patterned injury that may reflect a particular weapon or instrument

Findings indicating sexual assault

Extent of force delivered

Drug levels

The listing is open ended and depends to a great extent on the unique circumstances of death and on the proposed fatal scenario in the case being investigated.

The scene and autopsy room photographs provided to the profiler must be examined not only to confirm information presented as fact, but also to identify findings present that may not have been appreciated or described by the pathologist who performed the postmortem examination. Most forensic pathologists have had the experience of having completed an autopsy on a difficult homicide where photographs have been taken and diagrams and a narrative description of findings prepared, only to discover later when the photographic material is developed and reviewed that there, staring the pathologist in the face, is a patterned injury or other trauma that had been completely overlooked or misinterpreted at the autopsy table. We have had similar experiences in reviewing materials submitted for FBI criminal profiling. Patterned blunt force injury has, on occasion, not been previously recognized. Findings of asphyxia have been overlooked or misidentified. These errors of omission are not viewed as representing incompetence or inadequacy on the part of the local investigator or pathologist. In a complex, interpretive, interdisciplinary activity like death investigation, we should always reserve the right to be smarter and wiser today than we were yesterday.

It may sound simplistic to say that establishing the profile is the profiler's responsibility. Nevertheless, it would appear to be advantageous for the pathologist not to interject himself into the actual profiling process prior to completing his own analysis of the pertinent submitted materials. Objectivity can best be approximated in this fashion.

However, now that the forensic pathology findings have been evaluated, the time has come to discuss the case with the person whose responsibility it is to construct the profile. This activity may be accomplished either singly—that is, person to person or in a group profiling session. My strong personal preference is the latter arrangement, even though a group session may be more time consuming. If it is not yet an axiom of medical-legal death investigation, it ought to be, and it should be noted that here too two heads are invariably better than one. A small group of experienced investigators generates ideas of potential investigative import in geometrically beneficial fashion. By the same token and for the same reason, it was agency policy at the Washington, D.C., medical examiner's office to include additional medical examiners in any complicated case investigation, whether at the scene of death or in the autopsy room, for the express purpose of cross fertilization of ideas, as well as for documentation or endorsement of complicated case findings.

At the profiling session the case history, victimology, and forensic pathology findings are presented and discussed relative to their significance in terms of the specific issues of the case. Regarding forensic scientific input here, it will become obvious that most forensic pathology findings will be noncontributory to developing the profile. The discussion will most likely center around one or two parameters of particular forensic import, parameters that may have a significant bearing on the profile in progress, based not on the findings themselves but on the circumstances and unresolved issues of the case.

I would like to illustrate this point by posing several hypothetical questions that were raised in actual profiling sessions, with each question representing a different case (and with considerations of forensic pathologic or of profiling significance in parentheses):

How long could the victim have lived with the illness of diabetes insipidus following her abduction and prior to her death, with the medication that she required not being available to her? (Medical history, time of death and postmortem interval).

How much would the victim be expected to bleed with a wound of this type in this location, and is it more likely, given the relative paucity of blood on her clothing and at the scene, that she was killed elsewhere and dumped where she was found? (Anatomic wound location and extent of injury).

Is the incised wound of the neck in reality a postmortem injury, given the findings of conjunctival petechiae, as evidence of asphyxia, and the belt buckle mark of the neck, which may denote use of a ligature as a controlling device? (Was the sexual assault inflicted first, and the victim killed to avoid identifying her assailant?).

Item: A middle-aged woman, an alleged police informant, was found naked in her bedroom, jackknifed over the left side of her bed with her knees on the floor. Her throat had been slashed to the spine. However, considerably less blood was present on the bedclothes than would have been expected with a major incised wound of this type.

Careful examination of autopsy photographs of the deceased's neck revealed a patterned contusion or bruise of the right side of her neck just lateral to the right margin of the incised wound. The pattern was characteristic of a belt buckle, the belt ligature presumably having been employed as a controlling device and anteceding the slash wound of the throat. No mention of the patterned injury had been made in either the police report of the case or by the pathologist in the autopsy report.

Is the patterned injury present indicative of a particular type or class of weapon or instrument? (Did the subject bring his own weapon with him, implying forethought and planning?)

Item: A middle-aged female motel night clerk was found supine on the floor of the office behind the registration desk. Her clothing had been forcibly removed. A prominent complex ligature abrasion was present, involving nearly the entire front of her neck. Review of the scene photographs of the injury demonstrated a multiply repeating pattern of abrasion and contusion across the neck. The longer the injury was examined, the clearer the pattern became, much like the development in the darkroom of a photographic print, finally becoming recognizable as a square-shaped belt buckle. The pattern was specific enough that the buckle width could be estimated and the prong and vertical prong support areas could be approximated.

The point I would like to make here is that it is useful to set aside a block of time to examine all available wound photographs. Experience is of invaluable assistance in this regard. It is not enough just to say that an abrasion or contusion exists and to let it go at that. Much can be learned by active pondering, a process that takes time and effort.

Again, the listing of possible profiling issues related to forensic pathology is bounded only by the dynamics of the circumstances of the case. Let us next turn to a case study, which will illustrate a number of important forensic pathology principles.

Case Study

A twenty-one year-old male was found dead at the foot of the flight of stairs leading to the basement of the dormitory building to which he had been assigned at a federal reformatory. He was fully dressed. The criminal offense for which he had been convicted was interstate transportation of a stolen vehicle.

Rigidity was observed in the jaw. The only evidence of trauma, according to the prison infirmary physician, was an abrasion of the front of the neck "consistent with impact against the front edge of the basement steps" down which he allegedly fell. The case came in as an apparent accident. Figure 10–1 shows the front of the deceased's neck.

Diagnosis

Patterned ligature abrasion of anterior neck.

Discussion

The lesion present is characteristic of a patterned ligature abrasion, a belt in this instance, with the prong attachment represented by the vertical component present centrally. The buckle appears to be rounded, and the width of the belt can be estimated by the distance between the horizontal components at the left margin of the photograph.

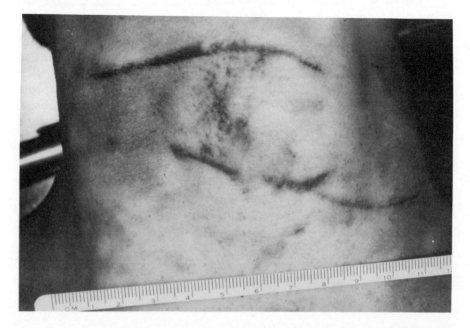

Figure 10–1. Abrasion at Anterior Surface of Neck

Also present at autopsy but overlooked by the infirmary physician were abundant petechial or pinpoint hemorrhages of the skin surfaces of the eyelids and orbits and of the conjunctival surfaces. Although petechiae are by no means diagnostic of asphyxia (they are commonly seen as a correlate of dependent lividity, for example, and in certain blood diseases, among a range of other clinical conditions), they are often present in adult victims of ligature strangulation, and in greater numbers than in other forms of violent asphyxia. Their origin is most likely the result of increased intracapillary pressure resulting from complete venous obstruction (by circumferential ligature pressure), with incomplete arterial compromise. In other words, the ligature is loose enough to permit passage of arterial blood (high pressure) into the head but sufficiently tight so that venous blood flow (low pressure) is stopped. Consequently, intravascular pressure above the ligature rises, causing petechial hemorrhage formation. Examination with dissection by layers of the strap musculature of the anterior neck and of the larynx and hyoid bone demonstrated regional soft tissue and intramuscular hemorrhage and a fracture of the cricoid cartilage at the base of the larynx or voice box.

Examination of the stomach at autopsy revealed it to be completely food filled, placing time of death within an hour or two (at the most) of the deceased's last prison meal. Smears prepared from swabs taken from the victim's anus demonstrated ovoid structures consistent with sperm heads (see figure 10–2), representing the situational matrix of death in this case—that is sexual assault.

An ensuing criminal investigation by the FBI corroborated the interpretations of the postmortem findings that have been presented here and resulted in the prosecution and conviction of the assailants.

Conclusion

It should be obvious by this point that there is more to the practice of forensic pathology and its relationship to criminal profiling than determining the cause and manner of death. In rationalizing the need for a medical examiner's office and for providing public funding for professional activities related to death investigation, the public benefit of such a program relates to the pathologist's ability to respond to the open-ended sequence of questions that are asked in each such case.

The questions come from the victim's family, from the police, from the press, from prosecutors and defense attorneys, and from a wide range of other interested persons. The questions, as we have seen, vary according to the case being investigated and range from issues of personal identification in a severely

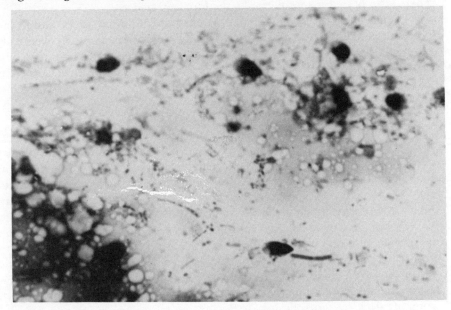

Figure 10-2. **High-Power View of Anal Smear Demonstration Ovoid Structures Consistent With Sperm Heads**

decomposed or skeletonized body, for example—from "Who are you?" if you will—to those of sequence of injury in a death where multiple forms of trauma may be present—that is, "What happened to you?" These and other queries form the basis of what Dr. Lester Adelson has aptly called his "dialogue with the dead." Dr. Adelson, the chief deputy coroner of Cuyahoga County (Cleveland, Ohio) for more than thirty years and author of one of the preeminent texts in the field, *The Pathology of Homicide*, has over the years and better than anyone, in my judgment, articulated the rationale for the discipline.

The questions posed in such cases continue to involve considerations of estimating time of death, postmortem interval and onset of illness (in a nonviolent or natural death, for example). They include estimating the age of an injury relative to the time of death. They involve identification of evidence of sexual assault. They involve correlation between the circumstances of violence and the autopsy findings. Dead men do, in fact, tell tales.

It is the responsibility of the forensic pathologist finally, to construct a scaffolding of factual information against which witnesses' and suspects' statements can be evaluated. For obvious reasons, the boundaries of the forensic pathology responses to the questions that are asked must be drawn in as conservative a fashion as is appropriate, based on the evidence provided. There is no place for speculation in the forensic sciences.

In many instances, this analytical exercise turns out to be simply an objective, independent, and impartial way to document what is already "known" in a given case. It is possible that no *new* information maybe generated by a medical-legal postmortem examination. Nevertheless, there is great benefit in knowing what happened and, from the perspective of law enforcement, in being able to corroborate or refute witnesses' and suspects' statements.

The most critical element in the practice of medical-legal death investigation is communication: communication between investigator and pathologist and among all of the investigative participants in a Siamese-twin relationship that absolutely requires communication and active participation to be effective. The operational aspects of this sort of interchange are no different in any medical-legal jurisdiction from what they are in the area of criminal profiling.

Criminal profiling is at the cutting edge of modern law enforcement. The involvement of forensic pathology in this exercise is an exciting new departure and represents the next dimension beyond jurisdictional medical examiner's office service caseload. As important as it is to know what happened to the victim in order to ascertain the type of person that would be most likely to have committed a given violent crime, to that extent it is also essential to include the forensic sciences, and forensic pathology in particular, within the criminal profiling methodology.

11
Interviewing Convicted Murderers

One goal of the study of sexual homicide crime scenes and patterns of criminal behavior was to explore how murderers commit their crimes. The interviews allowed us to retrieve, from the murderers themselves, first-hand information about patterns of values and beliefs, patterns of thinking, levels of recall on the crimes, and admission of responsibility for the murders.

Using interviewing techniques to secure the maximum information about a suspect or crime is highly valuable to law enforcement. As serial murders become more visible, the likelihood increases that law enforcement agents will be called upon to interview suspects during the course of an investigation. This chapter presents our experiences in interviewing convicted serial sexual murderers. Although the interviews were conducted with murderers already convicted and incarcerated, we believe that our observations provide insights for interviewing suspects during the process of apprehending a killer.

Terms of the Interview

A suspect is interviewed under various conditions. The condition is generally stated by the interviewer; in our case, the interview was conducted in order to understand what contributed to the criminal act.

Before beginning any interview, the interviewer needs to be fully familiar with any pertinent existing information, including crime scene photographs, records, and files. This information can be used not to draw conclusions but to establish a focused interest in the offender. From this interest respect is conveyed, an initial objective in establishing rapport. Conveying respect is often difficult in cases of violent and brutal crimes; however, it allows the interviewer to get to the point of the interview more quickly. Less time is spent by the subject in evaluating the interviewer if the interviewer exhibits respect.

The Communication Link

Rapport is the key communication link in an interview. Once established and recognized, it allows the interviewer to lead the interview and to reestablish communication if it breaks down. Rapport is gained when the investigator understands the subject's world.

Sections reprinted from *FBI Law Enforcement Bulletin*, 1985, 54:26–31.

From the investigator's perspective, establishing rapport during an interview requires ignoring personal feelings about the nature of the crimes in order to be open to the subject's answers to questions. One way to obtain this objectivity is to focus on the value of the information for law enforcement and protection purposes. Understanding why a suspect thinks and acts in a certain manner will help him in recalling the events and motivations of a crime.

Eliciting Information

Once communication has been initiated, and the suspect's thinking pattern and general rapport established, the questioning begins. In our study, the what/where/when sequencing and descriptions of places where the crime events occurred were sought first. Next, the interviewing agents asked questions about how the victim was chosen. Finally, questions about thoughts, feelings, and images were posed.

Questions were generally organized around four phases of the murder. These phases are: (1) the precrime phase, (2) the murder event, (3) the disposal of the body, and (4) the postcrime phase.

The Precrime Phase. Conscious motive for the murder was often elicited by asking the subject what triggered the murder. Those murderers with conscious intent were able to describe this in detail. Those murderers without conscious motive would usually say that they could not remember why they killed, but they were able to describe their feelings prior to the murder. Reconstructing the scene prior to the murder helped interviewing agents determine the cues that moved the offender's murder fantasy into action. For example, offenders were asked to describe their day prior to the murder and their thoughts and feelings before encountering the victim.

The Murder Event. Memory recall of details specific to the murders varied among the offenders we interviewed. Those murderers who deliberately planned the murder through a fantasy generally continued to remember details about certain aspects of the murder. During one interview, the agents remarked that the subject seemed to have almost total recall. The subject corrected the agents:

> Actually that's overblown because I really don't [remember everything]. I have shabby memory on things I don't want to remember, and things that are shocking or very vivid, I don't forget. I trip on those for years.

The areas that a subject avoids or refuses to talk about provide information about areas where strong emotions may exist. (In one case, the murderer began the interview by stating that he would not discuss his family.) Important aspects of the event to discuss include gaining access to the victim; conversation and behaviors involving the victim; transporting the victim from one location to another; what the murderer did sexually before, during, and after the victim's death; methods of torture; behaviors after the victim's death (such as mutilation or amputation); and thoughts and feelings during these acts.

Disposal of the Body. Our interviews with the murderers made clear the importance of fantasy in planning the disposal of the victim's body. Once the act was committed, the murderer had to decide what to do with the body. At this phase, the murderer may first consciously realize the reality of his act. Our questions concerning this phase included what was done with the body, how the offender left the scene, what (if anything) was taken from the body or the crime scene, and what thoughts and feelings the murderer experienced during the commission of these various acts.

The Postcrime Phase. A series of behaviors occurs after a murder. We asked each offender what he did right after the murder (did he wash or change clothes, go out with friends, go to sleep, or eat); how he thought and felt about it; whether he dreamed about it; whether he returned to the crime scene, attended the funeral, read about the murder in the newspaper, or talked to police. We were careful to include questions about recovery of the body (did the offender assist police in the recovery; was he present when the body was recovered; was his confession necessary for police to find the body).

Specific Techniques

Because of the importance of fantasy to sexual homicide, information about a subject's fantasy can be valuable. However, people with a long-standing fantasy life may not talk about it easily. Often a low-key approach is successful in encouraging the discussion of the fantasy. A fantasy contains great preoccupation and emotion. The person keeps going back to the thoughts. The subject may only be aware of images, feelings, and internal dialogue at certain heightened times.

One of the indications of the presence of a fantasy is the great amount of detail provided by a subject. These details provide the best information about how the subject operates. For many of the murderers we interviewed, their detailed planning was their statement of superiority, control, and cleverness. The fantasy life usually provided a sense of power and control as well as emotional stimulation. In some instances, the fantasy appeared to protect them from becoming totally disorganized or psychotic. We discovered this, through the interviews, in the subjects' reports of becoming enraged when victims interrupted their plans. These murderers were very sensitive to being called crazy or maniacal, for they associated those characteristics with carrying out acts in ways that are stupid, foolish and out of control.

The importance of the terminology used in the interview was illustrated in one case:

> *Agent*: Do you think your fantasy life was out of control?
> *Subject*: I'm going to have to change your terminology, not because I'm bantering words, but my fantasy world, no, I don't think it was out of control, I think my world of realism was out of control. My perception of the real world was distorted.

This exchange demonstrates how the murderer felt in control of his fantasy and out of control in the real world.

Our interviews revealed that, in contrast to murderers who plan a crime through fantasy, some murderers acted in response to external cues. Such people may not be able to answer why a particular act happened. These murderers were concerned with particular acts at certain times; suddenly they lost control. It is possible to talk about the existence of the fantasies without eliciting details of them and to obtain information about the serial murderer's blockage of certain memories:

> *Agent*: Did you have any unusual fantasies preoccupying you for any period of time or that you felt you were overinvolved in?
> *Subject*: Well, I can't say if I have or I don't. There are a lot of aspects of this crime I can't give an answer, cause I put up a mental block. I don't want to think of it. It makes me do bad time. I'm doing a long time and I just block it clear out.

The murderer confirms the likelihood that the fantasies are there; however, additional techniques such as hypnosis or therapy would be needed to access the information.

Continuum of Admission

An offender can take one of three positions regarding admission of guilt: admission of the crime, admission with lack of total recall, and not admitting the crime.

Admission of Guilt. In our study, the majority of murderers admitted their crimes. Some of the murderers turned themselves in to the police; others admitted to the crime when they were apprehended. Still others admitted guilt when confronted with evidence. As one murderer told the interviewing agents, "The police unwrapped the broomhandle and that did it."

Admission with Lack of Total Recall. Several murderers we interviewed were unable to remember actually committing the murder, but agreed the evidence incriminated them.

Non-admission of Guilt. One group of murderers we interviewed did not admit to their crimes even after their conviction for the murders. When confronted with such individuals, the interviewer needs to determine whether the individual is lying (which implies conscious intent) or whether he is denying (which implies unconscious intent).

To the offender, lying to an investigator provides a form of control. It may detour the investigator and waste valuable time, as when incorrect names and addresses are given.

One way investigators identify lies is on the basis of the amount of detail that a subject provides. Fantasy worlds or delusions are usually very detailed. However, when a subject tries to feign psychosis or delusion, his story usually appears inconsistent and lacking in detail. Investigators detecting this type of defense and bringing it to the attention of the offender may be successful. In one case the murderer claimed to have committed the murders because of instructions from a centuries-old dog. The agents refused to accept this ploy. They pointed out good-naturedly that the murders had been carefully planned and executed, which was a lot to expect from a dog. The murderer finally accepted the "credit" for the crimes and discussed them in detail with the interviewers. Even when suspecting that a subject is lying or denying, the interviewer should try to maintain an atmosphere of mutual respect.

There are reasons why a suspect might deny a crime. The denial might serve to protect the subject from legal action as well as from the psychological impact of admitting such a crime. One murderer interviewed denied any actual knowledge of committing the crime. He stated that he was coerced, forced to confess to the crimes, and possibly drugged before entering a plea of guilty. In the interview with the agents, he had an elaborate answer for each piece of evidence presented. He said that friends had given him the one hundred pairs of high-heeled shoes in his closet. He argued that photographs found in his possession were not his, because he would not be such a sloppy photographer. He presented extreme detail for each piece of evidence brought against him to "prove" why he could not have been the murderer.

There also may be cases in which the murderer justifies in his own mind the issue of admitting or denying guilt. The following statement from a serial murderer illustrates this position:

Agent: Could the police have done anything for you in order to get a confession?
Subject: Well, at first I didn't admit my guilt. I wouldn't admit to anybody. But I didn't really deny either.

We found that when someone outright denied that he had murdered or had had anything to do with the crime, the use of an imaginary third person was helpful. The Agents would go through the details of the crime and ask the subject why he thought this third person would commit such an act. This technique projected responsibility or guilt away from the subject and onto someone else. Note how this strategy is used in the following interview with a murderer:

Agent: Suppose we do it this way. Let's just divorce you from that situation. I'm sure you've thought about it a lot. Suppose it wasn't you involved and it was someone else. What, in your mind, would be the reasons for someone doing something like that?

Subject: I'd say she either said or did something extremely wrong.

Agent: Like what, for instance?

Subject: Well, it could have been that his [sexual] performance was inadequate. She might have thought it was. Or he might have thought it was and she said something about it.

This conversation shows how the murderer was able to provide a reason (sexual inadequacy) for the crime's having been committed and suggests that the intent to kill was triggered into action through an internal dialogue process within the offender.

Often someone who denies justifies his or her actions by blaming someone else. In our study, for example, a murderer justified his killing by describing the victim as a "tramp." One reason a murderer may not be able to admit the crime is that admission would destroy his premise of justification.

The following is one murderer's confession.

Judy

I learned that she was a model for both amateur and professional photographers from her roommate, who showed me her pictures. I called her about noon to ask if she was available for a modeling job that afternoon. I gave my name as Johnny Glen. She said she was free, and we made an appointment for 2:00 P.M. to meet at her apartment. She picked out some clothes, including extra ones that she said she needed for another assignment after we were finished. We left her apartment for my apartment, which I told her was fixed as a studio with lights and equipment there. She was agreeable. She said she didn't care where she was modeling as long as she was paid twenty dollars per hour.

We drove to my apartment, arriving around 2:15 P.M. I slipped the gun I usually kept in my glove compartment in my coat pocket before going into my apartment. Once inside I told her I wanted to take some pictures that would be suitable for illustrations for mystery stories or detective magazines and that this would require me to tie her hands and feet and put a gag in her mouth. She was agreeable, and I took a number of poses.

The last pictures that I shot had her tied and on the floor. She was getting a little restless. I finally made up my mind to go through with my intention [to rape her]. I went over to her and put my hand around her shoulder and just below her neck. I sat down on the floor beside her and propped her up to a sitting position and told her that I was going to keep her there a while and that I wouldn't hurt her if she did as she was told and didn't give me any trouble. I said I was going to have some fun with her and I also took the gun out of my pocket and showed it to her as a sign of seriousness and also to get her to a frame of mind where she would be docile. I also told her that I had a record and just by doing what I had done so far I was in serious trouble. This was to scare her into being submissive.

She motioned to me that she wanted to say something. I took out her gag and cautioned her to talk quietly and not to make any loud noises or scream. She said she was a nymphomaniac and that she was not going to cause trouble because she was estranged from her husband and that she had a custody suit pending which was due for a hearing in about a week. Any hint of her running around or engaging in any unusual activities might be used against her, as her ex-husband was trying to have her declared as unfit for custody of the child. She was saying this, I presume, to impress me that it was not necessary to threaten her with a gun.

I believed her, so I slipped the gun back into my pocket and picked her up and carried her into a little hallway adjacent to the living room where we had been taking pictures. I put her down and left her in there by herself in the same condition as she was on the floor in the living room. I went back into the living room and took the film out of the camera, put the camera and tripod away, went into the kitchen and got a glass of water and a piece of apple to eat. Then I went back where I left her in the hallway and sat down beside her. I started to run my hands over her body and squeeze her and I was kissing her around the neck and breasts. She seemed to be partially enjoying it. I don't recall how long we kept this up. Then I untied her hands and feet. I told her to remove her clothes. I think I said I had taken the film out of the camera. That is not correct. I had two or three shots left in the camera. I finished the roll of film then and took pictures of her sitting on the couch with her facing the camera, virtually naked and with one, I believe, leg on the couch and the other one dangling on the floor.

I left something out. While she was still tied and in the hallway, I had gone into the kitchen and when I came back she had a nosebleed for some reason. She was trying to hold her head back and her nose was bleeding. I don't know why. She hadn't been struck or anything unless in trying to move around slightly, she jarred her head against something. I just grabbed the first piece of cloth that was laying close by, and I used that to hold over her nose to stop the bleeding. It was bleeding quite freely, and I held her head back till it stopped. I mention this because the police did find a pillow case in my room after I was arrested and it had bloodstains on it, and one of the photographs of Judy show it.

Judy wanted to use the bathroom, and I let her. I told her she could get dressed, and she did and combed her hair and put on some makeup. When she came out I told her to sit on the couch and relax a while. I began to wonder just what I was going to do next, how I was going to resolve this. It was getting late in the afternoon, and I was trying to think could I release her and what would happen if I did and what would she do about reporting this. I asked her several times something like: "Judy, what are you going to tell your roommates when you get home?" "Do you think your roommates are very worried about you and would they call the police?" She indicated that she would try and cover this up and make up some story. She repeated that she could not afford any kind of scandal or improper activities, whether it was her fault or not, whether she was forced into something or whether voluntarily or not, as she thought it would hurt her chances to get her baby.

I questioned her intermittently like that, trying to decide in my own mind. The thought crossed my mind that the safest thing to do would be to kill her because she knew where I lived and the car and the color and the make and maybe the license plate. I was weighing one factor against another. My own fear of returning to prison and what the chances would be of her successfully making up a story. I don't recall how much time passed but maybe it was 7:30 or 8:00 P.M. I guess I finally decided I would not be able to take the chance and that I probably would kill her to cover up the other crimes that I already committed with her. I decided to take her out in the country somewhere. I wasn't too familiar with the area, but I knew there was some desert area. I waited until it was dark and a little later in the evening when things were pretty quiet on the street. I turned on the television to help pass the time. She was still sitting in the chair and had been dozing for a while. She woke up and wanted to know if I wanted her to sit on the couch with me. I said sure, and she came over and sat on my lap. It was 10:15 because I remember watching the 10:00 P.M. news. After the news I said we were going to leave the apartment. I told her I was going to drive her out in the sticks and then I was going to let her out of the car and give her the money. I promised her that would be more than enough for bus fare back. I told her I needed to tie her hands while on the way out as a precaution.

As we were driving, I kept debating with myself whether I could actually go through with it or not. I kept trying to justify it to myself and try to justify it by assuming that there just wasn't any other thing I could do except of being a sure risk to go back to jail. As a matter of fact, the actual thought I had was that if I was going to turn her loose, I might as well go down to the police station and just walk inside with her.

I finally reached the point where I said it was now or never, and I pulled off to the side of the road. I told Judy I wanted to have intercourse once more with her before I turned her loose. This was a pretext to get out of the car. She agreed to this but wanted to use the back seat of the car. I said it was pretty dangerous in the car because we were just on the shoulder of the road and not well off the road, and it would be embarrassing if someone stopped. I told her I had a blanket in the car and we could spread it on the sand. There was a railroad track running parallel with the road. I told her I wanted to tie her hands and she asked why and I said I didn't want her to argue. She didn't. I tied her wrists behind her while she was standing, and then I had her sit down and I tied her ankles. I had her roll over on her stomach and then I had a third length of cord, and I tied one end of that between her ankles and put a knot in that so it would hold firm, and then I bent her legs back at the knees as far as they would go, pulled her ankles back toward her head as far as it would go, and I put one knee in the small of her back and I lifted her chin off of the blanket with my hand and I just very quickly looped the rope around her neck twice and just pulled. I knew if she knew what was coming or what I intended to do she would have started begging and I wouldn't have been able to go through with it. I let go of her chin and put both hands on the end of the rope which I had in my hand, and I just pulled as tight as I could and as hard as I could and, of course, the other end was looped around her ankles so it was anchored there.

For an instant I wanted to undo what I had just done. I lifted her head up and called out her name. I assumed she was already dead. Then I sat there for a few minutes getting over the shock of it, and then I began thinking again and I noticed that we weren't too far from the railroad tracks, and I thought maybe I had better move her body back from the tracks a little further because someone on the train might see her. I just didn't want it found. First I took the rope from around her neck and then the ropes from her wrist and ankles and put them back in my pocket. I picked her up and carried her twenty to twenty-five yards further from the tracks to where there was soft sand. I started digging a depression and put her body in it. I took off her shoes. I remember thinking about possible fingerprints on the smooth leather and I wiped them off. I threw one away. I then took the other shoe, picked up the blanket, went back to the car, made a U-turn, and started back home.

Conclusion

Well-developed skills in interviewing can provide important information that can be linked with crime scene data. Through the use of various interviewing techniques, the investigation can receive maximum benefit from the interview process. Interview techniques discussed in this chapter have given members of the FBI's Behavorial Science Unit new insight for tapping into the fantasy systems of these criminals and for effectively dealing with their defenses.

12

The Police Artist and Composite Drawings

Horace J. Heafner

Television dramas of police work occasionally portray a police artist hurriedly brought to the scene of a crime to interview a witness or a victim in order to prepare a composite sketch of the perpetrator. The sketch is often completed in a few moments with the witness concurring as to the likeness of the drawing to the actual perpetrator. The investigator leaves with copy in hand to seek leads in the case while the police artist departs to other assignments. The scenario implies that preparing a composite drawing is an easy, quick assignment; in reality, developing a drawing from mental recall is often a very difficult task. Fear, trauma, and anxiety often hamper a witness's ability to recall the subject's face. In high-profile cases, pressure may be exerted to place a drawing on the street as quickly as possible even if the witness is vague about the description. Time is of the essence and the media are often seeking a copy for newspaper or television release.

Police artists may be called in to draw a composite in cases involving unsolved homicides and thus are part of the investigative team.

In this chapter there will be a brief look at the history of the use of this investigative tool. The chapter also looks at the role of the police artist and the details surrounding his work.

Historical Perspective of Composite Art

Man has been drawing the human face as long as history has been recorded. The face presents a set of intriguing characteristics that create a pattern of identifiable features. From the pattern created by facial features a person is able to recognize thousands of faces, often linking a name, personality, or background to them. In fact, a person can mentally encode a huge gallery of faces and store them for later retrieval.

Since no two faces are exactly alike, the facial features along with head shapes lend themselves to a classification system. In the 1880s Alphonse Bertillon, sometimes called the father of scientific detection, developed an identification system referred to as "Portrait Parle" that was a compilation of facial features taken from photographs with descriptive detail provided. Originally, Bertillon meant for the catalog to be an identification aid for the recognition of prisoners, but it was later found to be useful in obtaining descriptions of subjects from eyewitnesses. Bertillon's classification of features has provided a basis for modern recall systems that would aid the artist in producing sketches as well as the development of composite kits and catalogs. Currently in computer automation, a similar coding is being applied to facial imaging.[1]

A research of the FBI archives revealed an early use of the composite sketch. The sketch was done in 1920 for a bombing incident that took place at an office on Wall Street. The investigation developed a witness from a nearby blacksmith shop who had shod the horse of a stranger observed carrying a covered object in the back of his wagon. Subsequent interview of the black-smith indicated he felt capable of providing sufficient facial detail to have an artist prepare a drawing of the stranger. A commercial artist was hired to make a sketch that provided a sufficient likeness to develop leads with subsequent identification and arrest of the perpetrator (see figure 12–1).

Figure 12–1. Bombing Incident Suspect Sketch

Recognition versus Recall

Recall is much more difficult than recognition. As previously noted, a person can recognize an incredible number of faces and store them in memory. It is one of the first things learned and once stored, often remains for life. In recognition, young children are able to link names and faces not only from actually seeing the person but also from two-dimensional photographs. In recall, though, a person is confronted with a different challenge, and the process is considerably more difficult. Studies have shown that a witness's processing of sensory information involves input, storage, selection, and interpretation of information. This process can influence future decisions. The individual processing of information is also influenced by psychological factors of recognition, motivation, instructions, and attention. The factor of recognition involves memory, which is influenced by time and the number of events that occurred between the original memory input and the time when that memory is retrieved. We also find that memory is selective. A person does not take in all that is visual or auditory. If something isn't noticed then the response to an interview question will be unknown. In observing the human face, Liggett (1974) states: "Character of a face is determined by the unique pattern created by its features. It is not so much the details of these features nor even the individual spacing between one feature and another, so much as the interrelationship between all of them taken together, which enables us to recognize a face."[2]

The Interview and Eyewitness Description

Burne Hogarth points out that nothing is more complex for the artist than the drawing of the human head. Its varying form, relationship and subtlety of features, the effect of light and shadows on the face is a continuing challenge.[3] Therefore a police composite artist must possess good drawing skills. But a necessity often ignored is the ability to conduct an interview in order to elicit descriptive information. This means the ability to communicate effectively with the eyewitness. In this area, a lay knowledge of psychology is an asset.

Some people are incapable of describing another individual even though they may have been associated with them for some time. On the other hand, there are people who possess an innate perception of faces that allows them to recall in minute detail facial features such as racial grouping, age, skin tones. A police artist quickly realizes a witness of this ability is a unique individual, and the resulting sketch probably will be a good likeness of the subject.

This latter situation occurred in a major bank robbery case in Washington, D.C. The perpetrator walked into a large downtown bank and went directly to the manager, who was seated at his desk. The subject told the manager that his wife and daughter were being held captive by an accomplice and their safety depended on his cooperation. The manager, visibly upset but wanting to cooperate for the safety of his family, left the robber at his desk, walked to each teller's window, and obtained all available cash. The tellers were unaware that a robbery was in progress. When the manager was interviewed later by the artist, his mind was a blank regarding descriptive features. His concern for his family blocked out descriptive recall. Fortunately, a teller who had been about thirty-five to forty feet from the robber had looked at the robber's face out of curiosity. Her description was amazingly accurate, as shown in figure 12–2. With this sketch, the investigator eventually was able to identify the subject, who was subsequently arrested.

Getting the Most from the Interview

There are some basic procedures that should be followed in the interview in order to obtain a good description:

Leading the Witness.   A drawing must reflect only the description provided by the eyewitness. This is particularly true when a witness cannot furnish descriptive detail on a certain area of the face. The police artist must not lead the witness in any manner during the interview. If the witness cannot independently recall the features, the police artist will have to decide whether to proceed with the drawing.

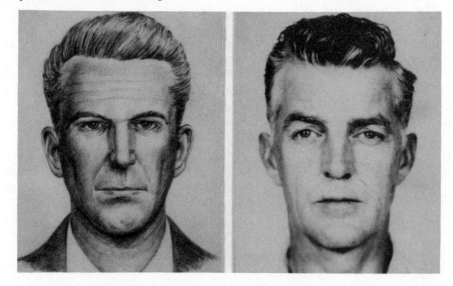

Figure 12–2. Bank Robber Sketch and Suspect

Demeanor and Communication Skills. A patient, cooperative attitude will go far in obtaining information. An interview for a composite sketch is meant to be a friendly encounter with a need to provide a time period to allow for maximum recall. From this interview, the witness may remember other information that will be helpful to an investigation.

Evaluation of the Witness. Prior to the interview, a brief discussion between the investigating officer and the artist may provide information regarding the witness that will aid the interview process. This is particularly important if multiple witnesses have seen the same subject. Determining which witnesses are more perceptive will save a considerable amount of time and produce a better composite.

Trauma. Witnesses or victims who have suffered trauma as a result of a crime should be handled with particular care. If such a person is brought to the artist immediately following the violent crime, he or she may not be physically, mentally, or emotionally capable of spending several hours in an interview situation. An investigator may think it advisable to rush a witness to the artist before the image begins to fade. However, if a period of time is allowed to elapse after the crime, the witness or victim may achieve an emotional stability that can aid the recall process.

Laboratory testing of facial memory shows no evidence to support the belief that a witness of a violent crime will be able to provide better descriptions of the incident than witnesses of a nonviolent crime.[4] However, a number of FBI cases have revealed that where a victim experienced shock caused by an unexpected or startling event, the remembered image was more vivid. Penry, inventor of the Photo-Fit system, said that "laboratory style facial memory testing is bound to operate on a different academic level without the genuine stimuli of threat, severe shock or acute fear. . . . If the face to be recalled has been confronted in a personally menacing or shocking way or is in anyway emotive situation, its imprint is far more likely to be vivid, detailed and long lasting."[5]

Children. Sometimes children are ignored as possible witnesses for a composite sketch. Although their verbal skills will be lacking, the use of a facial feature reference system can aid in providing descriptive detail. Davies, Ellis, and Shepherd noted that children eight and younger are poor at facial encoding but by age ten they approach, if not actually achieve a normal adult level.[6] The police artist must work patiently when attempting to facilitate a verbal response from a child. The child may need to be reassured that he or she doesn't *have* to remember something. This may prevent the child from providing information solely out of a desire to please the artist, which may result in a sketch dissimilar to the perpetrator.

Time and Witness Evaluation of Sketch. The composite artist must be judicious in the use of time during the interview. Too little time to develop a sketch is often the case, but too much time can also influence the drawing. Witness fatigue and the desire to get a sketch done sometimes results from a lengthy interview. Once the description and selection of features are made, the drawing should be developed rapidly, allowing input at any time from the witness. When the drawing is complete, the witness should rate it on a scale of one to ten. This can be important not only to communicate to the artist an evaluation of the accuracy of the sketch, but also to assist him if he is called to testify in a court of law. This places the responsibility of evaluating the drawing on the witness, not on the artist who has not even seen the person depicted in the drawing.

Facial Identification Catalog

The FBI has for a number of years successfully used the Facial Identification Catalog with eyewitnesses in order to aid recall. The catalog provides twelve major facial categories (figure 12–3 displays a page from the catalog) with the intention of bridging a gap that often occurs when a witness attempts to describe a subject. Each category is broken down into subcategories as shown in the display of the interview form (see figure 12–4). This process not only provides an organized method for the interview but involves the eyewitness in selecting individual features without any leading by the composite artist.

A number of psychological studies have been conducted concerning what features a witness recalls best. Pilot studies have revealed that most people use four main dimensions or descriptors to discriminate between faces. The features most used to distinguish between faces were the nose, eyes, face shape, hair color, and chin. This study is generally consistent with an FBI study made in 1978.[7]

During an interview an eyewitness will sometimes describe a face in such terms as honest, likable, homely, or attractive. These intangible terms are not easy to interpret artistically, but they are important in terms of recall. Gordon Bower and Martin Karlin noted in a 1974 study that "although a face hasn't a semantic meaning in the sense that a word does, it still may trigger a number of associations, such as the resemblance of the face to that of a friend or celebrity. Thus greater depth of processing of a face might correspond to a greater number of unique associations that a person retrieves from his memory."[8] In such instances, the Facial Catalog and look-alike photographs can aid the witness in helping define what is in his memory.

Hypnosis and the Composite Drawing

Hypnosis is sometimes used in criminal cases to enhance recall from a victim or a witness. In the hypnosis session, a witness may remember a face, license plate

Nose - Hooked

Male

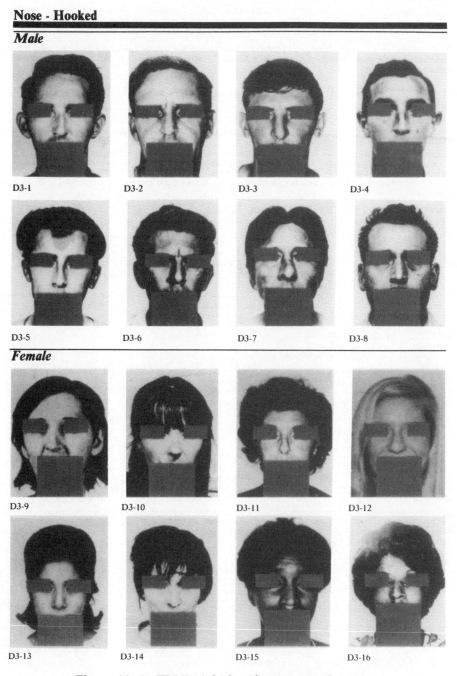

D3-1 D3-2 D3-3 D3-4

D3-5 D3-6 D3-7 D3-8

Female

D3-9 D3-10 D3-11 D3-12

D3-13 D3-14 D3-15 D3-16

Figure 12–3. FBI Facial Identification Catalog Page

FBI FACIAL IDENTIFICATION FACT SHEET

RETAIN ORIGINAL for your files. Send only LEGIBLE DUPLICATE COPY to Special Projects Section, Laboratory Division. To expedite transmittal of form send to Special Projects Section by facsimile machine 8:00 a.m. to 5:30 p.m. EST/EDT, FTS 324-2926.

CASE TITLE _____

DATE OF
INTERVIEW _____
BUFILE NO. _____
FIELD OFFICE NO. _____

NAME OF WITNESS _____

INTERVIEWING
AGENT _____

Before referring to Facial Identification Catalog obtain description of unknown subject from witness and check pertinent boxes in each category listed below.

Using this information, direct witness to appropriate sections of the catalog and enter final selections on lines provided in each category.

UNSUB NO. _____ SEX _____ AGE _____ RACE _____ COMPLEXION _____

HEIGHT _____ WEIGHT _____ BUILD _____ COLOR OF EYES _____ COLOR OF HAIR _____

A. HEAD _____
□ 1. oval
□ 2. round
□ 3. triangular
□ 4. long
□ 5. rectangular

B. EYES _____
□ 1. average
□ 2. bulging
□ 3. squint
□ 4. sunken or deep-set
□ 5. iris raised
□ 6. close-set
□ 7. wide-set
□ 8. heavy lid
□ 9. overhanging lid

C. EYEBROWS _____
□ 1. average
□ 2. thin
□ 3. heavy
□ 4. meeting

D. NOSE _____
□ 1. average
□ 2. concave
□ 3. hooked
□ 4. narrow base
□ 5. flared nostrils
□ 6. downward tip
□ 7. small
□ 8. large
□ 9. wide base

E. MOUTH _____
□ 1. average
□ 2. both lips thick
□ 3. both lips thin
□ 4. lips unequal
□ 5. large
□ 6. small

F. CHIN _____
□ 1. average
□ 2. jutting
□ 3. pointed
□ 4. receding
□ 5. square
□ 6. double chin
□ 7. cleft or dimple

G. EARS _____
□ 1. average
□ 2. protruding
□ 3. close-set

H. CHEEK AND
CHEEKBONE _____
□ 1. average
□ 2. prominent
□ 3. sunken cheek

J. HAIR _____
□ 1. straight
□ 2. curly or wavy
□ 3. balding or short cut-male
□ 4. long to short-female

K. FACIAL LINES
□ 1. forehead _____
□ 2. midface _____
□ 3. around eyes _____
□ 4. chin and neck _____

L. MUSTACHE
AND BEARD _____

M. SKIN
IRREGULARITIES _____

Furnish detailed description of hat, glasses, and clothing (from waist up). Include photos of drawings showing similar items, if possible. Use drawing of head to mark position of hairline, hat, scar(s), bandage(s), beard, mustache, etc.

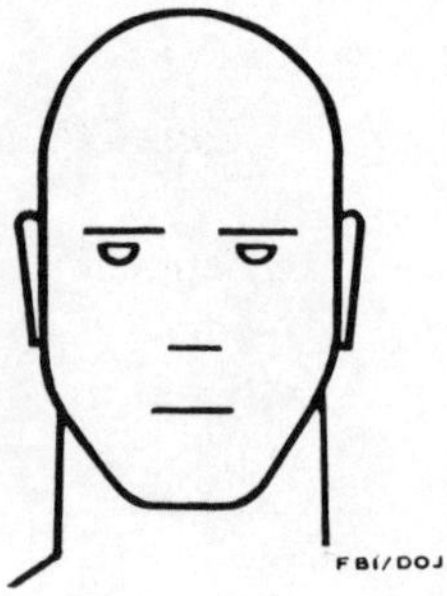

FBI/DOJ

Figure 12–4. FBI Facial Identification Fact Sheet

number, time shown on a wristwatch, and other details that could not otherwise be recalled. There have been instances when the use of hypnosis has been particularly effective in developing composite drawings.

One such case occurred some years ago in San Juan, Puerto Rico. A warehouse valued at over a million dollars was destroyed by fire. Subsequent investigation showed that the fire was the result of arson. The case remained unsolved for nearly five years until an arrest was made of the arsonist. He said he had been paid to set the fire but could not provide a description of the subject because of the passage of time. He also said he had only seen the subject once in his lifetime for only fifteen minutes. The arsonist agreed to submit to hypnosis, and, before the drawing was completed, the investigators knew who the subject was.

Preparing a drawing from a hypnosis session need only require minor adjustments in the routine of the police artist. In FBI cases only approved psychologists, psychiatrists, physicians, or dentists who are qualified hypnotists are used. Before the hypnosis session takes place it is necessary for the artist to discuss with the doctor when and where the interview portion for the drawing should begin. Some doctors prefer the police artist in the room from the beginning of the induction, others desire that they wait until after the hypnosis session is completed. When this is the case the witness is told to mentally view the subject and "freeze" the image for recall with the police artist. Once this has been done the witness can be taken through the Facial Catalog and note selection of facial features. The artist will observe that some witnesses appear a little vague when they first come out of the hypnosis session. If this is the case the artist should take care to proceed slowly and patiently.

Although hypnosis may be helpful in enhancing recall for the composite drawing, witnesses do provide incorrect information. Another problem encountered with the witness is the fear over the effects of hypnosis. The concern is strong enough, that some witnesses become nauseated before the hypnosis session begins. In such cases it would be important for the police artist to discuss with the investigator and hypnotist the alternative of doing the drawing without hypnosis. The result will generally be more satisfactory.

Skeletal Remains

Whenever human remains are found it is the responsibility of law enforcement agencies to seek to provide an identification of the person. Dentists have often assisted in the identification process, but there are many cases where dental work is missing or records unavailable. In cases where foul play is suspected, a forensic anthropologist becomes very important in the identification process. As an aid to the process, the composite artist can, by working with the anthropologist, provide a composite drawing or in some cases a sculpture of what the anthropologist sees through examination of the skull and other remains. Figure 12–5 shows the results of such an undertaking when an FBI artist worked with a forensic anthropologist from the Smithsonian Institution. The completed drawing was shown on television in Georgia, and the remains were subsequently identified. In cases handled by the FBI, the anthropologist is interviewed by the artist just as any other witness would be interviewed, using the Facial Identification Catalog. The facial features selected would be noted on the interview form and the drawing made for review by the anthropologist.

Computer Application

With the application of computer technology, it appears that many law enforcement agencies, both national and international, will likely turn to the computer to produce composite images. Although this method captures the imagination and interest of the law enforcement community and does offer advantages in time and money saved, there are several areas of concern to consider in making such a change.

The first area of concern deals with the interview process and personal rapport that can be developed between the composite artist and the witness. As previously noted, a victim or witness who has suffered stress, severe shock, or life-threatening situations requires special handling during the interview process. A trained police composite artist can provide the atmosphere conducive to eliciting needed descriptive detail. This key human contact can be quickly overlooked when a computer is used to obtain speedy results.

Figure 12–5. Sketch Made from Skeletal Remains and Identification

The second concern deals with the image produced by a computer. Systems that use illustrated features do not present this problem, but the composite depicting a photographic likeness of the subject produced from computer software using a database of photographic features can be a problem. Witnesses may tend to look at a photographic composite as an exact likeness, rather than viewing it as someone in the particular range of likenesses or similarities as is done with sketches. Such application narrows the matching of facial patterns and limits its application.

Conclusion

Composite drawing should never be overlooked as an investigative aid and though much depends on the ability of the witness, it may be the tool that unlocks a very difficult case and saves a considerable amount of investigative time. As noted before, how an image is matched with memory stored in the human mind is a mystery. Future systems should be designed so as not to frustrate the process but build upon those principles already known with a view to future application for law enforcement purposes.

Notes

1. *FBI Research Design and Training Unit Study*, Washington, D.C., 1978–87.
2. J. Liggett. *The Human Face*. New York: Stein and Day, 1974.
3. Burne Hogarth. *Drawing the Human Head*. New York: Watson-Guptill.
4. G. Davies, H. Ellis, J. Shepherd. *Perceiving and Remembering Faces*. London: Academic Press, 1981.
5. J. Penry. *Penry Facial Identification Techniques: News Bulletin 1975–1976.* Leeds, England: John Waddington of Kirkstall.
6. G. Davies, H. Ellis, J. Shepherd, *Perceiving and Remembering*.
7. *FBI Research Study*.
8. Gordon H. Bower and Martin B. Karlin. "Depth of processing pictures of faces and recognition memory," *Journal of Experimental Psychology*, 1974, *103* (4).

13
The Victim's Family and Its Response to Trauma

With the increase of violence and aggression in society, a new area of study is developing in the field of victimology in an attempt to identify and understand victim reaction to crime. Until recently, the literature was substantially focused on the offender, with little being written about the secondary victims of crime, the families of victims. This chapter constitutes an attempt to correct this situation.

Clinicians are in a key position to counsel families of crime victims because of their close association with facilities where victims are brought—the emergency wards. In cases where the victim is not brought to a hospital, law enforcement officers can be most helpful in referring a family for crisis counseling. We hope this chapter will increase clinicians' ability to assist families who experience their own trauma response following the news of the homicide of a relative.

Data for this chapter were collected from two studies. A pilot study of nine cases was undertaken to identify some general reaction areas of family members of homicide victims and to determine issues for further study (Burgess 1975). A second study included a survey of 331 members of Parents of Murdered Children support groups drawn from thirteen affiliate chapters in eleven states. The survey included two standardized inventories—that is, the Texas Inventory of Grieving and a modified Life Events Inventory (Rinear 1984). The findings from the studies are presented in terms of (1) the acute grief phase, and (2) the long-term reorganization phase, which includes reactions and posttrauma symptoms over time.

The Acute Grief Phase

No news items register as strong a reaction in people as that of a family member's being murdered. As families talk about their immediate reaction to the tragedy, two thoughts are noted: their loss of the family member (ego-oriented thought), and their horror at the manner in which the family member died (victim-oriented thought). Following this immediate reaction, families begin to ask a series of questions.

Immediate Thoughts

For many, the news of the homicide is a severe blow to the self. Losing a significant person leaves uppermost in their minds the sense of their own personal loss. One brother said, "I never felt so overwhelmed with emptiness before; it was as though someone cut my insides out." The somatic analogy reflects the tremendous impact implying that a part of the self has been lost through the victim's death. Or the survivor may react to the untimely and unexpected nature of the news . One widower talked of his reaction to people in general: "It is hard enough to accept natural death, but it's worse with violent death. It's so abrupt. So shocking. It's hard to trust people."

People are especially concerned about the physical injury inflicted on the victim, specifically, the brutality of the assailant and the varying degrees of trauma associated with the death. The assailant's method of killing may become a preoccupation, as may concern about the victim's suffering. One person said, "I mentally tried to put myself in my brother's position. Did he fight? How much agony did he go through?"

Who Did It?

There is an urgency to wanting to know the facts: Who did it? Who is the murderer? These questions correlate with the style of attack, the way in which the assailant gained access to the victim. The style may then determine whether the victim knew the assailant, whether it was a confidence attack or a blitz attack.

A blitz murder is committed suddenly and with few clues. If there is no suspect, the family must give considerable energy in working with the police to help determine leads, to reconstruct the victim's activities prior to the homicide, and to help reconstruct events during and following the murder.

The blitz style of attack is very difficult to come to terms with when someone is trying to find some reason for the murder. In one case, the widow spoke of the murder as being a case of "mistaken identity."

In a confidence murder, the assailant initiates interaction. The interaction or relationship that a homicide victim has with the assailant adds a complicated dimension to the dynamics of the case. One daughter said, "I can accept my father's death but not the way in which he died." The father was murdered by contract, and his family, except for the daughter, had resigned themselves to his violent death by the Mafia.

When an assailant with an established relationship is also known to the family, the family has to deal with their feelings about their own relationship with the assailant.

In cases where the style of attack is not clear-cut and the assailant is never apprehended, there is no feeling of closure to the crime. Families have been known to go through the incident themselves as part of the psychological settlement process. For example, one family went as a unit to the deserted area in the country where the daughter's body was found and tried to act out the scene. A cousin said,

> I tried to imagine how he did it and why she couldn't get away . . . she must have been in so much pain . . . I can't stand to think about it. . . . This might sound morbid to you, but it was just something I had to do.

What Can I Do?

One of the immediate reactions families describe is a wish to do something physically about the crime. An overwhelming feeling of helplessness may trigger this wish to action, usually against the assailant; however, people may take matters into their own hands only in strictly limited ways. Much media attention is given to rape victims who try to retaliate. One victim who sought out her assailant and shot him was convicted of second-degree murder (Fosburgh 1974); another victim who was convicted in a first trial was acquitted in a second (Meggs to try Barts again 1985).

Families will often describe feelings of outrage, anger, and aggression toward the assailant. The father of a murdered girl said, "I am overwhelmed with rage. I would kill him if I could." A brother who talked of his tremendous wish for revenge repeated how he wished to "get his hands on the guy." Later during the trial the brother became preoccupied with the defendant's hands and said, "I sat there and looked at his hands . . . remembering what he did. I wished so much that he would come near me so I would have the chance."

What Do I Do Now?

The next set of questions involves those reality issues the family must address. The aftermath of homicide includes all of the activities that are part of the grieving process, including funeral or memorial services.

Notification of Others. In a natural death, the family and friends take responsibility for notifying other people of the death and of the funeral plans. A homicide, however, usually receives media coverage that may further complicate the grieving process. One family complained of receiving "weird letters and crank calls" because of all the publicity given the murder. One niece reported the following:

> The news was on television immediately. . . . I couldn't stand all the phone calls and people saying such dumb things as, "That couldn't be your uncle that

was murdered, was it? What happened?" Who did they think it was with his name, occupation, and address blared out with all the details?

Viewing the Victim.   Someone has to identify the body; this can place an added psychological burden on the family member to whom the task falls. In one family, the daughter was the only person who felt psychologically strong enough. She said when the police first told her the news, she screamed. When she had to identify her father she was sick to her stomach.

Funeral Activities.   One of the duties that occupies the family's time the first week following the homicide is attending to the funeral details and arrangements. Such decisions as whether to have an open casket must be made. This may depend on the physical appearance of the body and can be a difficult decision for the family. Families must take into account how newspaper reporting has handled the situation to influence what peoples' mental images might be of how the victim was killed. Families must also consider the wishes, if they are known, of the victim. In one case, the victim had previously requested an open casket. This wish heavily influenced the family decision, even though the victim had been badly beaten and bruised.

The family of a homicide victim is involved in so much activity the first week after the news is received that they may not show an emotional reaction until after the funeral. A daughter of a victim reported her experience as follows:

> I had to go to the state where it happened. It was exhausting. When I went to the police, they talked and talked and talked, and I had to tell all I knew. I had to see pictures of the scene. He was slumped over in the car. I had to identify the car and then go to the morgue and identify the body. Had to claim the body and sign papers. Had to make all the funeral arrangements. Had to buy a suit, shoes, and such for my father. Had to write the notice for the newspaper. Then there were more questions by the police and FBI. Then I had to buy clothes for my family and go to the airport and pick them up. . . . The funeral was a long drive, and in the car it really hit me. . . . My grandmother started it by saying, "God, don't burn my baby." That really hit me. . . . I don't remember anything after that. . . . Except in the chapel I remember the body going into a furnace or knowing it was going in there. It was my father's wish. . . . My grandmother started up again.

Physical Signs and Symptoms.   Families are numb and confused and will describe a number of physical concerns. Insomnia, sleep pattern disturbances, headaches, chest pain, palpitations, and gastrointestinal upsets are quite common. Very often doctors will prescribe sedatives and tranquilizers in an attempt to relieve the physical symptoms. People will describe not feeling or remembering much about the first weeks or even months following the murder.

Reactions over Time

Two major themes were noted in the reorganization period following the acute grief period. Families have to deal with their own psychological reactions, and they have to deal with the sociolegal issues involved with the crime of homicide.

Psychological Issues

Grief Work. The family has to go through the process of grief work, which is the psychological process that moves the person from being preoccupied with thoughts of the lost person, through painful recollections of the loss experience, to the final step of settling the loss as an integrative experience (Parkes 1972). In describing the feeling of loss, one person said, "It is an awful loss that doesn't strike home for weeks and then the feeling of loss and wondering how to pick up the pieces."

Reviewing memories of the victim, as part of the grief work, is noted by one widower: "It was all sort of life from the movie, *Love Story*, the way things turned out. And now the only thing I can do is forget. . . . I can't go on thinking about it."

Contrasting the victim with the crime is a theme in many families. Many people talk of the contrast between the violent act committed against the victim and the victim's nonaggressive nature. One widow said, "He hated violence . . . and he died by it."

Settlement of the "if only" reaction is important to some people. As the families learn the details of the homicide, they begin to say to themselves, "If only I had [said something], this would not have happened." One person said, "If only I had stayed one more day, this never would have happened."

Dreams and Nightmares. Dreaming of the lost person in terms of wish fulfillment has been documented in bereavement studies (Parkes 1972). Wish fulfillment dreams are seen in survivors as a way of trying to save the victim. One person described a dream in which she tried to warn her cousin not to go with the murderer and woke up in the middle of the dream crying. Another person described the following dream in which he tried unsuccessfully to save his brother:

They were vivid dreams where I would be struggling. I was fighting and bouncing all over and would see the murder room and I would see my brother's face and it would be all contorted. I'd be in it and I couldn't move— I wasn't able to do anything. Then I would wake up and not be able to go back to sleep . . . that was eating me up . . . had them especially after a bad day.

Phobic Reactions. Like other trauma victims, these family members commonly manifest phobic reactions, which develop according to the specific circumstances surrounding the events of the crime. One sister of a murder victim whose case was unsolved developed a fear of having people, including her own boyfriend, walk behind her.

Families become very aware of the potential for a crime's occurring and cope by adding protective measures. They will take special precautions to protect themselves, such as obtaining permits to carry guns, or they will have guns at their bedsides. Some people will also put burglar alarms in their homes.

Identification with Tragedy. Identification with the dead person was noted as one way people dealt with the painful loss. One sister immediately began sleeping in her dead sister's bed and wearing her clothes. Widows, specifically, would identify with other women whose husbands had been murdered. These women talked of having something in common with Jacqueline Kennedy Onassis, Ethel Kennedy, and Coretta King. Or, in the case of a patrolman's wife, the remark was made, "She has joined the 'group.' "

Role Change. Death forces people suddenly into new roles for which they have little preparation. Loss of a wife changes a husband to a widower; loss of an only child or an only uncle or only cousin can totally eliminate the role from the life of the survivor. Being forced into assuming a new identity and giving up an important role adds difficult dimensions to the grief process.

Sociolegal Issues

The Court Process. All homicide cases will involve some degree of police and court procedure. There will be investigations in order to find the murderer. This entire process has a major effect on the grief reaction and crisis settlement. Many feelings are evoked during the process, but one of the hardest to bear, if the case goes to court, is the impersonal attitude of the court and the participants. One person described it clearly: "Here was a doctor . . . his life snuffed out and it was treated so casually. . . . Like, so what. . . . People forget . . . so much time elapses.

The Concept of Blame.   Murder undermines one's faith in the world as an ordered and secure place. Studies show that untimely natural deaths also shake people's confidence in this sense of security. Blaming someone for a tragedy is less disturbing than facing the fact that life is uncertain. It allows people to continue to be in control by putting the responsibility onto another person. The inability to explain a situation makes people feel helpless.

People look for a target onto which to project their feelings. The main target is usually the assailant. Families want justice; they want the assailant prosecuted. Some people believe in capital punishment; others see prison as the punishment for his unlawful actions. Some state that the assailant is a "sick" person and should be psychiatrically treated because they "don't want him to harm anyone else."

Another target is the criminal justice system. Families can become angry at the police for being unsuccessful in finding the assailant. Other people focus on the court process and become angry at the judges for "letting criminals right out the door after they are apprehended." Society is also a target for blame. One widower said, "I am a conservative by nature but this has made me somewhat of a radical . . . to think the society you live in produced a guy like that."

And not infrequently the victim may be blamed. The belief is that no victim is entirely innocent but rather participates to some degree in the crime (Amir 1967).

Parents of Murdered Children

Research focusing upon the effects of this type of bereavement among family members has been minimal, but one study was conducted by Dr. Eileen Rinear in a survey of members of Parents of Murdered Children support groups drawn from thirteen affiliate chapters in eleven states. The study sought to examine the postmurder symptomatology and patterns of bereavement among parents of murdered children. The term *child* referred to the relationship rather than to the victim's chronological age at the time of death (Rinear 1984). The sample of 237 completed questionnaires was furnished by respondents who were predominately female (67.9 percent) and white (92.8 percent), with a mean age of 51.5. The victims represented in the study were primarily males (61.6 percent) who were living away from their parents' home (63.7 percent) and had a mean age of 22.1 years.

The major symptomatology identified in this group of respondents began with the first weeks of the child's murder and persisted, in varying combinations and degrees of intensity, for as long as one to two years thereafter. The traumatic stress symptoms were consistent with symptoms of posttraumatic stress disorder and are described below, in rank order of the observed frequency:

1. *Sleep disturbance.* Surviving parents of homicide victims report, almost without exception, the onset of disturbed sleep patterns following the murder. Such sleep pattern disruptions include early morning awakening, insomnia, and sleeping more often than usual—all of which may occur singly or in various combinations.

2. *Constricted affect.* Almost all parents admit to feelings of numbness or emotional anesthesia following their child's death. The vast majority of such bereft individuals report an inability to experience emotions of any type, particularly those associated with intimacy, tenderness, and sexuality, as well as prolonged periods of constricted affect that often takes the form of depression. Comments offered by these surviving parents have included: "I haven't had much depth of feeling since the murder," "I can't feel anything—I feel like I am dead inside," "This year my defenses came down and I suffer from deep depression," and "I've changed emotionally—am unable to love or to respond to my other children."

3. *Diminished interest in previously enjoyed activities.* The majority of parents report a marked reduction in both their interest in, and their involvement with, one or more previously significant life activities. Such bereft parents have offered the following comments specific to this area of difficulty: "Once a devout churchgoer, I rarely attend services anymore," "After the murder, I lost all interest in my job," "I have ceased all relationships that I had prior to the murder."

4. *Recurrent and intrusive recollections of the murder.* The majority of parents report being preoccupied by thoughts of the extent of brutality and degree of suffering associated with their child's death. Such comments include: "Things are better if I am busy and not alone—otherwise, I can't turn off my thoughts," "There has not been one day since the murder that I have not thought of her and how she died, and why." One mother said:

   I keep thinking about my son lying there in the street with his head all bloodied. I was told he died instantly, but I still have fear that he may have suffered. It's been almost a year now, and these thoughts continue to haunt me.

5. *Feelings of detachment from others.* The majority of parents report feelings of detachment, estrangement, or alienation from others: "I always feel as though I am on the outside looking in," "I feel removed from my friends and co-workers because they have no concept of such a cruel experience," and "When a murder is involved, everyone stays away. That was our experience."

6. *Avoidance of activities that arouse traumatic recollections.* Many parents report avoiding situations that they somehow associate with their child's

murder. The comments include: "I rarely go to church anymore because when I go and I look up at the altar, all I see is my son's coffin up there," "I was unable to drive down the street where she was killed for almost a year after her murder," "I can't have sex with my husband anymore because every time he touches me, I think of my daughter and what the rapist did to her."

7. *Intensification of symptoms.* Parents reported an intensification of their postmurder symptomatology in response to a variety of events that for them serve to symbolize or remind them of their child's murder. Their comments included "I relive it each Sunday morning when I wake up. I can still remember the shock of not finding her in her bed," "Chance glimpses, remarks, TV programs all contribute to instant replay." One mother was quite specific:

I hate Halloween. My son's body was found in a desert area badly decomposed, a week after he was murdered. Each year when I see the skeletons at Halloween, they remind me of my son and what he must have looked like. This just stirs it all up for me again.

8. *Recurrent dreams of the murder.* Parents report recurrent dreams that take one of the following three themes: (*a*) wish fulfillment, in which the child is seen as being alive and well; (*b*) dreams focused on "undoing" the event, in which the parent attempts to defend physically, or at least warn, the child of the impending danger; and (*c*) dreams centered on some particularly painful or problematic aspect of the murder, in which the parent repeatedly relives the traumatic occurrences (for example, discovery of the child's body, notification of the child's death, confirmation of the child's identity).

9. *Memory impairment and trouble concentrating.* Many parents have difficulty concentrating following the murder. Some commented: "My husband's employer terminated him without his pension. He said he was 'preoccupied' with the murder," and "I find it hard to concentrate on my job duties since her murder, and I am now on a month's sick leave because of this problem."

Because of the many symptoms and enormous disruption of their lives, parents have found great assistance in support groups such as Parents of Murdered Children.

Special Intervention Situations

There is a conscious need by people to settle the incident, make some sense out of what has happened, explain it to themselves, classify it along with other life events, and make it somehow "fit" into their reorganized life-style. Families who had adequate emotional support through a social network or through crisis counseling tend to have a better chance of settling the acute crisis period and dealing with the long-term reactions. Some people, however, will have difficulty in settling the trauma syndrome because of the manner in which outside people treat them in regard to the situation. One case is where people *deliberately* avoid the family and consequently are not supportive. The second situation is where people *unwittingly* avoid the family and thus offer no support.

Deliberate Avoidance by the Social Network

For someone to be acknowledged as a victim means that other people must validate the crime as a crime. In some cases, people may have considerable ambivalence over viewing a crime as an actual crime (with a victim) because of the style of attack or the relationship with the murderer. When the victim has had a long-standing relationship or connection with the murderer, it is easier to place some blame on the victim.

A Case Study.   In this case, the victim belonged to a drug ring. Because he "squealed" to a federal agent, he received little recognition from people who knew him as a victim. His girlfriend had great difficulty grieving because no one acknowledged that her boyfriend was "worth it." The girlfriend and the victim were in counseling prior to the murder, and the therapy with the girlfriend after the homicide follows.

> Lori, age seventeen, and her twenty-two year old boyfriend, Mark, came to the community health center for counseling.
>
> Mark at one session requested to see the nurse individually to "talk over some things."
>
> The nurse saw him twice before he was murdered. He was very much involved in "dealing"—selling drugs, especially speed—and he also described mainlining speed. He talked of feeling confused and ambivalent about his life-style and especially wanted to talk about what he might change in himself. When he did not keep his last appointment, the nurse called him at home. He responded, "There are some heavy things going on here; I'll call you back." He never did call. He was shot in the heart by one of his housemates that afternoon.
>
> Lori contacted the nurse after the murder and expressed her desire to talk things over. The nurse saw Lori for crisis counseling for several sessions. The following are her reactions to a sequence of events.

"I can't believe I lost him." Lori was especially angry toward the housemates and said, "Those druggies make me furious." This reaction was in contrast to her prior feeling in that she rather enjoyed their life-style. Lori now said she did not want to have anything to do with them.

Lori said there was no one for her to talk to; her mother was just not interested. Her peers were very inquisitive but not supportive. They just wanted to talk of the murder and not of how she was feeling about her loss.

One of her fears was that the housemates might come after her. She said she was really afraid to talk to anyone but found she had to talk to someone. She had received a phone call warning her not to talk to the police.

Case Analysis of Crisis Intervention. Because Lori was deliberately shunned by her social network, she sought out the nurse to help her grieve her loss. Lori had a strong need to know the entire story and why Mark was killed even if that meant going to the narcotics agent. She talked this over with the therapist, decided to go, and was very glad she did. She was relieved to be able to trust someone with her information. She learned the facts of the case. Mark was importing drugs from Canada and selling them. He was arrested by federal agents and told that if he would testify against his housemates who had long histories of drug charges, he would receive a lighter sentence. Mark agreed to do this. However, his housemate found out and shot him in the heart.

Lori agreed to testify at the probable cause hearing in court, even though she was very frightened. Her emotions bothered her because she said "I felt more frightened for myself than upset for Mark." She found it difficult to deal with the fact that people looked on her as being a "rat."

When all the people involved with the murder were in jail, Lori returned to the house where the murder had occurred. She said, "I could see the whole thing happen as I stood there. . . . It was dreadful but real for me."

Lori struggled with two "if only" throughts: if only Mark had come to see her that fatal afternoon, and if only Mark had kept his appointment with the therapist.

Lori made some changes in her life-style following the murder. She moved from her apartment to her mother's house for several months. She isolated herself from people and said, "I can't stand to answer all their busybody questions, and they really don't care. They just want the goods." There was no memorial service for Mark, but Lori went regularly to the grave. She said, "I bring flowers; I talk to Mark and I cry." She expressed her grief at graveside and with the therapist.

This case illustrates the therapeutic influence that crisis intervention has when the murder victim is not socially acknowledged. The victim's girlfriend had no one in her social network to help her grieve and settle the crisis experience. She did seek out the therapist who had helped her with a previous crisis. Crisis counseling was initiated, and she was able to reorganize her life after several months. She indicated an adequate level of settlement, as her behavior verified, and said, "I've waked up to the world, and I am better for it."

Unwitting Avoidance by the Social Network

A Case Study. In some situations a murder or other crime may well be acknowledged, but for some reason the family of the victim receives no support in dealing with the crisis. The following case illustrates the devastating effects on a family who felt stigmatized and rejected by the unwitting avoidance of neighbors and friends and emphasizes the need for families to be referred for crisis counseling.

Pam, a twenty-one-year-old student, was presented at an outpatient psychiatric community clinic following referral from the student health service. As she talked during the interview, she would periodically dig her fingernails into her palms, and she acknowledged having cut her arm on several occasions.

Pam talked of having had feelings of "falling apart" and of not being able to control herself but that she currently felt more in control of her behavior. She felt her difficulties were caused by her being away from home for the first time. She would become more upset, however, when she went home because "mother is so sad and father so old."

Pam almost immediately began talking about her sister's death and murder six years previously. She did this with a great deal of intense emotion, explaining that it was very difficult for her to talk about it because they had been very close, with the sister being a "mother" to her.

Historically, the mother did not notice Pam's childhood problems, but her sister did and tried to help her. Pam views herself as having been a tomboy (because father wanted a boy and Pam had tried to please him), fat, very self-conscious, shy, and ugly because of a severe acne problem. The sister began helping Pam by getting her to lose weight and was about to take her to a dermatologist when she was murdered.

The nurse asked Pam to describe the events relevant to the murder. The sister went to work as usual the morning after a holiday. The employer called the house around 10:00 A.M. to find out where she was. The family became concerned and called the police, who felt it was not that serious a concern for alarm at 11:00 A.M. but stated they would begin a search. The father went to retrace his daughter's usual path to work. The father found his daughter strangled with her stocking in an isolated field that was part of the shortcut she took to work.

Pam wept at this point and said that the feelings she had were of hatred, and those feelings were difficult for her to think about as they upset her so much. The resentful feelings she had were toward the police department who wouldn't respond quickly to look for her sister; then when the father found the body, they sent their rookies to "mess up the clues so that the murderer was never found."

The hatred feelings were also for the townspeople who made the family feel like "freaks" and forced them to withdraw, as a family, into their house "like animals in a cage." The family did receive a lot of crank calls and weird letters at the time, and people continually talked about the incident in the town.

Pam saw this as the reason for her subsequent withdrawal from social contacts (she had one girlfriend) and for not dating in high school. Pam could recall feeling "numb" at the funeral and remembered looking at people to see their reaction. She then recalled her grandfather's funeral when she was seven when she did the same thing, and they had to take her out of the church. She did not cry at the time of her sister's death, but about two years later when a person whom she liked very much died, she cried with great feeling, realizing then that she was also weeping for her sister.

After the sister's death, Pam slept in her sister's bed (Pam's had been in the trundle bed), and she wore her sister's clothes. Her sister had been two years older than Pam.

Pam frequently had nightmares about a man coming in the window with a knife to stab her. Medication was prescribed and helped relieve the symptom. However, her fears of people walking behind her continued. She had been to her sister's grave only twice in the six-year period.

Case Analysis of Unresolved Homicide Grief.   One can readily make the diagnosis that the patient is suffering from unresolved homicide grief for two reasons:

1. The patient is unable to discuss with equanimity a death that occurred six years previously. With a supportive listener, she immediately began to discuss the death with intense emotion.
2. There was a history of failure to grieve at the time of the death.

There are two speculations: (1) the unwitting avoidance by social network and justice system and (2) identification with the sister. It becomes clear that the failure to grieve is related to unidentified feelings about (1) social system support and (2) the relationship to the sister. The data suggest two hypotheses. First, rather than providing comfort and support, neighbors avoid the family, and police are ineffective in solving the case. Rather than talking out the issues involved, the family becomes angry. Digging her fingernails into her palm and cutting her arm on several occasions were means of expressing frustration. As an alternative hypothesis, it may be suggested that Pam was so attached to her sister, as the only one who really cared, that for her to grieve would be to acknowledge that the sister really died. By Pam's not grieving, the sister is somehow still alive.

Whichever hypothesis is correct, the therapist must provide a supportive relationship that will allow the client to mourn her sister. In the process, the therapist will discover and help the client realize and understand human inadequacies and the nature of the relationship to the sister that made the grief process so difficult.

Conclusion

In summary, the increase of violence in society will undoubtedly place demands on mental health facilities that provide services to the families of homicide victims. Family reaction to the murder of a family member reveals a two-phase process. The crisis phase consists of an acute grief process, including immediate reactions to the murder questions about the assailant, the funeral details, and the police investigation. The long-term reorganization phase includes the psychological issues of bereavement and the sociolegal issues of the criminal justice system.

Two specific intervention situations are discussed; one involves helping someone grieve when the victim has been socially excluded, and the other involves helping someone whose grief was unresolved because of a lack of crisis intervention and social network support. Front-line responders such as police officers and emergency room staff can help family members by offering resources for referral.

Notes

Amir, A. Victim precipitated forcible rape. *Journal of Criminal Law* 1967, 58:

Burgess, A.W. Family reaction to homicide. *American Journal of Orthopsychiatry*, 1975, 45: 391–98.

Fosburgh, L. Women convicted in "rape slaying," *Los Angeles Sunday Herald Advertiser*, October 6, 1974.

Meggs to try Barts again. *Tallahassee Democrat*, May 7, 1985.

Parkes, C. *Bereavement: studies of grief in adult life*, New York: International Universities Press, 1972.

Rinear, E.E. Parental response patterns to the death of a child by homicide. Unpublished doctoral dissertation, Temple University, 1984.

14
Victims: Lessons Learned for Responses to Sexual Violence

Daniel L. Carter
Robert A. Prentky
Ann W. Burgess

T he past decade has seen considerable advances made in (1) raising consciousness about sexual violence, (2) developing victim services, (3) apprehending suspects, (4) convicting suspects, and (5) empirical research on sexually aggressive behavior. Indeed, Chappel and Fogarty (1978) referred to publicity about rape within the last decade as a "veritable explosion." This publicity, and, by inference, an attendant increase in social awareness, has led to noteworthy advances in the development and provision of victim services (McCombie 1980), rape law reform (e.g., Marsh, Geist & Caplan 1982), and research on the sexual victimization of women (e.g., Walker & Brodsky 1976; Holmstrom & Burgess 1978; Chapman & Gates 1978; Russell & Howell 1984).

Also, the past decade has observed a steady increase in the numbers of reported rapes and a parallel acknowledged fear of rape (Warr 1985). Studying fear of rape among 181 urban women using a mail survey in 1981 revealed that two-thirds of the women under age thirty-five ranked fear of rape on the top half of the scale. Warr's (1985) data suggest the majority of women will experience moderate to high levels of fear of rape through adolescence to mid-thirties. He contends fear of rape continues to be a problem of considerable magnitude and consequence. Russell and Howell (1984) conclude from their San Francisco interview survey that sexual violence against women is endemic.

However, one area that has remained embedded in controversy is advice about how to deal with dangerous human situations. There has been a great deal of debate over what a person should do when confronted by an assailant. The literature suggests two polarized views of what to do when confronted

*Reprinted, with changes and permission, from *Journal of Interpersonal Violence*, 1 (1) 1986: 73–98.

with a rapist: (1) acquiesce, or do not resist, and (2) resist and/or fight. We wish to bridge this polarization by reviewing the victim resistance data from our sexual homicide study and from a study of convicted rapists. The data analysis from surviving rape victims assists in defining strategies according to type of assailant.

Sexual Homicide Study

We analyzed from our study of sexual homicide the offenders' perceptions of victim response to their attacks as a way to add to the data base on victim resistance.

Victims of Thirty-Six Sexual Murderers

There were 118 victims in this study; 109 were fatally injured and nine survived the murder attempt. Most victims in this sample were white (92 percent), female (82 percent), and not married (80 percent). The age ranged from six to seventy-three for 113 victims (five cases provided no victim age). Fourteen, or 12 percent, were fourteen or younger; eighty-three, or 73 percent, were between fifteen and twenty-eight years old; and sixteen, or 14 percent, were thirty years or older. Thus, most victims (73 percent) were between fifteen and twenty-eight, which matches the age range for rape victims in general.

Close to half (47 percent) of the victims were closely related in age to the offender. More than one-third of the cases (37 percent) involved a younger victim than offender. In 15 percent of the cases, the victim was older than the offender. More than half of the victims came from average or advantaged socioeconomic levels (62 percent), 30 percent had marginal incomes, and 9 percent had less-than-marginal incomes.

In more than one-third of the cases, the victim had a companion at the time of the assault, with 63 percent being alone at the time of the murder.

Victim Resistance

Any cause-effect determination in victim resistance reports needs to include the total series of interactions between a victim and an assailant, including the dynamic sequencing of victim resistance and offender attack. Offenders were asked to report on their victims' resistance in terms of whether they tried to verbally negotiate, verbally refuse, scream, flee, or fight. The offender was then asked to report his own response to the victim's behavior. It is important to keep in mind that these data represent only the offender's perceptions of the victim-offender interaction.

In the eighty-three cases with data, twenty-three victims (28 percent) acquiesced or offered no resistance as perceived by the offender. One murderer said, "She was compliant. I showed her the gun. She dropped her purse and kind of wobbled a second and got her balance and said, 'All right; I'm not going to say anything. Just don't hurt me.' " Twenty-six (31 percent) victims tried verbal negotiation; six (7 percent) tried to refuse verbally; eight (10 percent) screamed; four (5 percent) tried to escape and sixteen (19 percent) tried to fight the offender.

The reaction by the offender to the victim's resistance showed that while in thirty-one cases the offenders (34 percent) had no reaction, fourteen (15 percent) threatened the victim verbally, twenty-three (25 percent) increased their aggression, and twenty-four (25 percent) became violent. Thus, in two-thirds of the cases, the assailant countered the victim's resistance; often (50 percent) it was met with increased force and aggression. Thus it appears with most offenders interviewed, both physical and verbal (or forceful and nonforceful) resistance played a part in triggering a reaction by the offenders.

It is important to note that almost equal numbers of victims in the homicide sample were said to have resisted physically (N = 25) as were said to have made no attempt at resistance (n = 23). Both types of victim actions resulted in death.

The FBI special agents interviewed the murderers about deterrence to killing. Murderers who were *not* consciously aware of their motives to kill were the only ones able to identify factors that might deter their killing. They stated such prevention factors as being in a populated location, having witnesses in the area, or cooperation from the victim. Those murderers who had a conscious plan to kill said that factors such as witnesses and location did not matter because the murder fantasy was so well rehearsed that everything was controlled ("I always killed in my home, and there were no witnesses."). Or as one murderer said, "The victim did not have a choice. Killing was part of my fantasy." Also, the murderer with the planned fantasy generally believed he would never be caught.

Convicted Rapists Study: Massachusetts Treatment Center

A study was conducted on data from 108 convicted rapists committed to a treatment center and 389 of their victims. The study examined the amount of expressive aggression before, during, and after the offense specifically by rapist type. The Massachusetts Treatment Center rapist classification system is concerned with the interaction of sexual and aggressive motivation. Although all rape clearly includes both motivations, for some rapists the need to humiliate and injure through aggression is the most salient feature of the offense, whereas for others the need to achieve sexual dominance is the most salient feature of the offense. In abbreviated fashion, four of the subcategories of rapists follow.

For the *compensatory* rapist, the assault is primarily an expression of his rape fantasies. There is usually a history of sexual preoccupation typified by the living out or fantasizing of a variety of perversions, including bizarre masturbatory practices, voyeurism, exhibitionism, obscene telephone calls, cross-dressing, and fetishism. There is often high sexual arousal accompanied by a loss of self-control, causing a distorted perception of the victim/offender relationship (for example, the rapist may want the victim to respond in a sexual or erotic manner and may try to make a "date" after the assault). The core of his fantasy is that the victim will enjoy the experience and perhaps even "fall in love" with him. The motivation derives from the rapist's belief that he is so inadequate that no woman in her right mind would voluntarily have sex with him. In sum, this is an individual who is "compensating" for his acutely felt inadequacies as a male.

For the *exploitative* rapist, sexual behavior is expressed as an impulsive predatory act. The sexual component is less integrated in fantasy life and has far less psychologic meaning to the offender. That is, the rape is an impulsive act determined more by situation and context than by conscious fantasy. The assailant can best be described and understood as a man "on the prowl" for a woman to exploit sexually. The offender's intent is to force the victim to submit sexually, and hence, he is not concerned about the victim's welfare.

For the *displaced* rapist, sexual behavior is an expression of anger and rage. Sexuality is in the service of a primary aggressive aim, with the victim representing, in a displaced fashion, the hated individual(s). Although the offense may reflect a cumulative series of experienced or imagined insults from many people, such as family members, wife, girlfriends, it is important to note that there need not be any historical truth to these perceived injustices. This individual is a misogynist; hence, the aggression may span a wide range from verbal abuse to brutal murder.

For the *sadistic* rapist, sexual behavior is an expression of sexual-aggressive (sadistic) fantasies. It appears as if there is a fusion (i.e., no differentiation) or synergism between sexual and aggressive feelings. As sexual arousal increases, aggressive feelings increase; simultaneously, increases in aggressive feelings heighten sexual arousal. Anger is not always apparent, particularly at the outset, wherein the assault may actually begin as a seduction. The anger may begin to emerge as the offender becomes sexually aroused, often resulting in the most bizarre and intense forms of sexual-aggressive violence. Unlike the displaced anger rapist, the sadist's violence is usually directed at parts of the body having sexual significance (breasts, anus, buttocks, genitals, mouth).

Study Findings

The results of data analysis indicated that for all rapist types, there was a higher incidence of brutal aggression associated with combative resistance than with noncombative resistance. Of the four rapist types, there were important differences in victim resistance and physical injury and amount of expressive aggression before, during, and after the sexual act, thus implying the need to adjust a resistance strategy to the type of rapist encountered. This chapter defines the four types of rapists and outlines a strategy derived from the analyzed data.

Clinical Observations of Victim Response

While we cannot infer causality from the correlative data analyzed (i.e., it cannot be ascertained whether a victim's combative response precipitated or contributed to an increase in violence or was a reaction to violence), the data strongly suggest that it is important to explore strategies that are viable alternatives to physical combativeness, particularly in situations where such resistance proves to be ineffective and may increase the risk of serious injury or even death. Knowledge of alternative strategies may serve to enhance the effectiveness of resistance.

The following discussion is an attempt to provide an overview of possible strategies for resisting rape. The observations and conclusions derive from our joint clinical experience, including extensive contact with victims and offenders as well as the detailed evaluation of more than three hundred offender files. This experience allows us to observe a large number of effective and ineffective responses to rape, sometimes with the same offender. While there is a conceptual and clinical foundation for the recommendations that follow, there is, at present, little supportive empirical evidence.

Response Strategies Defined

Studies have examined coping behaviors of victims (e.g., Burgess and Holmstrom 1976, 1979), strategies of rape avoiders and rape victims (e.g., Bart and O'Brien 1984) and victim behavior signaling vulnerability (e.g., Grayson and Stein 1981). Analysis of the various strategies defined in the literature, combined with our clinical experience with both convicted offenders and rape victims, allows us to define a typology of response strategies as follows: escape, verbally confrontative resistance, physically confrontative resistance, nonconfrontative verbal response, nonconfrontative physical resistance, and acquiescence.

Escape

We emphasize that escaping the assailant is always the optimum response *when it can be employed successfully*. However, deciding whether an escape attempt will be successful is very difficult. If the victim is alone in the woods with nowhere to run or is assaulted by multiple offenders, escape attempts may not only be unsuccessful, but may also be hazardous. If weapons have been brandished, the possible consequences of attempting to escape—and being caught—may make it not worth the risk. If the offender appears to be young and athletic, the probability of a successful escape diminishes.

In general, in a city or urban location, if there are no weapons, if there are other people somewhere in the vicinity, and if there are no encumbrances (i.e., no clothes tied or tangled around the ankles), the probability of successful flight will be increased. Caution must be exercised, however. There is a small percent of individuals (i.e., sadists) for whom unsuccessful flight may only serve to increase arousal and, in so doing, increase the brutality of the attack.

Verbally Confrontative Resistance

This strategy includes screaming or yelling ("Leave me alone! Get away!") as a means of attracting attention or asserting oneself against victimization. These verbal responses are strictly confrontative and are intended to convey the message at the outset of the assault that the victim will not acquiesce.

Physically Confrontative Resistance

Confrontative physical resistance ranges from moderate responses (fighting, struggling, punching, or kicking) to violent responses (attacking highly vulnerable areas—face, throat, groin—with lethal intention). These responses are dictated by many critical situational factors, such as the location of the assault, the presence of a weapon, the likelihood of help, the size and strength of the offender, and the degree of violence of the assault. When employed successfully, such responses often occur quickly and make use of surprise. The victim can expect that in many cases physical resistance will be met with increased aggression.

Nonconfrontative Verbal Responses

These responses are intended to dissuade the attacker ("I'm a virgin," or "I have my period or cramps."), create empathy (engaging the offender in conversation and listening and attempting to respond in an understanding way), inject reality ("I am frightened.") or negotiate ("Let's talk about this," or "Let's go have a beer.") to stall for time and devise another strategy (set the stage for an escape). Talking tends to be the safest and most reliable means of reducing the degree of violence (once it is determined that the offender is intending to use violence), though it may not be effective in stopping the assault completely.

In general, nonconfrontative dissuasive techniques do not work (McIntyre 1978). In the heat of an attack, most rapists will not be concerned about the victim's menstrual cramps or virginity if, in fact, they even believe her. Victims should avoid such references as "I have VD" or "I'm pregnant," as such statements may support the offender's pathological fantasy that the victim is "bad" or promiscuous and thus deserves to be raped. Also threats of reprisal ("You will be caught and go to jail.") should be avoided.

The safest way to engage the assailant through dialogue is for the victim to appeal to his humanity by making herself a real person and by focusing on the immediate situation ("I'm a total stranger. Why do you want to hurt me? I've never done anything to hurt you," or "What if I were someone you cared about? How would you feel about that?" and not "This is going to ruin my life."). The attacker can easily dismiss what may happen sometime in the future. He cannot as easily dismiss what the victim is telling him is happening right now. The victim should avoid asking "What if I were your daughter or sister?" because she will not know what meaning such an individual has for the offender.

Nonconfrontative Physical Resistance

This technique involves active resistance that does not actually confront the attacker (as in the case of physical confrontation). Nonconfrontative physical responses may be feigned or quite real and uncontrollable. Feigned responses might include fainting, gagging, sickness or seizure. Uncontrollable or involuntary responses may include crying, gagging, nausea, and loss of sphincter control. In general, these responses may work on occasion, but they are highly idiosyncratic and thus are not reliable. In one important situation (with a displaced-anger rapist), this strategy could be dangerous.

Acquiescence

Acquiescence implies no counteractive response (offensive or defensive) to thwart the attack. The victim might say something to the effect of "Don't hurt me and I'll do what you want." Acquiescence is often the result of paralyzing fear, abject terror, or a belief that such a response is necessary to save one's life. In most cases, acquiescence need only be a last resort when attempts to stop the attack have failed. Acquiescence may be interpreted by the offender as participation and exacerbate the intensity of the attack.

In general, the decision to submit or acquiesce to an attacker is a difficult one, determined as much by the violence of the assault as by the victim's emotional state and specific fears (such as death or rape). Some women will be able to cope much better than others with the knowledge that they submitted. Acquiescence can invoke, in some victims, postassault rage and/or guilt, while other victims may be able to accept and feel comfortable with whatever actions they felt were necessary to survive the assault with a minimum of physical and emotional injury. If, after other strategies have failed, acquiescence is deemed to be the optimum response to protect life and reduce physical injury in a given situation, it is important that the victim be comfortable with such a choice and be aware that postassault guilt feelings will probably arise.

We operate on the assumption that aggression begets aggression. When the amount of rage and aggression obviously exceed what is necessary to force compliance, a violent confrontative response on the part of the victim will generally increase the violence in the assault and place the victim at increased risk for serious physical injury. Gratuitous violence on the part of the rapist places the victim in dangerous, volatile, and unpredictable situations. For that reason, we recommend that the *first* response to violence *not* be violent. If direct dialogue does not begin to neutralize the attacker (reduce the intensity of the aggression), then the victim will have no recourse but to employ any means available to object. The offender believes that he is entitled to sex under any condition, and hence has a callous indifference to the comfort or welfare of the victim. Both verbal resistance and nonconfrontative resistance strategies are appropriate. Once it has been demonstrated that the rapist will likely use whatever force necessary to gain victim compliance, confrontative physical resistance would be unwise unless the victim is confident that it will work. The best strategy, then, is to encourage the rapist to start talking about himself (playing on his narcissism) so that the victim becomes real rather than a sexualized object. Nonconfrontative physical strategies may also work, but they tend to be unreliable and are highly idiosyncratic to the individual rapist. As noted earlier, some of these responses (crying, nausea, gagging) may be involuntary, in which case the victim may have to overcome the response if it is aggravating the situation.

Many exploitative rapists will certainly be given a moment's pause if the victim appears undaunted and immediately says, "You what? Here? Now? Come on, let's sit down here and talk." While admittedly this requires extraordinary presence of mind on the part of the victim, it has the advantage of momentarily catching the rapist off guard. It may not avoid the rape, but it might decrease the amount of physical injury that could result from the assault as well as give the victim time to assess options and set the stage for possible escape.

If the victim is unable to engage the offender in conversation, and the physical attack continues, escalates, or appears to be lethal, the victim should fight with every means available (attack eyes or groin, hit the offender with a rock or stick, etc.) to escape and/or avoid serious injury.

If the assailant remains after verbal confrontation, has no weapon, and responds with threats or retorts, the victim should immediately resist physically by punching, hitting, kicking. Such physically confrontative resistance is often successful with compensatory rapists and is sometimes successful with exploitative rapists.

If the attacker responds to victim physical confrontation with increased anger and/or violence, the victim should cease physical resistance. If he responds by immediately ceasing his aggressive/violent behavior and is willing to engage the victim in conversation, he is also likely to be an exploitative rapist and the victim should use verbal strategies.

If the attacker continues to escalate aggression/violence, the victim should attempt to begin verbal dissuasive techniques. Again, the object is to break the confrontation, reduce tension, and defuse the violence. If verbal dissuasion is unsuccessful and the violence continues in spite of the victim's attempts, the victim again must do anything to get out of the situation. If verbal dissuasion is successful and the violence seems to diminish, those same responses should be continued, with specific statements tailored to what the rapist is saying.

For the *displaced-anger rapist*, the victim is a substitute for and a symbol of the hated person(s) in his life. The primary motive is to hurt and injure the victim. Aggression may span a wide range from verbal abuse to brutal assault. Continued physical confrontation, unless the victim is reasonably certain that she will be able to incapacitate the attacker, may only justify in the offender's mind the need to "punish" the victim and thus escalate the violence.

In general, nonconfrontative responses are also not recommended. A displaced-anger rapist will not respond empathically to the victim's evident pain or discomfort. Such responses as nausea, gagging, or crying are evidence that the rapist is achieving the desired result. Moreover, acquiescence is not an appropriate response to this type of rapist. Because sexual intercourse is not this offender's primary motive, deterrence of the rape will not be accomplished by acquiescing.

The recommended response to such a rapist is verbal, and the words must be carefully chosen. The victim must convince the offender that she is not the hated person ("It sounds like you're really angry at someone, but it can't be me. We've never even met before."). The victim should avoid statements that may justify the assault in the mind of the rapist. Challenging the fantasy is critical.

Statements such as "How do you know that I'm a bitch? You've never met me before. We're strangers. I could be a nice person," may be along the lines of what is appropriate.

For the *sadistic rapist*, the victim is a partner who has been recruited to play out sexual-aggressive or sadistic fantasies. Needless to say, this rapist is an extremely dangerous individual. Because these assaults are brutal and can end with serious physical injury to the victim, it may be a matter of life and death to escape.

If escape is not possible, there are few recommendations we can make. If the victim acquiesces, the sadistic offender may perceive her as an active participant in the assault. This will function to increase his arousal, and hence, his anger. If the victim is physically confrontative, struggles, or otherwise seeks to protect herself, the rapist may also perceive her as an active participant, which also will increase his anger and arousal. Passivity or submission may also serve to intensify feelings of rage in the offender. Once the fused sexual-aggressive feelings are activated, sadists generally will not hear attempts at negotiation, empathy, or dissuasion. Finally, nonconfrontative physical resistance is not effective, as there is a high probability that these behaviors may also be interpreted as participation in the assault.

Because there are no reliably safe and effective responses, the victim must do *anything* necessary to get out of the situation. That may mean feigning participation and, at a critical moment, making maximum use of surprise, attacking the offender's vulnerable areas as viciously as possible. This requires the victim to convert fear into rage and a sense of helplessness into a battle for survival.

Decision-Making Process

We realize that most of our recommendations may be forgotten at the moment of panic when the victim is confronted by a would-be rapist. The victim may not have the presence of mind—and perhaps not even the time—to evaluate different responses to rapist types. Believing, however, that knowledge brings an added sense of confidence to an unpredictable and volatile situation, we have tried to reduce much of the foregoing discussion to a systematic decision-making process (see figure 14–1).

The *first* response should always be to attempt to escape. If escape is not possible, the *second* response is firm verbal confrontation. If the attacker persists, there is no weapon present, and no physical violence is occurring, the victim should immediately initiate the *third* response: offensive physical confrontation. If the attacker flees, he probably is compensatory. If he does not flee and responds with physical aggression, the victim should start talking, keeping conversation in the present. The victim should attempt to reduce the

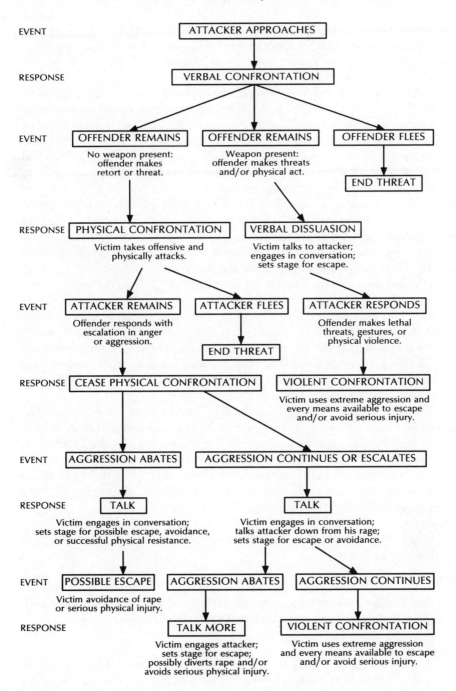

Figure 14–1. Victim Response Strategies

aggression, talk the assailant down from his rage, and convey the message that she is a stranger, and that there are other ways to find a sex partner or express anger. The intent is to disrupt the fantasy and, in so doing, challenge the rapist's symbolic conceptualization of the victim.

If the response is positive (the offender stops, listens, or talks), the same course of action should be continued. If he pays no attention and persists in his attempts to force the victim to submit to sexual activity and if the amount of aggression does not extend beyond that force, the attacker is probably exploitative. The victim should persist in verbal attempts to make herself real by diverting the offender with questions about himself.

If there is a clear escalation in aggression, the victim should try to distinguish between a displaced and a sadistic motive. If the primary intent seems to be to humiliate and demean by word or deed, the offender is more likely to be a displaced-anger rapist. If none of this is present, and the rapist is making demands that are both eroticized and bizarre, then he is probably sadistic. With a displaced-anger rapist, the victim should keep conversation in the here and now and underscore the message that she has not abused him. Because these men have a history of perceived abuse by women, the victim should try to demonstrate some sense of interest, concern, or caring. If the victim determines that the individual is a sadist, she should use extreme violent confrontation and do whatever possible to escape. There is no single response that is likely to deter a sadistic assault, and because these assaults are potentially lethal, the victim must do *whatever* is in her power to survive the attack and attract help.

We have been discussing in the abstract what to do in a highly traumatic situation, and it may seem cavalier or even insensitive to suggest that a victim should perform a quick mental status exam as she is being assaulted. However, all rapes are *not* "blitz" assaults, and victims have often been noted to use multiple strategies over time until one works (Bart and O'Brien 1984). As an overview, as well as an attempt at simplification, the strategies that we have recommended can be briefly summarized as follows:

Step 1. *Firm verbal confrontation.* Firmly tell the attacker to get away and leave you alone.

If step 1 is unsuccessful:

Step 2. *Physical confrontation.* Immediately take the offensive and attack the assaulter with moderate physical aggression (hit, kick, punch, etc.).

If step 2 is unsuccessful:

Step 3: *Nonconfrontative Verbal Responses.* Attempt to calm the assaulter and talk him down from his rage. Engage him in conversation, and make yourself a real person to him. Challenge his fantasy that you are the person he wants to harm. Set the stage for an escape attempt (e.g., try to talk him into taking you to a more populated area: "Let's go have a drink" etc.).

If step 3 is unsuccessful in neutralizing the violence:

Step 4: *Violent confrontation.* Use extreme aggression, and take any action within your means (kick, punch, bite, strike with rock, etc.) to incapacitate the assaulter and avoid rape or mortal physical injury.

In sum, knowledge may be the only weapon a victim has in a highly dangerous situation. As such, knowledge can provide a sense of power, as well as the confidence necessary to *act* rather than resign out of helplessness.

Notes

Bart, P.B., and O'Brien, P. Stopping rape: Effective avoidance strategies. *Signs: Journal of Women in Culture and Society*, 1984, *10*, 83–101.

Burgess, A.W., and Holmstrom, L.L. Coping behavior of the rape victim. *American Journal of Psychiatry*, 1976, *113*: 413–418.

Burgess, A.W., and Holmstrom, L.L. Adaptive strategies and recovery from rape. *American Journal of Psychiatry*, 1979, *136*: 1278–1282.

Chapman, J.R., and Gates, M. (Eds.) *The Victimization of Women.* Beverly Hills: Sage Publications, 1978.

Chappell, D., and Fogarty, F. *Forcible rape: A literature review and annotated bibliography.* National Institute of Law Enforcement and Criminal Justice, Law Enforcement Assistance Administration, U.S. Department of Justice. Washington, D.C.: U.S. Government Printing Office, 1978.

Grayson, R., and Stein, M.I. Attracting assault: Victims' nonverbal cues. *Journal of Communication*, 1981, *31*: 68–75.

Holmstrom, L.L., and Burgess, A.W. *The Victim of Rape: Institutional Response.* New York: Wiley, 1978.

Marsh, J.C., Geist, A., and Caplan, N. *Rape and limits of law reform.* Boston: Auburn House Publishing Company, 1982.

McIntyre, J.J. Victim response to rape: Alternative outcomes. Final Report to the National Institute of Mental Health, Grant #R01 MH29045, 1978.

McCombie, S.L. (Ed.) *The rape crisis intervention handbook: A guide for victim care.* New York: Plenum, 1980.

Russell, D.E.H., and Howell, N. The prevalence of rape in the United States revisited. *Signs: Journal of Women in Culture and Society*, 1983, 84.

Walker, M.J., and Brodsky, S.L. *Sexual assault*, Lexington, Mass. DC Heath and Co., 1976.

Warr, M. Fear of rape among urban women. *Social Problems*, 1985, *32*: 238–250.

15
Murderers: A Postscript

I n reviewing the lessons learned from this study, the previous chapter dealt
with suggestions for strategies in confronting dangerous sexual situations.
This chapter now looks to the murderer for suggestions regarding prevention of sexual aggression and violence.

Murderers: Circa 1987

Our first step was to determine the status of these thirty-six men since they
were interviewed. A brief update revealed the following:

Four of the murderers died in prison: two were executed, one committed
suicide, and one died of natural causes. One murderer is in a mental institution
and appealing his "not guilty by reason of insanity" sentence in hope of serving
the remainder of his sentence for robbery (committed in conjunction with the
murder and for which he was not found insane) in prison. The remaining
thirty-one murderers remain in prison.

Most of the murderers have made use of the appeal process. One has been
appealing every opportunity since 1952. In two cases, the murderers have
exhausted all appeal processes. One murderer was persuasive in obtaining a
commutation; however, community and professional pressure was intense and
the governor reversed his decision.

All the murderers have parole hearing dates and, to date, all petitions have
been denied. However, several men are believed to be strong candidates for
being paroled in the next decade.

We now turn to implications from the study in terms of crime classification, childhood sexual trauma, deviant fantasies, and further research.

Crime Classification

Our work and the research of others (Prentky et al. 1985) suggest a typology of
murderers is essential to investigate for a variety of reasons. First, any
understanding of the typology may enhance law enforcement efforts both at
persuading certain offenders to turn themselves in and at more narrowly

focusing investigative efforts. Second a classification system will give professionals working to curtail violent behavior a focus for intervention efforts that address the need to monitor, evaluate, and change salient personality characteristics. Measurements of these characteristics and methods of evaluating positive change are essential to prevent the tragic reality of released violent criminals' repeating their crimes. Third, a classification system would facilitate dialogue between the various disciplines working with offenders and would encourage research into profiling of suspects from crime scene evidence, a technique in progress at the National Center for the Analysis of Violent Crime. Further, behavioral research efforts by law enforcement agencies is important to their development of additional skill in reading the seemingly inert characteristics of crime scene evidence. Understanding the motivational and behavioral matrix of the offender increases law enforcement's use of the connection between patterns of thinking and behavior.

The classification of crimes from crime scene analysis provides an opportunity to expand and advance the psychosocial framework for studying murderers that is sometimes criticized for its unproved theories, obscure interpretive level, and lack of attention to cultural factors (Wolfgang and Ferracuti 1967) to include measurable behavioral indicators from analysis of crime, such as presence or absence of a weapon, or injury to victim. The law enforcement typology used in this study is based on discrete, verifiable concepts and behavior. It does not rest solely on controversial statements of motivation derived from a complex theory of subconscious motivation. Consequently, the typology has the potential for verifiable classification of acts and visual evidence, enhancing the investigation and study of murderers. For example, to hypothesize that a serial murderer killed a young woman to destroy his female identification with his sister is cumbersome and cannot be substantiated by analysis of crime scene evidence or other data available before his capture and evaluation. What is clear is the pattern of killing of young women of a certain age range in a repeated and particular systematic style. Analysis of these data from the crime scene may be useful in understanding the psychosocial nature of the murderer, and may assist in his capture.

Childhood Sexual Trauma

One important area for prevention involves early identification and intervention with formative traumatic events. The examples of childhood sexual abuse and subsequent symptoms and criminal behaviors suggest that several variables, such as daydreams, isolation, cruelty to children and animals, play an important part in the subgroups (i.e., rape-murder and murder-mutilate) of sexual murderers. There is every indication that the motivation for murder is a complex developmental process that is based on a need for sexual dominance at the expense of the victim. It appears from this study of convicted killers that there is an important difference in the symptom constellation among those with a history of sexual abuse and those without such a history. Although it is not clear whether there is a difference in psychological motivation for sexual murder, what is apparent is an early onset of specific behaviors that are noted in the subgroup of murderers who mutilate.

The association of the specific impact of sexual molestation in the lives of these offenders and subsequent mutilation of their victims requires further investigation. To speculate on a possible link between the adolescents who were sexually abused and those who mutilate the body suggests a premeditated pattern where acts of self-mutilation are then transferred and carried out on others.

Deviant Fantasies

For the men who repeat sexual murder, their internal processing and cognitive operations appear to sustain and perpetuate fantasies of sexually violent actions. These fantasies are the primary source of emotional life for these men. As a result, clinicians are urged to take careful note of patients reporting sadistic as well as criminal fantasies and record a systematic history on the content, duration, progression, and effect triggered by the fantasy. For law enforcement, murder that appears to be motiveless—that is, the victim is a stranger and there is no profit to be gained from the death of the victim— suggests that the victim and offense must be seen as having symbolic meaning to the offender reflecting violent sadistic fantasies.

This study raises concern of how to deal therapeutically with the notion of fantasy in the criminal population. We note that dwelling on fantasies escalates rather than diminishes the power of the fantasy and the need to act it out. Unless one alters the structure of the fantasy that moves toward the aggressive acts, repetition of violence occurs.

Understanding the reinforcing quality of actions, be they in fantasy, play, or acting-out behaviors, may lead to different notions regarding not only motivation but also behavior change. Exploratory efforts by clinicians are needed for methods to alter the structure of these fantasies. For example, the offender might be forced to relate to the victim position in the fantasy as a way to stimulate compassion for rather than violence to the victim.

Further Research

This study raises far more questions than it answers. Current understanding of disclosed childhood sexual abuse has focused on the initial treatment and prevention efforts. Yet our understanding of undisclosed childhood sexual abuse and its long-term effects is limited in regard to gender difference and behavioral outcomes. It becomes even more imperative, given our findings on behavioral differences, that we not only learn how to detect cases of child sexual abuse early but also delve further into behavioral outcomes, particularly in the noncriminal abused adults.

Basic research in biological and psychosocial factors are necessary to explore the biochemical hormonal sensory levels associated with deviant fantasies of both youth and adults. We know that pessimistic cognitions are associated with lowered epinephrine levels in endogenous depression; research might suggest the biological underpinnings of violent sexualized fantasies.

Basic research on the sensory arousal levels of people during fantasy might answer the question: Is there a basis of hormonal release addicting the person to violent fantasy and violent acts? And does the structure of fantasy differ between various groups of deviant offenders?

Longitudinal research on children's response to and recovery from sexual and physical/psychological abuse and research on the social context in which the child survives and recovers from abuse are important to any understanding of motivational factors in those who become offenders. In this context, a control group of abused males who do *not* commit criminal acts is essential to identify the factors that help the victim recover and survive the abuse.

Notes

Prentky, R.A., Cohen, M.L., and Seghorn, T. Development of a rational taxonomy for the classification of sexual offenders: Rapists. *Bulletin of the American Academy of Psychiatry and the Law*, 13 1985, 39–70.

Wolfgang, M.E., and Ferracuti, F. *The subculture of violence.* Beverly Hills: Sage, 1967.

FD-676 (Rev. 3-11-86)
OMB No. 1110-0011

U.S. Department of Justice
Federal Bureau of Investigation

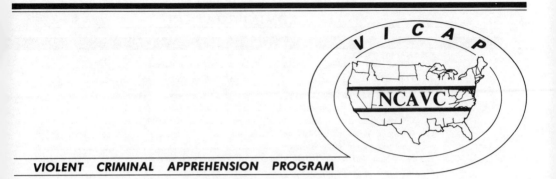

VIOLENT CRIMINAL APPREHENSION PROGRAM

VICAP
Crime Analysis Report

VICAP NCAVC FBI ACADEMY Quantico, VA 22135 (703) 640-6131

NATIONAL   CENTER   FOR   THE   ANALYSIS   OF   VIOLENT   CRIME

P

I. ADMINISTRATION

CASE ADMINISTRATION

FOR VICAP USE ONLY

1. **VICAP Case Number:** _____ 2. **FBI Case Number:** _____

3. **FBI OO:** _____ 4. **VICAP Assignment:** _____

5. Reporting Agency: _____

6. Address: _____ 7. City: _____

8. County: _____ 9. State: _____ 10. ZIP: _____

11. Reporting Agency's ORI Number: _____

12. Reporting Agency's Case Number: _____

13. NCIC Number If Victim Is 1) Missing or 2) an Unidentified Dead Body: _____

14. Investigator's Name: _____

15. Investigator's Phone Number: _____ - _____ - _____

16. VICAP Crime Analysis Report Type:

    1 ☐ Original Submission of This Case

    2 ☐ Supplement to Previously Submitted Information

    3 ☐ Correction of Previously Submitted Information

17. Investigating Agency's Case Status:

    1 ☐ Open (active investigation)   4 ☐ Cleared by Arrest

    2 ☐ Suspended (inactive investigation) 5 ☐ Exceptionally Cleared (by UCR definition)

    3 ☐ Open —— Arrest Warrent Issued

CRIME CLASSIFICATION

18. This VICAP Crime Analysis Report Pertains to the Following Type Case (check one only):

    1 ☐ Murder or Attempted Murder —— Victim Identified (go to Item 19)

    2 ☐ Unidentified Dead Body Where Manner of Death Is Known or Suspected to Be Homicide (go to Item 19)

    3 ☐ Kidnapping or Missing Person with Evidence of Foul Play (victim still missing) (go to Item 20)

19. Based on Your Experience and the Results of the Investigation of This Case, Do You Believe This Offender Has Killed Before?

    1 ☐ Yes (explain in Narrative Summary)   99 ☐ Unable to Determine

    2 ☐ No

20. There Is an Indication That This Case Is Related to Organized Drug Trafficking:

    1 ☐ Yes   2 ☐ No   99 ☐ Unable to Determine

DATE AND TIME PARAMETERS

21. Today's Date: ____/____/____
                   (mo) (da) (yr)

	Date	Military Time	Exact	Approximate
22. Victim Last Seen:	____/____/____ (mo) (da) (yr)	_____	☐	☐
23. Death or Major Assault:	____/____/____ (mo) (da) (yr)	_____	☐	☐
24. Victim or Body Found	____/____/____ (mo) (da) (yr)	_____	☐	☐

II.   VICTIM INFORMATION

VICTIM STATUS

25. This Is Victim _____ of _____ Victim(s) in This Incident.
     (number)   (total)

26. Status of This Victim:
    1 ☐ Deceased (as result of this incident)
    2 ☐ Survivor of Attack
    3 ☐ Missing

VICTIM IDENTIFICATION

27. Name: _____
            (last, first, middle)

28. Alias(es) (including maiden name and prior married names):
    _____
    _____

29. Resident City: _____ 30. State: _____ 31. ZIP: _____

32. Social Security Number: _____–_____–_____ 33. FBI Number: _____

PHYSICAL DESCRIPTION

34. Sex:
    1 ☐ Male   2 ☐ Female   99 ☐ Unknown

35. Race:
    1 ☐ Black   3 ☐ Hispanic   5 ☐ Other
    2 ☐ Caucasian   4 ☐ Oriental/Asian   99 ☐ Unknown

36. Date of Birth: ____/ ____/ ____
                   (mo) / (da) / (yr)
    99 ☐ Unknown

37. Age (or best estimate) at Time of Incident: _____
    99 ☐ Unknown   (years)

38. Height (or best estimate): _____ feet _____ inches
    99 ☐ Unknown

39. Approximate Weight: _____ lbs.
    99 ☐ Unknown

40. Build (check one only):
    1 ☐ Small (thin)   3 ☐ Large (stocky)
    2 ☐ Medium (average)   99 ☐ Unknown

41. Hair Length (check one only):
    1 ☐ Bald or Shaved   4 ☐ Shoulder Length
    2 ☐ Shorter Than Collar Length   5 ☐ Longer Than Shoulder Length
    3 ☐ Collar Length   99 ☐ Unknown

42. Hair Shade (check one only):
    1 ☐ Light   3 ☐ Neither 1 or 2 Above
    2 ☐ Dark   99 ☐ Unknown

43. Predominant Hair Color (check one only):
    1 ☐ Gray and/or White   5 ☐ Black
    2 ☐ Blond   6 ☐ Other
    3 ☐ Red   99 ☐ Unknown
    4 ☐ Brown

If your victim is either a missing person or an unidentified dead body, respond to Items 44 through 48. Otherwise, go to Item 49.

44. Abnormalities of Teeth:
    - 1 ☐ None
    - 2 ☐ Braces
    - 3 ☐ Broken or Chipped
    - 4 ☐ Crooked
    - 5 ☐ Decayed
    - 6 ☐ Noticeable Gaps
    - 7 ☐ Some or All Missing
    - 8 ☐ Stained
    - 9 ☐ Other (describe): _____
    - 99 ☐ Unknown

45. Glasses or Corrective Lenses Normally Worn by or Associated with Victim:
    - 1 ☐ None
    - 2 ☐ Prescription
    - 3 ☐ Contacts
    - 4 ☐ Bifocals
    - 5 ☐ Plastic Frame
    - 6 ☐ Metal Frame
    - 7 ☐ Rimless
    - 8 ☐ Other (describe): _____
    - 99 ☐ Unknown

SCARS AND/OR BIRTHMARKS

46. Location of Noticeable Scars or Birthmarks (not tattoos):
    - 1 ☐ None
    - 2 ☐ Face, Head, or Neck
    - 3 ☐ Arm(s) or Hand(s)
    - 4 ☐ Torso
    - 5 ☐ Buttocks
    - 6 ☐ Feet or Leg(s)
    - 7 ☐ Other (describe): _____
    - 99 ☐ Unknown

TATTOOS

47. Tattoo Locations:
    - 1 ☐ None
    - 2 ☐ Face, Head, or Neck
    - 3 ☐ Arm(s) or Hand(s)
    - 4 ☐ Torso
    - 5 ☐ Buttocks
    - 6 ☐ Feet or Leg(s)
    - 7 ☐ Other (describe): _____
    - 99 ☐ Unknown

48. Tattoo Designs:
    - 1 ☐ Initials or Words
    - 2 ☐ Number(s)
    - 3 ☐ Picture(s) or Design(s)
    - 4 ☐ Other (specify): _____
    - 99 ☐ Unknown

OUTSTANDING PHYSICAL FEATURES

49. Did the Victim Have Outstanding Physical Features (crossed eyes, noticeable limp, physical deformity, etc.)? (Do not repeat information reported in Items 44 through 48, above.)
    - 1 ☐ Yes (describe): _____
    - 2 ☐ No
    - 99 ☐ Unknown

CLOTHING OF VICTIM

50. Generally Preferred Clothing Style (this item deals with general style of dress typically preferred by the victim, not a detailed clothing description):
    - 1 ☐ Business Suit
    - 2 ☐ Casual
    - 3 ☐ Gaudy or Garish
    - 4 ☐ Sport or Athletic
    - 5 ☐ Western Wear
    - 6 ☐ Work Clothes or Uniform
    - 88 ☐ Other (describe): _____
    - 99 ☐ Unknown

51. Generally Preferred *Predominant* Color Tone of Clothing (check one only):
    - 1 ☐ Whites
    - 2 ☐ Yellows
    - 3 ☐ Greens
    - 4 ☐ Blues
    - 5 ☐ Purples/Violets
    - 6 ☐ Reds/Oranges
    - 7 ☐ Browns/Tans
    - 8 ☐ Grays/Blacks

52. If This Victim Is a Missing Person or Unidentified Dead, Give a Detailed Description of Clothing:

_____
_____

MISCELLANEOUS

53. Victim's Residence (check one only):
    - 1 ☐ Single-Family Dwelling
    - 2 ☐ Multi-Family Dwelling
    - 3 ☐ Temporary or Transient Housing
    - 4 ☐ Motor Vehicle
    - 5 ☐ Street
    - 99 ☐ Unknown

54. Current Occupation(s): 1) _____

2) _____

III. OFFENDER INFORMATION

OFFENDER DEFINED. As used in this VICAP Crime Analysis Report, "offender" includes arrestees, perpetrators, or persons the investigator has reasonable cause to believe are responsible for the commission of the crime.

OFFENDER STATUS

55. This Is Offender _____ of _____ Offender(s) in This Incident.
    (number)   (total)

56. The Offender Is (check one only):
    1 ☐ Unknown——Not Seen (go to Item 85)
    2 ☐ Unknown——Seen
    3 ☐ Identified (named)——Not in Custody
    4 ☐ In Custody
    5 ☐ Deceased

OFFENDER IDENTIFICATION

57. Name: _____
            (last, first, middle)

58. Alias(es) (including maiden name and prior married names):

    _____

    _____

59. Resident City: _____   60. State: _____   61. ZIP: _____

62. Social Security Number: _____—_____—_____   63. FBI Number: _____

PHYSICAL DESCRIPTION

64. Sex:
    1 ☐ Male   2 ☐ Female   99 ☐ Unknown

65. Race:
    1 ☐ Black   3 ☐ Hispanic   5 ☐ Other
    2 ☐ Caucasian   4 ☐ Oriental/Asian 99 ☐ Unknown

66. Date of Birth: ___/ ___/ ___
                    (mo) / (da) / (yr)
    99 ☐ Unknown

67. Age (or best estimate) at Time of Incident: _____
    99 ☐ Unknown   (years)

68. Height (or best estimate): _____ feet _____ inches (to _____ feet _____ inches)
    99 ☐ Unknown

69. Build (check one only):
    1 ☐ Small (thin)   3 ☐ Large (stocky)
    2 ☐ Medium (average)   99 ☐ Unknown

70. Hair Length (check one only):
    1 ☐ Bald or Shaved   4 ☐ Shoulder Length
    2 ☐ Shorter Than Collar Length   5 ☐ Longer Than Shoulder Length
    3 ☐ Collar Length   99 ☐ Unknown

71. Hair Shade (check one only):
    1 ☐ Light   3 ☐ Neither 1 or 2 Above
    2 ☐ Dark   99 ☐ Unknown

72. Predominant Hair Color (check one only):
    1 ☐ Gray and/or White   5 ☐ Black
    2 ☐ Blond   6 ☐ Other
    3 ☐ Red   99 ☐ Unknown
    4 ☐ Brown

73. Was Wearing Glasses:
   1 ☐ Yes   2 ☐ No   99 ☐ Unknown

74. Facial Hair (check all that apply):
   1 ☐ None   3 ☐ Beard   99 ☐ Unknown
   2 ☐ Mustache   4 ☐ Other

75. Appeared Generally Well Groomed:
   1 ☐ Yes   2 ☐ No   99 ☐ Unknown

76. Offender Wore a Disguise or Mask:
   1 ☐ Yes   2 ☐ No   99 ☐ Unknown

SCARS AND/OR BIRTHMARKS

77. Noticeable Scars or Birthmarks (not tattoos):
   1 ☐ Yes   2 ☐ No   99 ☐ Unknown

TATTOOS

78. Noticeable Tattoos:
   1 ☐ Yes   2 ☐ No   99 ☐ Unknown

OUTSTANDING PHYSICAL FEATURES

79. Other Outstanding Physical Features of the Offender Not Reported Above
   (crossed eyes, noticeable limp, physical deformity, etc.):

   1 ☐ Yes (describe): _____
   2 ☐ No
   99 ☐ Unknown

IV.   IDENTIFIED OFFENDER INFORMATION

If you have an offender in custody or identified in this case, complete Items 80 through 84. Otherwise, go to Item 85.

OFFENDER BACKGROUND

80. Cities and States of Residence during Last 5 Years (exclude current city of residence):
   1) _____   3) _____
   2) _____   4) _____

81. List the States the Offender Has Visited during Last 5 Years (attach separate sheet if necessary):
   1) _____   3) _____
   2) _____   4) _____

82. Foreign Countries Lived or Traveled in:
   1) _____   3) _____
   2) _____   4) _____

PROPERTY OF OTHERS

83. Offender Was in Possession of Property of Others (check all that apply):
   1 ☐ Body Parts   4 ☐ Jewelry
   2 ☐ Clothing   5 ☐ Photo(s)
   3 ☐ Credit Card(s), Checks, or other   88 ☐ Other (specify): _____
      I.D.

OFFENDER'S ADMISSIONS

84. Offender Admits Other Similar Crime(s) of Violence:
   1 ☐ Yes (attach details)   2 ☐ No

V. VEHICLE DESCRIPTION

VEHICLE USED IN THIS INCIDENT

85. Is a Vehicle Known to Have Been Used in This Incident?

    1 ☐ Yes   2 ☐ No or Unknown (go to Item 96)

    NOTE: Complete vehicle information if 1) a vehicle was used by the offender in this incident; or 2) this is a missing person case and the vehicle is missing; or 3) this is an unidentified dead case and the vehicle has been connected with the victim; or 4) the vehicle is in any way significantly involved in this incident.

86. Did the Vehicle Belong to, or Was It under the Civil Control of, the Victim?

    1 ☐ Yes   2 ☐ No

87. The Vehicle Would Normally Be Described as Being:

    1 ☐ Exceptionally Well Maintained ("sharp")   3 ☐ Neither 1 or 2 Above
    2 ☐ Not Generally Well Kept ("beat-up")   99 ☐ Unknown

88. The Vehicle Would Normally Be Described as Being:

    1 ☐ Newer/Late Model   3 ☐ Neither 1 or 2 Above
    2 ☐ Older Model   99 ☐ Unknown

89. License Number: _____   90. License State: _____

91. Vehicle Year: _____   92. Make: _____   93. Model: _____

94. Body Style:

    1 ☐ Passenger Car   6 ☐ Motorcycle
    2 ☐ Van   88 ☐ Other (specify): _____
    3 ☐ Pick-up Truck
    4 ☐ "Jeep" Type (i.e., Bronco, Blazer, etc.)   99 ☐ Unknown
    5 ☐ Tractor-Trailer

95. Color: _____   _____
              (top)   (bottom)

VI. OFFENSE M. O.

OFFENDER'S APPROACH TO VICTIM AT TIME OF INCIDENT

96. The Victim or a Witness Reported That the Offender's Approach to Victim Was:

    1 ☐ No Living Victim or Person Witnessed the Offender's Approach to Victim
    (go to Item 100)
    2 ☐ By Deception or Con: Openly, with Subterfuge or Ploy (e.g., offers assistance or requests direction) (go to Item 97 and then go to Item 100)
    3 ☐ By Surprise: Lay in Wait or Stepped from Concealment
    (go to Item 98 and then go to Item 100)
    4 ☐ By "Blitz": Direct and Immediate Physical Assault (go to Item 99)

97. If the Offender Initiated Contact with the Victim by Means of Deception, Indicate the Type of Deception Below:

    1 ☐ Posed as Authority Figure   7 ☐ Asked for or Offered Assistance
    2 ☐ Posed as Business Person   8 ☐ Caused or Staged Traffic Accident
    3 ☐ Asked Victim to Model or Pose for   9 ☐ Phony Police Traffic Stop
         Photos   10 ☐ Solicitation for Sex
    4 ☐ Offered Job, Money, Treats, or Toys   11 ☐ Offered Ride or Transportation
    5 ☐ Implied Family Emergency or Illness   12 ☐ Other Deception
    6 ☐ Wanted to Show (something)

98. If the Offender Initiated Contact with the Victim by Means of Surprise, Indicate the Type of Surprise Below:

    1 ☐ Lay in Wait——Out of Doors   4 ☐ Victim Sleeping
    2 ☐ Lay in Wait——In Building   5 ☐ Other Surprise
    3 ☐ Lay in Wait——In Vehicle

99. If the Offender Initiated Contact with the Victim by Direct and Immediate Physical Assault, Indicate the Type of Direct and Immediate Physical Assault Below:

   1 ☐ Immediately and Physically Over- 3 ☐ Choked Victim
   powered Victim (picked up, carried 4 ☐ Stabbed Victim
   away, etc.) 5 ☐ Shot Victim
   2 ☐ Hit Victim with Hand, Fist, or 6 ☐ Other Direct Assault
   Clubbing Weapon

EXACT GEOGRAPHIC LOCATION

100. Last Known Location of Identified Victim or Location of Unidentified Dead Body Recovery Site:
   a. ☐ City of (if within incorporated city, town, etc.)

   _____

   b. ☐ County of (if not within incorporated city, town, etc.)

   _____

   c. State: _____ d. ZIP: _____

LOCATION OF EVENTS

BODY RECOVERY SITE

101. Description of General Area of the Body Recovery Site (check one only):
   1 ☐ Rural 3 ☐ Urban
   2 ☐ Suburban 99 ☐ Unknown

102. The Neighborhood of the Body Recovery Site Is *Predominantly* (check one only):
   1 ☐ Business, Industrial, or Commercial 4 ☐ Uninhabited or Wilderness
   2 ☐ Farm or Agricultural 99 ☐ Unknown
   3 ☐ Residential

103. The Body Recovery Site Was (check as many as apply):
   1 ☐ Any Residence 7 ☐ In an Open Field
   2 ☐ At or Near a School or Playground 8 ☐ In a Vehicle
   3 ☐ In a Retail Shopping District 9 ☐ On Public Transportation
   4 ☐ On a Public Street 88 ☐ Other (specify): _____
   5 ☐ In a Vice Area
   6 ☐ A Densely Wooded Area 99 ☐ Unknown

104. The Body Recovery Site Was Victim's Residence:
   1 ☐ Yes 2 ☐ No 99 ☐ Unknown

105. The Body Recovery Site Was Victim's Work Place:
   1 ☐ Yes 2 ☐ No 99 ☐ Unknown

106. Potential Witnesses at the Time the Offender Left the Body at the Body Recovery Site:
   1 ☐ Other People Were Present in the 2 ☐ Area Was Essentially Deserted
   Immediate Area 99 ☐ Unknown

MURDER OR MAJOR ASSAULT SITE

107. Was the Murder or Major Assault Site the Same as the Body Recovery Site?
   1 ☐ Yes (go to Item 113) 2 ☐ No or Unknown

108. Description of General Area of Murder or Major Assault Site (check one only):
   1 ☐ Rural 3 ☐ Urban
   2 ☐ Suburban 99 ☐ Unknown

109. The Neighborhood of Murder or Major Assault Site Is *Predominantly* (check one only):
   1 ☐ Business, Industrial, or Commercial 4 ☐ Uninhabited or Wilderness
   2 ☐ Farm or Agricultural 99 ☐ Unknown
   3 ☐ Residential

110. The Murder or Major Assault Site Was (check as many as apply):
   1 ☐ Any Residence 7 ☐ In an Open Field
   2 ☐ At or Near a School or Playground 8 ☐ In a Vehicle
   3 ☐ In a Retail Shopping District 9 ☐ On Public Transportation
   4 ☐ On a Public Street 88 ☐ Other (specify): _____
   5 ☐ In a Vice Area
   6 ☐ A Densely Wooded Area 99 ☐ Unknown

VI. OFFENSE M. O. (cont.)

111. The Murder or Major Assault Site Was Victim's Residence:
    1 ☐ Yes   2 ☐ No   99 ☐ Unknown

112. The Murder or Major Assault Site Was Victim's Work Place:
    1 ☐ Yes   2 ☐ No   99 ☐ Unknown

113. Potential Witnesses at the Time of the Murder or Major Assault:
    1 ☐ Other People Were Present in the   2 ☐ Area Was Essentially Deserted
       Immediate Area   99 ☐ Unknown

SITE OF OFFENDER'S INITIAL CONTACT WITH VICTIM
114. Was the Site of the Offender's Initial Contact with the Victim the Same as the Murder or Major Assault Site?
    1 ☐ Yes (go to Item 120)   2 ☐ No or Unknown

115. Description of General Area of Initial Offender-Victim Contact (check one only):
    1 ☐ Rural   3 ☐ Urban
    2 ☐ Suburban   99 ☐ Unknown

116. The Neighborhood of Initial Offender-Victim Contact Is *Predominantly* (check one only):
    1 ☐ Business, Industrial, or Commercial   4 ☐ Uninhabited or Wilderness
    2 ☐ Farm or Agricultural   99 ☐ Unknown
    3 ☐ Residential

117. The Initial Offender-Victim Contact Was (check as many as apply):
    1 ☐ Any Residence   7 ☐ In an Open Field
    2 ☐ At or Near a School or Playground   8 ☐ In a Vehicle
    3 ☐ In a Retail Shopping District   9 ☐ On Public Transportation
    4 ☐ On a Public Street   88 ☐ Other (specify): _____
    5 ☐ In a Vice Area
    6 ☐ A Densely Wooded Area   99 ☐ Unknown

118. Initial Offender-Victim Contact Was Victim's Residence:
    1 ☐ Yes   2 ☐ No   99 ☐ Unknown

119. Initial Offender-Victim Contact Was Victim's Work Place:
    1 ☐ Yes   2 ☐ No   99 ☐ Unknown

120. Potential Witnesses at the Time of the Initial Offender-Victim Contact:
    1 ☐ Other People Were Present in the   2 ☐ Area Was Essentially Deserted
       Immediate Area   99 ☐ Unknown

VICTIM'S LAST KNOWN LOCATION
121. Was the Site of the Victim's Last Known Location the Same as the Site of the Initial Contact between the Victim and Offender?
    1 ☐ Yes (go to Item 127)   2 ☐ No or Unknown

122. Description of General Area of Victim's Last Known Location (check one only):
    1 ☐ Rural   3 ☐ Urban
    2 ☐ Suburban   99 ☐ Unknown

123. The Neighborhood of Victim's Last Known Location Was *Predominantly* (check one only):
    1 ☐ Business, Industrial, or Commercial   4 ☐ Uninhabited or Wilderness
    2 ☐ Farm or Agricultural   99 ☐ Unknown
    3 ☐ Residential

124. The Victim's Last Known Location Was (check as many as apply):
    1 ☐ Any Residence   7 ☐ In an Open Field
    2 ☐ At or Near a School or Playground   8 ☐ In a Vehicle
    3 ☐ In a Retail Shopping District   9 ☐ On Public Transportation
    4 ☐ On a Public Street   88 ☐ Other (specify): _____
    5 ☐ In a Vice Area
    6 ☐ A Densely Wooded Area   99 ☐ Unknown

125. The Victim's Last Known Location Was Victim's Residence:
    1 ☐ Yes   2 ☐ No   99 ☐ Unknown

126. The Victim's Last Known Location Was Victim's Work Place:
    1 ☐ Yes   2 ☐ No   99 ☐ Unknown

EVENTS AT ASSAULT SITE

127. There Is Evidence That the Offender Disabled the Telephone, Other Utilities, or Security Devices:
    1 ☐ Yes   2 ☐ No   99 ☐ Unknown

128. The Property at the Crime Scene(s) Was Ransacked, Vandalized, or Burned:
    1 ☐ Yes   2 ☐ No   99 ☐ Unknown

129. There Are Indications That the Offender Took Steps to Obliterate or Destroy Evidence at the Scene:
    1 ☐ Yes   2 ☐ No   99 ☐ Unknown

OFFENDER'S WRITING OR CARVING ON BODY OF VICTIM

130. Writing or Carving *on Body:*
    1 ☐ Yes (describe): _____   2 ☐ No

131. Instrument Used to Write or Carve *on Body:*
    1 ☐ Knife or Other Sharp Instrument   4 ☐ Writing Instrument (pen, etc.)
    2 ☐ Blood   88 ☐ Other (specify): _____
    3 ☐ Lipstick   _____

OFFENDER'S WRITING OR DRAWING AT THE CRIME SCENE

132. Writing or Drawing *at Crime Scene(s):*
    1 ☐ Yes (describe): _____   2 ☐ No

133. Instrument Used to Write or Draw *at Crime Scene(s):*
    1 ☐ Knife or Other Sharp Instrument   4 ☐ Writing Instrument (pen, etc.)
    2 ☐ Blood   88 ☐ Other (specify): _____
    3 ☐ Lipstick   _____

SYMBOLIC ARTIFACTS AT CRIME SCENE

134. Was There Evidence to Suggest a Deliberate or Unusual Ritual/Act/Thing Had Been Performed on, with, or near the Victim (such as an orderly formation of rocks, burnt candles, dead animals, defecation, etc.)?
    1 ☐ Yes (describe): _____   2 ☐ No
    _____   99 ☐ Unknown

OFFENDER'S COMMUNICATIONS

Item 135 deals with communications initiated by the offender with respect to the crime. Examples would be: an offender sending a letter or tape recording to the police or media claiming responsibility for the crime; a ransom note; or a suspicious communication received by the victim prior to the crime. (This item does not refer to conversation between the offender and victim during commission of the crime.)

135. Was There Any Communication from the Offender Before or After the Crime?
    1 ☐ Yes (enclose a copy or synopsis   2 ☐ No
          of the communication)   99 ☐ Unknown

VII.   CONDITION OF VICTIM WHEN FOUND

BODY DISPOSITION

136. There Is Reason to Believe the Offender Moved the Body from the Area of the Death Site to the Area of the Body Recovery Site:
    1 ☐ Yes   2 ☐ No   3 ☐ Unable to Determine

137. Evidence Suggests the Offender Disposed of the Body in the Following Manner:
    1 ☐ Openly Displayed or Otherwise   3 ☐ With an Apparent Lack of
       Placed to Insure Discovery   Concern as to Whether or Not the
    2 ☐ Concealed, Hidden, or Otherwise   Body Was Discovered
       Placed in Order to Prevent Discovery   99 ☐ Unable to Determine

138. It Appears the Body of the Victim Was *Intentionally* Placed in an Unnatural or Unusual Position *after Death* Had Occurred (e.g., staged or posed):
    1 ☐ Yes   2 ☐ No   3 ☐ Unable to Determine

139. Body Was Discovered...
    1 ☐ Buried   5 ☐ In a Container (e.g., dumpster, box
    2 ☐ Covered   refrigerator)
    3 ☐ In a Body of Water (stream, lake, river,   6 ☐ In a Vehicle
       etc.)   7 ☐ Scattered (body parts)
    4 ☐ In a Building   8 ☐ None of the Above

140. If the Body Was Discovered in Water, Was It Weighted?
    1 ☐ Yes —— With What? _____   2 ☐ No

RESTRAINTS USED ON VICTIM

141. Was the Victim Bound?
    1 ☐ Yes   2 ☐ No (go to Item 146)

142. Article(s) Used to Bind or Restrain the Victim or the Body:
    1 ☐ An Article of Clothing   4 ☐ Chain
    2 ☐ Tape   5 ☐ Handcuffs or Thumbcuffs
    3 ☐ Cordage (e.g., rope, string, twine, wire, 88 ☐ Other (specify): _____
       leather thong, etc.)   _____

143. The Evidence Suggests That the Restraining Device(s) Was (check one only):
    1 ☐ Brought to the Scene by the Offender   3 ☐ Both 1 and 2 Above
    2 ☐ An Article Found at the Scene by   99 ☐ Unknown
       the Offender

144. Parts of Body Bound (check as many as apply):
    1 ☐ Hands or Arms   5 ☐ Hands and Ankle(s) Bound Together
    2 ☐ Feet, Ankle(s), or Legs   88 ☐ Other (specify): _____
    3 ☐ Neck   _____
    4 ☐ Arms Bound to Torso

145. The Bindings on the Victim Were Excessive (much more than necessary to control victim's movements):
    1 ☐ Yes   2 ☐ No   3 ☐ Unable to Determine

146. The Body Was Tied to Another Object:
    1 ☐ Yes   2 ☐ No

147. Was a Gag Placed in or on the Victim's Mouth?
    1 ☐ Yes (describe):_____   2 ☐ No
       _____   99 ☐ Unknown

148. Was a Blindfold Placed on or over the Victim's Eyes?
    1 ☐ Yes (describe):_____   2 ☐ No
       _____   99 ☐ Unknown

149. Was Victim's Entire Face Covered?
    1 ☐ Yes —— With What? _____   2 ☐ No
       _____   99 ☐ Unknown

CLOTHING AND PROPERTY OF VICTIM

150. Clothing on Victim When Found:
    1 ☐ Fully Dressed
    2 ☐ Partially Undressed
    3 ☐ Nude
    88 ☐ Other (specify): _____

151. There Is Evidence the Victim Was Re-dressed by Offender:
    1 ☐ Yes
    2 ☐ No
    3 ☐ Unable to Determine

152. There Is Evidence to Suggest That Any or All of the Victim's Clothing had been *Ripped* or *Torn*:
    1 ☐ Yes
    2 ☐ No
    3 ☐ Unable to Determine

153. There Is Evidence to Suggest That Any or All of the Victim's Clothing had been *Cut* from the Body:
    1 ☐ Yes
    2 ☐ No
    3 ☐ Unable to Determine

154. Items of the Victim's Clothing Were Missing from the Body Recovery Site:
    1 ☐ Yes (identify):_____
    2 ☐ No
    99 ☐ Unknown

155. Victim's Clothing (not on the body) Recovered at the Body Recovery Site Was:
    1 ☐ Piled Neatly
    2 ☐ Scattered
    3 ☐ Hidden
    4 ☐ Not Applicable

156. Based on the Investigation, There Is Evidence to Suggest That the Offender Took Small Personal Items (other than clothing) From the Victim (these items may or may not be valuable, e.g., photos, driver's license, real or costume jewelry, etc.):
    1 ☐ Yes (specify):_____
    2 ☐ No
    99 ☐ Unknown

VIII.   CAUSE OF DEATH AND/OR TRAUMA

CAUSE OF DEATH

If victim is a survivor, go to Item 158.

157. Medical Examiner's or Coroner's Officially Listed Cause of Death:
    1 ☐ Gunshot Wound(s)
    2 ☐ Stab Wound(s)
    3 ☐ Cutting or Incise Wound(s)
    4 ☐ Blunt Force Injury
    5 ☐ Strangulation —— Manual, Ligature, Undetermined (circle one)
    6 ☐ Smothering
    7 ☐ Airway Occlusion —— Internal
    8 ☐ Torso Compression
    9 ☐ Hanging
    10 ☐ Drowning
    11 ☐ Burns —— Fire
    12 ☐ Burns —— Chemical
    13 ☐ Burns —— Scalding
    14 ☐ Hypothermia or Exposure
    15 ☐ Malnutrition or Dehydration
    16 ☐ Electrocution
    17 ☐ Crushing Injury
    18 ☐ Explosive Trauma
    19 ☐ Undetermined
    88 ☐ Other (specify): _____

TRAUMA

158. *Major* Trauma Location(s) (check as many as apply):
    1 ☐ Head / Face / Neck
    2 ☐ Arm(s) / Hand(s)
    3 ☐ Torso
    4 ☐ Leg(s) / Feet
    5 ☐ Breast(s)
    6 ☐ Buttocks
    7 ☐ Genitalia
    8 ☐ Anus
    88 ☐ Other (specify): _____
    99 ☐ Unable to Determine

159. Extent of *Blunt Force* Injury:
    1 ☐ None
    2 ☐ Minimal   (minor bruising only, possibly caused by offender's slapping to control the victim)
    3 ☐ Moderate (injury inflicted which in itself could not have caused death)
    4 ☐ Severe   (injury which in itself could have caused death, whether it was the cause of death or not)
    5 ☐ Extreme   (injury inflicted beyond that necessary for death. Overkill)

VIII. CAUSE OF DEATH AND/OR TRAUMA (cont.)

160. Estimated Number of Stab Wounds: _____

161. Estimated Number of Cutting Wounds: _____

162. Number of Entry Gunshot Wounds: _____

163. Range of Gunfire:
     1 □ Not Applicable
     2 □ Distant (no stippling / tattooing)
     3 □ Intermediate (stippling / tattooing)
     4 □ Close (powder residue / tattooing)
     5 □ Contact

BITE MARKS ON VICTIM

164. Bite Marks Were Identified on the Victim's Body:
     1 □ Yes
     2 □ No (go to Item 166)

165. Location of Bite Marks:
     1 □ Face
     2 □ Neck
     3 □ Abdomen
     4 □ Breast(s)
     5 □ Buttocks
     6 □ Groin
     7 □ Genitalia
     8 □ Thigh(s)
     88 □ Other (specify): _____
     _____

ELEMENTS OF TORTURE OR UNUSUAL ASSAULT

166. There Is Evidence to Suggest That the Offender Disfigured the Body of the Victim in Order to Delay or Hinder Identification of the Victim (burned body; removed and took hands, feet, head; etc.):
     1 □ Yes
     2 □ No

167. Elements of Unusual or Additional Assault upon Victim:
     1 □ None
     2 □ Victim Whipped
     3 □ Burns on Victim
     4 □ Victim Run Over by Vehicle
     5 □ Evidence of Cannibalism / Vampirism
     6 □ Offender Explored, Probed, or Mutilated Cavities or Wounds of Victim
     88 □ Other (specify): _____
     _____

168. Body Parts Removed by Offender:
     1 □ None (go to Item 170)
     2 □ Head
     3 □ Scalp
     4 □ Face
     5 □ Teeth
     6 □ Eye(s)
     7 □ Ear(s)
     8 □ Nose
     9 □ Hand(s)
     10 □ Arm(s)
     11 □ Leg(s)
     12 □ Breast(s)
     13 □ Nipple(s)
     14 □ Anus
     15 □ Genitalia
     16 □ Internal Organs
     88 □ Other (specify): _____
     _____

169. Dismemberment Method:
     1 □ Bitten Off
     2 □ Cut —— Skilled/Surgical
     3 □ Cut —— Unskilled/Rough-Cut
     4 □ Hacked / Chopped Off
     5 □ Sawed Off
     88 □ Other (specify): _____
     _____

SEXUAL ASSAULT

170. Is There Evidence of an Assault to Any of the Victim's Sexual Organs or Body Cavities?
     1 □ Yes
     2 □ No (go to Item 178)
     3 □ Unable to Determine

171. Type Sexual Assault, or Attempt (check all that apply):
     1 □ Vaginal
     2 □ Anal
     3 □ Victim Performed Oral Sex on Offender
     4 □ Offender Performed Oral Sex on Victim
     88 □ Other (describe): _____
     _____
     99 □ Unable to Determine

172. Semen Identification In a Body Cavity of the Victim:
    1 ☐ No   3 ☐ In Anus   5 ☐ Unable to Determine
    2 ☐ In Vagina   4 ☐ In Mouth

173. Evidence of Other Ejaculation:
    1 ☐ No   3 ☐ Elsewhere at the Scene
    2 ☐ On Body of Victim   4 ☐ Unable to Determine

174. There Is Evidence to Suggest Postmortem Sexual Assault:
    1 ☐ Yes   2 ☐ No   3 ☐ Unable to Determine

175. Is There Evidence of Sexual Insertion of Foreign Object(s) (other than the penis) into the Victim's Body?
    1 ☐ Yes   2 ☐ No (go to Item 178)

176. Evidence of Sexual Insertion of Foreign Object(s) *Still in Body* When First Discovered (e.g., rocks, twigs, knife, clothing):
    (object)   (object)

    1 ☐ Vagina _____   4 ☐ Mouth _____
    2 ☐ Penis _____   88 ☐ Other _____
    3 ☐ Anus _____

177. There Is Evidence of Sexual Insertion of Foreign Object(s) into Victim's Body, but the Object Was *Not In The Body* When the Body Was First Discovered:
    1 ☐ Yes —— _____ into _____
    2 ☐ No   (describe object)   (body cavity)
    3 ☐ Unable to Determine

IX.   FORENSIC EVIDENCE

WEAPONS

178. Weapons Used by Offender in This Assault:
    1 ☐ None   5 ☐ Ligature
    2 ☐ Firearm   6 ☐ Hands or Feet
    3 ☐ Stabbing or Cutting Weapon   88 ☐ Other Weapon (describe): _____
    4 ☐ Bludgeon or Club

179. Assault Weapon(s) Used by Offender:
    1 ☐ Weapon of Opportunity (offender finds weapon at or near scene)
    2 ☐ Weapon of Choice (offender preselects weapon and brings to scene)
    3 ☐ Both 1 and 2 Above
    99 ☐ Unknown

180. Recovery of Assault Weapon(s) (check as many as apply):
    1 ☐ Not Recovered   3 ☐ Recovered Elsewhere —— Where? ____
    2 ☐ Recovered At Scene

181. Type Firearm Used:
    1 ☐ Handgun   88 ☐ Other (specify): _____
    2 ☐ Rifle
    3 ☐ Shotgun   99 ☐ Unknown

182. Caliber or Gauge of Firearm(s) Used: _____

183. Number of Grooves and Direction of Twist of Recovered Bullet or Firearm: _____

184. Size of Shotgun Shell Pellets Recovered or Used: _____

BLOOD

185. What Is the Offender's Blood Type?
    1 ☐ A   3 ☐ AB   99 ☐ Unknown
    2 ☐ B   4 ☐ O

186. What Is the Rh Factor of the Offender's Blood?
    1 ☐ Positive   2 ☐ Negative   99 ☐ Unknown

Index

About the Authors

Ann Wolbert Burgess, R.N., D.N.Sc., is the van Ameringen Professor of Psychiatric Mental Health Nursing at the University of Pennsylvania School of Nursing and associate director of nursing research at the Department of Health and Hospitals, Boston, Mass. She was a member of the 1984 U.S. Attorney General's Task Force on Family Violence and on the planning committee for the Surgeon General's Symposium on Violence in October 1985. She has coauthored a number of books, including *Child Pornography and Sex Rings* (Lexington Books, 1984).

Daniel Lee Carter, B.A., serves in a clinical role and is grant research coordinator at the Massachusetts Treatment Center in Bridgewater, Mass. He also serves as a research associate in the psychology department at Brandeis University. Mr. Carter has been conducting programmatic research on sexual aggression for eight years.

John E. Douglas, M.S., is a supervisory special agent of the FBI and serves as program manager of the bureau's Criminal Profiling and Consultation Program, which includes crime analysis. Mr. Douglas supervises a staff of FBI Special Agent investigative profilers who provide investigative support to law enforcement agencies throughout the world. He is also an adjunct faculty member of the University of Virginia and the University of Houston Law Center, National College of District Attorneys, as well as a senior research fellow at the University of Pennsylvania.

Horace J. Heafner joined the FBI in 1945, where he served as a fingerprint technician for approximately five years. Upon graduating from the Abbott School of Fine and Commercial Art in Washington, D.C., he was accepted into the FBI Cartographic Section, where he assisted in some of the early research in the design and use of courtroom exhibits. During this period Mr. Heafner provided assistance in designing and implementing a composite art system for use by the field divisions. Mr. Heafner currently serves as a supervisor in the Special Projects Section of the Laboratory Division at FBI Headquarters.

James L. Luke, M.D., attended Yale and Columbia universities and Case Western Reserve University School of Medicine. He received his pathology training at the Yale-New Haven Hospital and at University Hospital in Cleveland, Ohio. He received his training in forensic pathology at the Office of the Chief Medical Examiner in New York City (1965–1967) and served as chief medical examiner of the state of Oklahoma (1967–1971) and of Washington, D.C. (1971–1983). His present position is that of chief medical examiner of the state of Connecticut. He has been a consultant in forensic pathology to the Behavioral Science Investigative Support Unit at the FBI Academy in Quantico, Va., since 1984.

Robert Alan Prentky, Ph.D., is director of research at the Massachusetts Treatment Center in Bridgewater, Mass. He is also an assistant professor at Boston University School of Medicine and serves as a research associate in the psychology department at Brandeis University. He has been conducting programmatic research on sexual aggression for eight years.

Robert K. Ressler, M.S., is a supervisory Special Agent with the FBI and has served the bureau for eighteen years. He has served as an instructor and criminologist at the FBI's training academy in Quantico, Va., since 1974. He is on the faculty of the FBI Academy in the Behavioral Science Unit, and also holds adjunct faculty status with the University of Virginia and Michigan State University, and is a senior research fellow with the University of Pennsylvania. Prior to entering the FBI, he served ten years with the U.S. Army as a military police and criminal investigation officer, and he currently holds the rank of colonel in the U.S. Army Reserves. Mr. Ressler has testified as an expert witness in many criminal cases and has lectured to, and consulted with, police officers and agencies throughout the United States and abroad in the areas of hostage negotiation, criminology, abnormal criminal psychology, and criminal personality profiling. He pioneered in the formulation of the process of criminal profiling and in the creation of the FBI's National Center for the Analysis of Violent Crime. He created the NCAVC Research and Training Programs and is currently the program manager of the Violent Criminal Apprehension Program (VICAP). Special Agent Ressler initiated, designed, and supervised the FBI's Criminal Personality Research Project, which was the basis of the research that made this book possible.